The
BEST
of the
GRAPEVINE

———◆———

Volume 2

BOOKS PUBLISHED BY AA GRAPEVINE, INC.

The Language of the Heart (& eBook)
The Best of the Grapevine Volumes I, II, III
The Best of Bill (& eBook)
Thank You for Sharing
Spiritual Awakenings (& eBook)
I Am Responsible: The Hand of AA
The Home Group: Heartbeat of AA (& eBook)
Emotional Sobriety — The Next Frontier (& eBook)
Spiritual Awakenings II (& eBook)
In Our Own Words: Stories of Young AAs in Recovery (& eBook)
Beginners' Book (& eBook)
Voices of Long-Term Sobriety (& eBook)
A Rabbit Walks Into A Bar
Step by Step — Real AAs, Real Recovery (& eBook)
Emotional Sobriety II — The Next Frontier (& eBook)
Young & Sober (& eBook)
Into Action (& eBook)
Happy, Joyous & Free (& eBook)
One on One (& eBook)
No Matter What (& eBook)
Grapevine Daily Quote Book (& eBook)
Sober & Out (& eBook)
Forming True Partnerships (& eBook)
Our Twelve Traditions (& eBook)
Making Amends (& eBook)
Voices of Women in AA (& eBook)
AA in the Military (& eBook)
One Big Tent (& eBook)
Take me to your Sponsor (& eBook)

IN SPANISH

El lenguaje del corazón
Lo mejor de Bill (& eBook)
El grupo base: Corazón de AA
Lo mejor de La Viña
Felices, alegres y libres (& eBook)
Un día a la vez (& eBook)
Frente A Frente (& eBook)
Bajo El Mismo Techo (& eBook)

IN FRENCH

Le langage du coeur
Les meilleurs articles de Bill
Le Groupe d'attache: Le battement du coeur des AA
En tête à tête (& eBook)
Heureux, joyeux et libres (& eBook)
La sobriété émotive

The
BEST
of the
GRAPEVINE

———◆———

Volume 2

AAGRAPEVINE,Inc.
New York, New York
WWW.AAGRAPEVINE.ORG

AA Preamble

Alcoholics Anonymous is a fellowship of men and
women who share their experience, strength
and hope with each other that they may solve their common
problem and help others to recover from alcoholism.

The only requirement for membership is a desire
to stop drinking. There are no dues or fees
for AA membership; we are self-supporting through
our own contributions. AA is not allied with
any sect, denomination, politics, organization
or institution; does not wish to engage in any
controversy, neither endorses nor opposes any causes.

Our primary purpose is to stay sober
and help other alcoholics to achieve sobriety.

Contents

CHAPTER ONE

That We May Solve Our Common Problem

(Identification and recovery—the many kinds of people who share one disease; the many different details that tell a common story)

CHAPTER SIX

Neither Endorses Nor Opposes Any Causes

*(Trends and issues in AA—an overview of problems and
controversies within the Fellowship; with emphasis on the
Twelve Traditions)*

CHAPTER SEVEN

Alcoholics Anonymous Is a Fellowship

*(The Fellowship as a whole—past, present, and future;
historical glimpses; our Third Legacy, Service, and the General
Service Conference)*

Foreword

Readers of the AA Grapevine magazine have called it their "meeting in print" since the first issue came off press in June 1944. In this second volume of *The Best of the Grapevine,* scores of those readers, along with the writers, artists, and editors who joined them in putting the book together, welcome you to a marathon meeting—a collection of articles selected by Grapevine enthusiasts as those that best nurtured their sobriety and developed their understanding of AA principles.

So sit back, relax, keep an open mind, and "listen" to AA friends from all over the world. Prepare to meet co-founders Bill W. and Dr. Bob; come to know the men and women who through trial and error forged AA's Steps and Traditions; welcome some non-AA friends into your hearts and minds; and widen your circle of friends among the AAs new and old who keep our Fellowship, and therefore ourselves, alive and growing.

You are invited to enter the world of the Grapevine, a sober world filled with the love and laughter, the hard work and spiritual growth, that stand at the heart of the life-saving Fellowship of Alcoholics Anonymous.

Turn the pages, and let the meeting begin.

"'Alcoholics Anonymous is a fellowship of men and women who share their experience, strength, and hope with each other...'"

ONE

That We May Solve Our Common Problem

———————— ◆ ————————

Then I Saw Charlie
December 1953

I had just jacked up another job and I felt unstable and insecure and very, very sorry for myself.

I thought, What the hell is the use? What am I trying to accomplish?

A year and a half without a drink and worse off than I had ever been as a lush!

What the hell am I staying sober for? So that I could make a lot of money—or so that I could have a new car—or so that the neighbors would stop talking? None of these things had taken place. For my wife? She didn't help any. What did she know about an alcoholic? You would think, from the way she talked, that she had been the drunk in the family.

"Why don't you stick to one of these jobs, honey? You'll be back at your old desk some day. But stick to any job for now." What the hell did she know about it? What did she know about the resentments and the envies and the fears that built up inside me? What did she know about my pride and my self-pity?

And all these other problems—wow! I had thought all I had to do was to stay sober. Hah—what a laugh that was!

Stay sober for what? So some pink-cheeked, simple-minded personnel man, fresh from the security of school, could scowl at my work application and say, "What does a man with your background want a job like this for?"

Or so that the State Department would title me "eligible" for a job with the Voice of America and then, because I had declared myself an alcoholic, label me "unsuitable"? Why the hell did they have to classify me with commies and perverts and bad risks?

My wife came into the room and I stared down into the copy of Marcus Aurelius's *Meditations* I had been holding open.

"Leo." I knew what was coming and I hated it. "Leo, Johnny was telling me that they are hiring down at Brice and Sloan's right now. You can run those machines, can't you? Johnny says they are paying good wages, too."

"Yeah, he was telling me," I muttered. "I'll take a walk over there Monday morning."

"Why don't you go over this afternoon, dear? Maybe Johnny will give you a ride home when he gets through."

"Look." This was just the excuse I had been looking for. I slammed shut Marcus Aurelius and his meditations. "Why don't you let me work these things out for myself? What the hell do you know about it? What do you have to keep harping on this job business for?"

"I was only thinking of the children, honey," she said. "With the holidays coming—"

"Damn it! I told you I would take care of things, didn't I?" I got up quickly and strode over to the closet where my coat hung. "You never did believe I had any work problem anyway. Why the hell don't you say so? Why the hell don't you tell me I'm just lazy? That's what you're thinking, isn't it?"

I put on my hat and coat.

"Now, honey, don't go flying off the handle." She'd try to smooth things off now. "If you are going out why don't you call up some other AA members and arrange to meet them somewhere?"

"To hell with other members and to hell with AA and to hell with you!" I yanked open the front door.

"When will you be back, honey?" She was worried now and I felt a childish sense of elation.

"When I get here—if ever." I knew it hurt her and I slammed the door and started down the street.

The beer and ale sign hung out over the sidewalk at the foot of my street and I turned toward the familiar open door. The odor of the bar and spilled beer and sawdust floor disinfectant blended into my senses with the sounds of disconnected conversations and the TV.

The utter futility of what I was trying to do with my life without the crutch of booze was overwhelming.

What the hell is the use? Where am I going? What am I accomplishing in life?

I tried to appear nonchalant as I strode in and the familiar habit of reaching for the price hit me and I plunged my hand into my trousers pocket. I had exactly fifteen cents to my name!

What the hell good would fifteen cents do me? Buy one beer?

I didn't want one drink, I wanted to get drunk—and I couldn't do that on fifteen cents!

Then I saw Charlie!

He was sleeping with his head cradled on his arms, sprawled across one of the tables. He looked awful. He hadn't shaved since God knew when and his clothes were a mess. And he'd been sober with us for seven or eight months.

"How long has he been at it?" I asked the bartender.

"About six days now. Started Saturday afternoon," he said.

He busied himself polishing the well-polished bar. "Can't you get him home or to a hospital or somewhere?"

I looked down at Charlie and something strange and strong and good welled up inside me and surged through me and washed all the self-pity and resentment and futility clean out of me.

"Sure. I'll get him out of here, Sam," I said.

I walked over to the wall phone and dropped in a nickel of my fifteen cents. I'd better get a couple of bucks from the wife, I thought. I might need cab fare. She'd walk down with it...and she'd be glad to know what I was doing.

I turned and looked at Charlie and the age-old AA slogan ran

through my mind, "BUT FOR THE GRACE OF GOD." And, strangely, it
sounded like a prayer of thanks.

And I knew why I was sober and what I was trying to accomplish
and where I was trying to go. And I was very, very glad for the year
and a half of sobriety.

L. W., Providence, R.I.

Remembering a Girl—Defeated Except Once
March 1947

T oday I am remembering. Remembering a girl of twenty-five
who was buried not so long ago. This remembering is a form
of insurance for me, insurance for more days like today. I
don't want to forget the conflict, the frightening struggle she and I
had. I don't want to forget how often she won. I do not resent her,
and I do not fear her any longer, for now she will have to fight both
God and me. And God never loses.

I want to remember the day she acknowledged with quiet despon-
dency that she was hopelessly addicted to alcohol, that it was no mere
beverage, but the food and drug of her soul. And with that acknowl-
edgment began the fear of source of supply far more than the fear
of inevitable consequences. Intellectually she knew the outcome—
emotionally she could not see far enough ahead to care. And a drink
always pushed the care aside temporarily.

I want to remember the nights I talked to her—talked, threatened,
pleaded, ridiculed, and condemned her. How often we tried to get together to whip this thing! I told her no one else drank as she did, that
she had everything she wanted, so why didn't she stop? I watched
her try to pray, saw her fumbling to remember the words of the De
Profundis: "Out of the depths I have cried to Thee, O Lord." And then
we would resolve that tomorrow would be different—we would start
with a clean slate.

But tomorrow was no different. She arose full of determination, but ridden by fears of almost certain defeat. There was grit, but small hope. And before long, our time-worn game of duplicity was being played. We fenced with one another, and her strokes became more and more forceful until she won. And with her victory, again I had to sit as an onlooker, with pity but no strength to help in my heart, and watch this awful thing she was doing to herself. I watched her as she slipped beyond my reach, into the never-ending flight, chasing an ideal, and not knowing what she wanted or why, but wanting it desperately. I watched her as she rode the highway of fantasy. She was a great writer; she called her book The Battle of the Bottle, but the first line of her message for posterity was never written. She was a great pianist, but her genius was thwarted by the affliction she bore. She was the personification of the perfect wife, and would be the perfect mother, too, if only given a child to prove it. She was a well-balanced, cultured, charming young woman, an inspiration to all who knew her. She was artistic, creative, enthusiastic, bountiful, and compassionate—oh, infinitely compassionate. But misunderstood, and alone. So alone. I followed in her shadow and thought, like Miniver Cheevy, she too was ..."born too late,

Scratched her head and kept on thinking,
She, too, coughed, and called it Fate,
And kept on drinking."

I watched her slide from the fantasy of the perfect to the figure of the downtrodden reformer. Why must there be wars'? Why were children starving'? Who were the fools who ran things and how did they get there? And why didn't they have the intelligence of a chicken? A chicken for president! No—she was losing her grip. That wasn't sensible—she'd have to pull herself together. Do the housework, that was it. No—better read something first—elevate the mind. Too much superficiality in the world today. Not enough people read Shakespeare and the Bible. Why, did you know if you really knew Shakespeare and the Bible, you need never know another thing? Those two books had everything—all wisdom, all knowledge. She'd read the Book of Job.

She was like Job herself—everything was wrong.

And then I watched the indignation at life come upon her. The world was run by ignoramuses. She knew! She had worked at a war plant! And oh, the waste! She'd call the president. She dialed the White House. National 1414. He was busy. He couldn't talk to her. Some democracy!

And then the remorse and self-pity. I watched as she vaguely recognized her condition. Here she was, drunk, and only this morning she had been so full of determination to do better. She had tried— oh, yes, she had tried. In fact, all her life she had strived to be a real person. Lots of people floated along never giving a thought to the meaning of Life, but as far back as she could remember, she had consciously worked on herself. She had worked harder than most, she had read more, she had studied, everything from Greek to millinery. She had known what she wanted and had bent all energies and capacities to get it, whatever it was. Oh, the cruelty of it all! What a dastardly trick Fate had played on her. She was of no use to herself or anyone else. And for a few minutes she got a morbid pleasure from these thoughts. How tragic! But sort of pathetically, beautifully tragic! Here she was, so young, so gifted, and the world would never benefit because of her cursed malady.

And then I watched the fear set in. At first, a mild rage at the unfairness of it all. But later, I saw her wracked in stark fear and hopelessness. She was frantic with fright—fright for her sanity, fright for her life. What was to become of her? I was as one on the outside, a spectator to this horrible transformation, and was helpless. She watched the door, furtively, anxiously, knowing it to be locked, yet afraid. She dared not look out the window for fear of vague faces. She dared not answer the telephone for fear of unknown voices. She could not read. She could not sleep. She could not pray. And she heard music—a fragment of a haunting theme, repeated and repeated, ending each time in a discord. And the oblivion.

No, I do not want to forget the girl. I want to remember that she is only one drink away. I don't want to forget what time was to her.

She suffered through yesterday a thousand times in her remorse. She feared tomorrow with terror, and hoped by some means she could escape it. Today never existed for her. I am glad she is dead.

And who has taken the place of that girl? Quite a different person altogether. I find I am a simple person—no thwarted genius after all. That great American novel will have to be written by someone else. I find, after sober practice, that the concert stage can do without this average parlor pianist. I find that being a perfect wife requires some exertion other than dreams. I find that today builds into tomorrow. I find that we don't just "get somewhere"—we go there, one day at a time. I find it a luxurious sensation to be sane.

And what is time to me now? It is a most precious asset. I have the luxury of being able to cherish the memory of yesterday, to live today with serenity, to wait for tomorrow. I find great contentment in just knowing where I was and where I am. And I am grateful; grateful for the existence of Alcoholics Anonymous; grateful to my God for leading me to the doors of AA and to himself; grateful for hope. I am grateful for this minute. My eternity may be in it.

C.M., Arlington, Va.

The Minister Says the Password
February 1976

My name is George, and I'm an alcoholic. That's the standard beginning for every AA talk I've ever heard. "I'm Joe, and I'm an alcoholic." "I'm Billy, and I'm an alcoholic." We're all alcoholics. This admission is vital, for it keeps us honest and keeps us aware of who we are and what we must do.

But it's only part of the story. I am a sober alcoholic, thanks to the gracious help of my Higher Power and the Fellowship and support of AA. It is every bit as important to remind myself of that as it is to remember my disease.

For many of us, the admission that we were alcoholics was so difficult, painful, embarrassing, and shocking that we feel we arrived in the program just by finally saying the words "I'm an alcoholic." Some of us held back, afraid to let the words out. Others of us were defiant, obstinately refusing to be railroaded by a bunch of eager beavers with the Big Book in hand. When the moment of admission finally came, it was a milestone of immeasurable importance.

I had my problems with it, even though the realization that I was an alcoholic came easier for me than for some. I was incredibly blessed, for as a minister I had been invited to participate in the Al-Anon program that met in my church. There, wives, husbands, and friends or relatives of alcoholics shared their experience, strength, and hope with me long before I had any notion I might need help for myself. I received a grounding in the subject that few "civilians" have.

The day of my last drink, I was suffering one of the few hangovers I ever had and wondering what was happening to me. I found myself praying, "Do you think my drinking is out of control, God?" Quickly, I rejected the notion as ridiculous. But I was concerned enough that I asked him to give me a sign all the same.

I went on drinking the rest of that day, with little thought of my prayer, but when I woke the next morning, I had my answer. I heard these clear and unmistakable words: "George, George, you've gone too far!"

Looking back on it, I can place all kinds of interpretations on what happened that morning. Voice of God or voice of conscience? It doesn't really matter. I had been called to account for my drinking, and the diagnosis had been pronounced: I was an alcoholic. Though I am an ordained Presbyterian minister, though I was active as a citizen in my community, though I had never been arrested, never lost a job, never been locked out of the house, never been asked to leave anybody else's home because of my drunkenness, though I came to AA with job, family, and reputation all intact—I was an alcoholic and the fear, panic, helplessness, and self-loathing I felt could not have been worse if I had just discovered that I had leprosy.

I thought of friends I had let down. I thought of my church position and the possibility that I would be defrocked. I thought of my AA friends and how I had to talk to somebody. Boy, will this shock 'em! I thought. And immediately I revised that idea. "Shock 'em, hell! They've probably known it all along." How could I face them? But I had to face them. I was sick. I was an alcoholic. A quick inventory of the symptoms I had learned left me no doubts. I had an incurable disease, and I had to have help.

On top of the fear were the resentment and the anger. Why me? What did I do wrong? Just when everything was looking up, why did this have to happen? It wasn't fair.

And what would I tell my wife? How would she take the news? She didn't suspect anything yet—not really. Oh, she had blown her top at me once for coming in plastered and passing out on her, but that was only once. This was different. This was an admission of guilt. And what's more, there was no going back, no undoing it, no saying, "I'm sorry. I'll never let it happen again. Now let's hurry up and forget all about it." No, this time I was in for it, and I knew it.

I could not face the AAs in my hometown. What if people found out about me? Instead, I went to a nearby town to see a clergyman who, I had been told, knew something about alcoholism and AA. I told him my plight, hoping to hear the reprieve: "Oh, George, you're not an alcoholic! You've just let your imagination run away with you." But the reprieve did not come. Instead, he said, "I don't know if you're an alcoholic or not. I only know how I drank, and I can tell you that everything I did is what you've just got through telling me you've done."

So I went to my first AA meeting—not as an observer, and not in my own hometown, but in a neighboring town. I was very much aware that I had an incurable disease, but that night, I didn't say, "I'm an alcoholic." I softened it a little and said, "If I'm not an alcoholic, I sure have a funny way of drinking."

That was the way I made my first public admission that I'm an alcoholic. To me, it was very shameful. But as the months went by, it became easier. After all, I was no different from anyone else in the room. They all said, "I'm an alcoholic," so what was the big deal? It was almost like the password at a fraternal meeting. I even got over my embarrassment and joined my hometown group.

Now, when I hear the password repeated again and again at our meetings, I want to object. Yes, we're alcoholics. Yes, it was vitally important that we come to that awareness. Yes, we've got to be honest with ourselves and one another. But we're more than alcoholics. Much more.

We're alcoholics who are living sober lives! Alcoholics who have a choice whether or not to take that first drink. For the first time in our lives, we are really alive! Our message is good news, and we need to say so.

Some of us hint at this by saying, "I'm a recovered alcoholic," as if we had just been cured. Others say "arrested alcoholic," which conjures up images of a policeman holding us captive in handcuffs! "Nonpracticing alcoholic," "dry alcoholic," you name it—we have a number of ways to indicate that we are more than just alcoholics. None of them tells the story very well, but all are better than the flat statement "I'm an alcoholic." There's nothing very remarkable about being an alcoholic. We're a dime a dozen. The good word is that we're *sober* alcoholics.

I'm an alcoholic, sober today, thanks to my Higher Power and the fellowship and support of AA. That's my good news for you. It's not a very fancy statement. There's a lot more that needs to be said—words about my Higher Power, about the incredible love AA people have for one another, about struggling with the Steps, about black battles with our own private demons. Yes, it's a whole new way of life we're talking about.

I know most of you will continue to start your AA talks with the words "I'm an alcoholic." But remember to add the good news: "I'm sober." *That's* what's worth talking about.

                                                                G.M., Okla.

The Kid Who Came In from the Cold
September 1986

I first came to AA on December 5, 1964. I was taken to AA by a clergyman. I did not want to be an AA member or quit drinking, but I did want to be reunited with the family. I was twenty-five years old.

At first, I attended meetings regularly. I read the Big Book. The family and I were reunited. Life began to get good again. It's unfortunate that some of us equate physical well-being and getting back on our feet with mental and spiritual soundness. I began to attend meetings less and less.

I began to say to myself, "You know, you might have been a little rash in coming to AA so soon." Hardly anyone was under forty, much less twenty-six. Being the only Hispanic, I decided alcoholism was an Irish disease. I didn't qualify.

There were those who also were only too glad to show me the way out by their comments. They were the men who sat around the club and told war stories about their drinking. "Boy," they would say. "I spilled more whiskey on my tie than you ever drank." Or, "Kid. How many times did you go to jail? Do you still have your family? You do! Well, what are you doing here?" Then, they would hit you with the killer. "It's a good thing that you didn't have to go through what *we* had to suffer, Kid." No question about it. They were the "real" men. When they said "Kid," and gave me that disdainful stare, I knew that I did not measure up; that down deep inside I was a closet wimp.

I took a nearly full-time job in the evenings, and when friends came to invite me to go with them to meetings, I declined. Oh, certainly I would plan to attend some of the functions once in a while. I could be a source of inspiration to all those less fortunate than I, which was nearly everyone from my point of view. I was different. I knew that I was an undiscovered natural resource whose time had not yet come. "Drink again? Why, that is utterly out of the question." Perhaps, in the past, I had been a bit bizarre on occasion, but that's expected when a great mind is subjected to the mundane trivialities of life such as having to work for a living. I was the most surprised one of all when I got drunk.

Something that rarely fails to impress nearly every newcomer is what my sponsor calls "the magic of AA." We meet clean, well-dressed people who seem genuinely warm and friendly. We find firm hand-shakes and compassionate hearts. Here, at last, are people who understand exactly how we have felt. They give of themselves unselfishly, offering to take us to meetings and giving us their phone numbers. They tell us that they care. And most importantly, they say, "Come back. We need you." No matter how insincere you might be when you arrive, you cannot help but be impressed by the love and acceptance that you find. An overwhelming sense of hope is experienced, perhaps for the first time, as we are welcomed into the Fellowship.

If, like me, you happen to drink again and are fortunate enough to return to AA you may find that there is a little less of the magic than you first experienced. I was one of those who bounced in and out of AA for quite some time. I was never sober for more than three weeks at any one time and that only occurred once. Each time I returned, there was less and less of the magic.

There were all those who had gotten sober since I had first come in. I especially hated them. As time went on, I began to notice a few things. I noticed that when I got up to get my tenth "white chip" of the month, the applause wasn't quite as enthusiastic as I remembered it. It occurred to me that no one had offered their phone number to me for quite some time. Whenever one of those newly sober members rushed up to save me, their sponsor called them away.

It wasn't that I lacked a desire to stop drinking. Each time I returned, I returned with all the sincerity I could muster. The problem was that I had lost the ability to control my drinking and was not able to stay sober on my own resources. Those of us who are sober sometimes forget that lack of success does not necessarily mean lack of sincerity.

There comes a time when nothing matters anymore. There was no magic left. It all dissolved in a sea of alcohol. I was coming to AA because I had nowhere else to go. I had run out of alternatives.

It was December of 1968. The family was gone. So were the house, the car, and everything else. I was living in what had once been chicken coops and were now "remodeled" for people such as myself. I was alone. I wandered in and out of AA almost mechanically, getting a white chip if they offered it.

At the time, I weighed about 100 pounds. I couldn't sleep. I couldn't eat anything that would stay down. I was impotent. I was so sick, mentally as well as physically, that I could not maintain a conversation with anyone. After a few minutes, most people just got up and left. It was at this time that I went to a meeting with a man whom I had asked to be my sponsor during one of my brief periods of sobriety. He never gave up on me. That night, when the group secretary did the chip system, I got another white chip. It was January 20, 1969. I have not gotten another one since.

The point of this story is that there is no such thing as a "hopeless slipper." There are "slippers" that we label "hopeless" when we don't want to bother with them anymore. My first sponsor never gave up on me. He knew that repeatedly getting drunk did not mean that I had no desire to stop drinking. Sincerity of desire cannot be judged by amount of success. I should know that as well as anyone, yet, in sobriety, I too have been guilty, at times, of casting the same judgment upon others. How quickly we forget!

Part of the magic of AA is that the Fellowship, like the "loving God who presides over us all," never gives up hope for the suffering alcoholic. My first sponsor knew this. He knew that unconditional love is what often makes the difference between living and dying for the man or woman who seeks shelter in Alcoholics Anonymous. He knew that when we gave up all hope for those still "out there," we had lost the magic of AA ourselves. And, we had lost it sober.

C.C., West Palm Beach, Fla.

Without a Secret High

March 1986

I led my first AA meeting and qualified myself as an alcoholic exactly ninety days after I put down my last drink. But I was still smoking marijuana at the time.

Why?

I knew I was powerless over alcohol and that I couldn't stay stopped without help. Surrendering to the experience of the people in AA and having nowhere else to turn, I decided to take their suggestions—regarding not drinking, that is. It seemed to me that *was* "the program."

What I didn't accept was all the fellowship-of-drunks stuff. I wanted no part of that coffee-shop socializing, adolescent romanticizing, and a hug at first sight. What do you mean you love me? You don't even know me!

I was separate and different as always. Besides, I didn't need any new friends. There were plenty of friends just waiting out there who were as sure as I was that people like us couldn't live on this planet full time without escaping via some drug or another.

Besides, I wasn't powerless over these other substances; I could stop whenever I wanted. It was booze and booze alone that brought me to AA.

But just staying away from booze, even with the "help" of the other drugs, was still so hard that I had to go to meetings every day to share the pain. Through that grinding process I came to learn the first few things about trusting people and surviving feelings—in spite of myself.

It was two of those feelings—shame and fear—that finally brought me to surrender. The last straw came when a patient in a detox meeting asked me incredulously, after I had made my pitch for AA (yes,

I was speaking all around town about not drinking): "Do you mean to tell me you don't get high on anything?" I nodded my head with a fake smile and lied to give him the "party line." I finally knew I was in trouble.

While I wasn't sure I had to stop drugging, I knew I had to stop lying. So I started sharing in meetings that I was still smoking grass.

My confession didn't elicit many bravoes for honesty. In fact I got enough disapproval that it was impossible for me to be comfortable in meetings. I especially hated hearing that I couldn't be high and sober at the same time. I didn't understand it; to me being sober meant not being drunk.

But I was terrified of drinking again. So I finally buckled under the pressure and decided to take the suggestions of people I had come to trust, and to try another ninety days without any mood-changers at all.

The rewards were virtually immediate. For the previous six months I had spent my time feeling paranoid, fighting the obsession to pick up a drink, and demolishing the self-esteem that I was slowly building up in AA. Conversations with myself went something like: "Who are you kidding? You're never going to make it. You're different because you're crazy. You've always been crazy." Now each day clean and withdrawing from the last chemical substances brought a new kind of revelation.

In addition, being clean and dry meant I could get a sponsor, one from whom I didn't have to hide.

But it also meant that I had to sit and watch the people who came in after me celebrating their anniversaries before me. And because I put down the drink exactly six months before I finally got sober, my first anniversary was a kind of stutter of false pride and genuine humility. There were many I could hardly believe had more sober time than me. Hadn't I been making coffee when they first wandered in?

But my second "true" anniversary sat more easily and it felt less like time was being "taken away" from me. And since the third, I have accepted that I honestly celebrate the date that I finally surrendered

and brought my disease and my secret into the rooms of AA because
I wanted to be sober.

A.D., New York, N.Y.

I'm Unique—But I Want to Belong
September 1970

Wwhat can match the emotional impact of a classical AA
story? It's so easy to recognize the power of the AA
program when the speaker's words give you a picture
in Technicolor and 3-D of the personal hell he lived in during his
drinking days, and the way the AA program led him from the darkness into the light. But who wants to listen to my story? How can I
help a suffering alcoholic with my pantywaist drinking experiences?

You see, I belong to a group of "second-class citizens" in AA. Are
there many of us? I can't tell. Most of us feel too apologetic about
our histories to talk much about them. If we do, we have to resist the
temptation to embroider our stories so as to be "one of the gang."

AA seemed to recognize this problem some years back. Many alcoholics who hadn't reached skid row had been able to grasp the
program, but it wasn't always easy for them to identify with the
former down-and-outers. So the second edition of the Big Book
added a group of stories entitled "They Stopped in Time." Now, that
should have been tailor-made for my type of alcoholic. (Do alcoholics come in types? Types seem to blend into a harmonious whole as
understanding increases, but at the beginning this thought is too
big to grasp.) Eagerly, I read those new stories. But I couldn't find
myself anywhere! The thought struck me: Could it be that I stopped
too soon? That would have made a dandy excuse for acquiring a
more colorful drinking history. But I was lucky. The program was
working for me, and I stayed. Maybe my story didn't fit into the Big
Book, but somehow I seemed to fit into AA. At least, no one told me
to go out and do some more drinking. If they had, it might not have

changed anything, anyhow—I never was too good at taking advice.

How can my story help anyone? I wasn't even an alcoholic when I came in! (That was certainly my conviction at the time.) What's more, I came in by the back door—or, perhaps, the side door. I had made a mess of my life, and most of it was caused by my behavior while under the influence, but I had no addiction, no compulsion. I always stopped drinking as soon as I threw up—sooner, if I was lucky. (In that respect, at least, I "stopped in time.") And I never started drinking the morning after, because the safety valve in my stomach kept me relatively free of hangovers. But, for some reason, my wife told me to get out, and I came up with a promise: I would never drink again! I really believed that by myself I could stop forever. No problem! What is worse, from the standpoint of my prestige as an AA speaker and as a scientist, I have no evidence to show that I couldn't have stopped without AA, because AA did come along at that moment. I had never tried to stop before, so I can't prove anything! (Except that I haven't had a drink since. Actually, I can't prove that, either, but I don't have to.)

My solemn promise never to drink again wasn't good enough for my wife. In my own estimation, I always maintained strict adherence to the truth, but my moral credit rating had been dropping, and there was a credibility gap. I would have to come up with something stronger than a promise. So I called AA.

This was before we had a central office in this county, but there were three numbers listed under AA in the local phone directory. I almost got out of having to do anything more about it, because it was a Sunday, and the first two numbers didn't answer. But the third one did. It was a good thing I didn't realize that I was talking to an answering service. I expected them to send someone right over. Instead, they told me where I could find a meeting nearby that evening. I felt a little let down. But at any rate, the order to leave home was suspended temporarily. When I got to the meeting, there were more surprises: No committee at the door asked me for my credentials; nobody even turned around to stare when I sneaked in, a little after the meeting had started. I was glad. The last thing I wanted at that time was a lot of attention.

I hadn't come to the meeting to learn how to stop drinking. After all, I had already decided to quit, so that was taken care of! I had come just to prove that I was serious about stopping—not to myself, but to my wife.

A funny thing happened to me at that meeting. I heard a lot about drinking, of course, and what AA can do about it. But what I took home with me, and into my heart, was something very different, very unexpected. Alcoholics Anonymous had a formula for living. They had taken the message of the Bible, I decided later, and transformed it into a set of simple, do-it-yourself directions. I loved the Bible, but I had never been able to let it reach me. The Twelve Steps got to me fast. I wanted what you had!

The literature I brought home soon made us a husband-and-wife team of beginners. We started going to discussion meetings. And I faced a new problem. As each person had his turn to speak, he gave his name and announced that he was an alcoholic. Was I going to be different? Was I going to say, "My name is E., and I want your program, but I'm not really an alcoholic"? Of course not! I was too much of a coward. Besides, I didn't have that much honesty yet. And I wasn't thinking that clearly about myself. I didn't want to admit to myself that I didn't qualify. I wanted to belong. I wasn't worried about my drinking, but I wanted to learn how to live. I wanted what you had.

It's ironic! As I started getting enough honesty to admit my own doubts about being an alcoholic, I also got honest enough to start recognizing symptoms of the disease in myself, and to start identifying with others' stories, even though they had progressed much further down the ladder—*outwardly*. I began to recognize the significance of inward degradation, of moral bankruptcy. And then my own outward behavior, which I had stoutly defended to myself as "normal," began to appear in its true colors. Eventually, I realized that normal drinkers rarely vomit over the boss's living room rug in front of a large audience, that blackouts are not the hallmark of every normal drinker or even of a "he-man" drinker. When I had a nightmare about getting drunk again, I didn't get shook up. I was happy. Now I knew I belonged in AA.

Nevertheless, I still have an inferiority complex about my story. No arrests. No hospitalization even remotely connected with drinking. No time lost from work. No brawls. Not much of a story! My kind of story doesn't wind up in the Big Book. To make that grade, you've got to be a red-blooded alcoholic, even if you did "stop in time."

A frequent problem for an alcoholic is that he may think he's unique. He can't believe others have had the same experiences, the same problems. He thinks he's different. Not me! I think there are many like me, but they don't get heard. Some of them may be listening for a sign that they, too, can belong, Well if I can do it, anyone can do it. And I do belong. AA is my life. Why shouldn't it be? Before, I had only a sort of existence; I only thought I was living. l was wrong. AA gave me life.

Having trouble with the First Step?—Relax. All the program asks is enough honesty to get started—just what we are capable of at the moment. At the beginning, that's very little honesty. Each day, there will be a little more. It will come. Because, you see, the AA program works for anyone who wants it.

E.S., Corona del Mar, Calif.

Rock 'n Roll Sobriety
May 1986

I was very apprehensive but decided to loosen up a bit and go to the rock concert anyway. I felt I had grown out of a lot of that loud, deafening music, but since my sister really wanted me to go I agreed. What the hell, I was still young—twenty-three years old that is, and flexible enough to fit in with just about any group of people. I decided to make it a good time so I threw out my negative feelings and geared myself with a positive attitude. Thus was my mental state when I headed for the Riverfest on Harriet Island to rock with REO Speedwagon.

We got there early enough to get good seats, and I sat back to observe the throngs of people that filed past. Their eyes sparkled with anticipation and their faces gave evidence of the excitement they felt. Raw energy hung low like a heavy fog and mixed with the warm, damp air left over from the muggy day. Multicolored, greased-up hair, six-inch chain earrings, black leather studded outfits, and bright, bold, colorful sunglasses caught my eye. Nothing was unexpected, however. I was merely a spectator enjoying the show as my continuous grin would suggest to those passing by.

The concert was finally getting under way and my friends needed more beer, so off they trotted to battle the crowds and long lines while I attempted to save their seats. Of course they missed the first song, and almost lost their seats. While I was dancing and clapping to the music I could see them off in the distance as they jostled their way through the crowd, trying to save their sacred beer from spillage. It seemed an eternity, but everyone finally settled in.

By this time the band was working up a sweat and the crowd's intense energy was growing. It didn't take long before the familiar smell of marijuana played on my senses. Oh, God! I decided right then and there to thank God for my sobriety. It seemed only yesterday when at this same concert I was too stoned to even realize what songs were played. Hard rock is tough to figure out anyway, yet at least tonight my mind was intact and I could actually distinguish one instrument from the next and figure out the rhythm.

Unfortunately my enthusiastic, absorbed state was interrupted. "What d'ya want?" I screamed at my sister over the grating sound of heavy metal.

"We have to go to the bathroom," she yelled. I had forgotten the wretched curse of beer drinking.

"Okay," I shouted, "but hurry back. I can't be saving seats all night." Off they went again while I continued to enjoy the show. Yes, by God, I was enjoying this concert.

All around me people were losing their balance and falling off benches because of the effects of alcohol and drugs. Yet I firmly held my ground and confidently stepped up my movements in the tiny spot I inhabited. I was amazed at the amount of control I felt amid all this unleashed energy. Sweating bodies were pushed and shoved in the whirlwind of mass chaos, while endless screaming mingled in the air with pounding drums and electrifying acoustics—still, I was in control! My thoughts were soon disturbed by the scrawny kid next to me.

"Do you have an extra joint?"

"What?" I exclaimed, clearly flabbergasted. He was maybe fifteen or sixteen.

"Do you have any extra weed, man?" he repeated, somewhat hesitant this time.

"I wouldn't even have a match to light one for you," I answered. He didn't seem to believe me, but I really couldn't help him. I looked at him again and smiled.

Half an hour passed before I saw the familiar faces of my sister and her friends. They were having trouble getting through the wild crowd. Too bad they were missing the whole show. When they finally made it, I informed her that they had played her favorite song. "Don't go to the bathroom," she shouted in my ear, uninterested in my comment. "You wouldn't believe how long the lines are."

As she continued to be preoccupied with lighting her cigarette and carefully guarding what beer she had salvaged, I absorbed myself in the excitement of the live music and the fact that I was seeing—really seeing—REO Speedwagon for the first time.

The thoughts and emotions that coursed through me that night are almost inexpressible. I recognized a year and a half of growth amid the blaring, screeching, deafening sounds of electric guitars and synthesizers, and saw for the first time that this was what self-esteem was all about. I was not afraid to do my own thing in this crowd. I was not worried about how I looked, nor intimidated by how others looked. I was not comparing myself to others; I was not crazy, and felt no need to act crazy; I was definitely not unhappy; and I was not thirsting for attention and acceptance, or trying so hard to feel that I belonged. I was not inside looking out, rather I was outside looking in.

I stood in the middle of 35,000 people and felt free to be a different, unique individual. The most important part of it all is that my Higher Power was with me and I was conscious of him. How many other people in this rowdy, rambunctious crowd were thinking of a God and feeling the greater effects of his energy and power? How many times while I was drinking did I become conscious of my Higher Power and my inner feelings? I can't think of one. The only times I remember being aware of that is when I cried out in pain and desperation. He was there then, but I couldn't see him through my tears, my darkness, my raw pain.

"Did you have a good time?" I asked my sister when it was all over.

"Yeah, it was great," she answered, but quickly changed the subject to the amount of beer that was spilled on her. I could plainly see the effects of the concert were short-lived. Tomorrow she would not remember the real music, only a loud, undistinguishable sound and a lot of people. I, however, had discovered a new dimension to my sobriety, and it was well worth a hard-earned six bucks!

B.Z., St. Paul, Minn.

My Name Is Bertha...
March 1969

My name is Bertha. I am an Afro-American alcoholic. I don't know when I became an alcoholic, but I do believe I became one because I drank too much too often.

I always blamed my drinking on being poor, or on anything other than that I liked what booze did for me, that when I had a drink I was as big and had as much as the next person. I would never admit that I was drinking too much, or spending money that I should have used to buy food for my two little boys.

As time went on, I drank more. I was not able to hold a job—no one wants a drunk around. I was always able to get a boyfriend who had a joint, or sold whiskey, but it didn't last long. I would embarrass everyone by coming in drunk or passing out. Then it got to the place I couldn't drink without getting in jail. On one of these trips, the judge must have thought I was worth saving, for instead of sending me to jail he sent me to AA for one month.

I went to AA. At least, my body went. I hated every minute of it. I couldn't wait until the meeting was over to get a drink. I was afraid to drink before the meeting. I thought if they smelled whiskey on my breath they would lock me up, and I couldn't live without my bottle. I hated that judge for sending me to a place with all those drunks. I wasn't an alcoholic! Oh, I might drink too much at times—everyone I knew drank. But I don't ever remember that any of them went to sleep in joints and woke up with no shoes on in the winter, or fell out of chairs. But I did. I don't remember any of them getting put out in the winter because they didn't pay their rent, but to me whiskey meant more than a home for my sons.

Things got so bad I was afraid to go on the street, so I turned to Mothers' Aid. That was one of the worst things that could have happened to an alcoholic woman. I would wait for the mailman each month, like any good mother, but as soon as he handed me my check, I put on my best dress and went looking for my alcoholic friends. Once I started drinking I didn't care that the rent wasn't paid, or that there was no food in the house, or that my boys needed shoes. I would stay out until my money was gone. Then I would go home full of remorse, and wonder what I was going to do until I got my next check.

In time, I began to go out and forget the way back home. I would wake to find myself in some beat-up rooming house, where roaches were crawling over everything. Then the time came when I couldn't afford whiskey, so I turned to wine. Finally, I got so lowdown I was ashamed of my friends seeing me, so I went to the worst joints I could find. If it was daylight, I would go down alleys to make sure no one saw me. My father was and still is a minister, and I was afraid that I might run into him, or that someone might tell him where I was, and

I could still remember what he had done to me when I got drunk one Christmas when I was very young.

I felt that I didn't have anything to live for, so I tried suicide many times. But I would always wake up in the psychiatric ward to begin another long treatment. After a while, I found that the psycho ward was a good place to hide when I had taken something stolen to the pawnshop. I thought if the cops did come to the hospital the doctors would tell them I was crazy and didn't know what I was doing. But then one good doctor told me there was nothing wrong with me except drinking too much. He said if I came back again they would send me to the state hospital. I didn't want that, so I stopped going to the psycho ward.

Now I had gotten to the place where I would wake up with black eyes and not know where I got them, or wake up with a lot of money and not know where I got it. Later, I found out that I went into stores and stole clothes, then sold them. One morning I woke up with a thousand dollars. I was trying to remember where it came from when two of the biggest cops I ever saw walked in and took me to jail. It came out that I had sold a woman a fur coat. The cops picked her up, and she told them she had bought it from me. I got out on bail right away, but when I went to trial the judge gave me thirty days. When my thirty days were up, I started back on my rounds. I didn't last long. They tell me that I killed a man during that period, but I can't remember anything. It was a total blackout. Because I had been drunk, the judge gave me only a twelve-year sentence in prison.

By the grace of God, I only served three years. It was there that I really found out what AA was. I had rejected AA on the outside, but now it came to me in prison. Today, I thank my Higher Power for giving me another chance at life and AA and being able to try and help some other alcoholic. I have been home since March, and have not taken a drink in four years.

Since I have been in AA, I have more friends than I ever had in my life—friends who care about me and my welfare, friends who don't care that I am black and that I have been in prison. All they care about is that I am a human being and that I want to stay sober. Since I've been home, I have been able to gain the respect of my two sons again. So many wonderful things have happened to me that at times I can't believe this is me. I think I am dreaming and will soon wake up.

The only thing that bothers me is that there are only about five blacks in AA in Louisville [in 1969). Even those don't take part in AA functions as I would like to see them do. I don't know if it's force of habit or something else that keeps them in one place, but I do know that in AA there is much work to do, and none of us can do it standing still. I hope I haven't hurt anyone's feelings, but maybe we could all grow and change.

I do think that some of the blacks here—and other places, too—are afraid to go to other meetings. I just want to say that you don't have to be afraid, because no one at any AA meeting will bite you. There are no color bars in AA. If you give us a try, you will see that we really are human beings, and we will welcome you with open arms and hearts. I am talking about AA people, who have gone through some of the same things that you might be going through now.

I'm writing this in my room at the Ken-Bar Inn, Gilbertville, Ky. I am at the Eighth Tri-State AA Convention, where I have spent the weekend with nothing but white people. They haven't eaten me yet! I have not seen a black face but mine since I've been here, and if I didn't look in the mirror I wouldn't know that I *was* black, because these people treat me as one of them, which I am. We all have the same sickness, and in helping one another we are able to stay sober.

I am hoping that writing this may bring some poor, mixed-up soul into the program. It's time to stop finding excuses for drinking and getting into trouble, because now there is a way out, and if you want what we have, try coming around and giving the program a chance.

B. D., Louisville, Ky.

Condemned to Live an Underground Life
July 1976

The group was a medium-sized one in a residential suburb of a large Western city. It was the weekly speaker meeting, and I was introduced as "one of our younger members from the — Group."

I stood up, identified myself as an alcoholic, and launched into the story of what I used to be like, what happened, and what I'm like now. Well, *almost*. For there is a vital part of my story that I could not tell those fine people.

"I am an alcoholic, *and* I am a practicing homosexual. I don't look it; I don't mince when I walk or wear outlandish clothes; I don't go around the room after the meeting soliciting good-looking male AAs. But the fact remains, I am a practicing homosexual." I've often speculated on the reactions of those people had I made that statement and told them the parts of my past and present that I left out or glossed over in my pitch.

For that matter, what would *your* reaction be?

Throughout the darkest depths of my drinking, I tried desperately to come to terms with the fact that I was a homosexual, a member of a minority group looked upon by great segments of society as "revolting," "disgusting," "unnatural," "queer." I lived in a triple world: the facade of a normal man; the self-abasement of alcoholic drinking; the secret knowledge of my homosexuality.

Toward the end, quantities of booze would wash away the barriers between the worlds, and I would go on a wild, alcoholic trip, motivated by my desire to be with others like me. It always ended in disaster. One trip ended in my discharge from the service as "undesirable"; another caused untold embarrassment and heartache for my family and the firm that then employed me.

No matter how hard I tried, I sank deeper and deeper into the guilt-filled whirlpool of alcohol and sexual desire. Then, one day, alcohol became the most important thing. I was drinking to be drinking, not to numb the inhibitions of social behavior so I could be what I really wanted to be. My homosexual companions and friends rejected me as an untrustworthy drunk who might give away their own secret. Several of them tried to protect me from what seemed to be eventual self-destruction. This time, I rejected them—the very people I wanted to be with. I was really all alone.

I had tried AA several times, each time for a different physical or material reason. When sober in those periods, I put on a bright mask of confidence, but I lived in fear and frustration. I got nowhere with AA. I couldn't be totally honest with myself or anyone else. I was a homosexual. So I found myself utterly alone in the world, a lousy "drunken queer."

But something changed. I wanted to get sober, because I wanted to be sober more than I wanted to drink. I went to the AA office and club in a daze, hoping that somehow, somewhere, I could get sober and stay sober. For the very first time, I asked my Higher Power to help me.

But the specter of my homosexuality was still there. "Sure, you're sober in AA again. That's nothing new," I said to myself. Then came the burning question: "But how are you going to accept the fact that you're a homosexual and, as such, must always be condemned to living an underground life, *even with your AA comrades?*"

At first, I concentrated strictly on staying sober and attending meetings. I said nothing to anyone about my "other" life. I asked the Higher Power each day to show me the way to a solution. About a month or two after I came on the program, I met another homosexual, a man much older in years and sobriety than I. One Sunday afternoon, we drove out of town to an institution to see an AA inmate. Without actually realizing I was doing it, I told this man my *real* story and told him how desperate I was to stay sober and be able to make a life for myself. I was breathless with apprehension and fear, but I *had* to tell it.

When I finished, he glanced at me with a smile on his face and said, "Welcome to AA." He told me then several things I'll never forget. The first was that it was possible to stay sober and live the life of a homosexual. There were others in the AA program; I would meet them in time. He said to me, "You didn't ask to be a homosexual, but you *are*. Short of long, difficult, and expensive psychiatric treatment, there is little chance that you can change your sexual life and desires, *even if you wanted to*. Your Higher Power knows what you are, and so do I. Your job now is to learn to live with your homosexuality, to make the best of a difficult bargain."

What a great day! I had a glimmer of hope for the first time in many years. Here was someone who understood my life, someone who knew *exactly* how I felt. It was as if a whole new life had begun. I knew it was possible to be myself and stay sober!

That was over ten years ago, and I wish I could honestly report that life has been smooth and calm since then . But, of course, that isn't true. It took months of difficult inventory-taking and many wild, emotional discussions to accept the fact that I was a homosexual. It took a couple of years of fearful experimentation to discover that I could lead a normal life. What is normal for me sexually is repugnant to the majority of people. But I have to live basically for me if I am to continue to stay sober and work this program. There have been many periods of terrible doubt and darkness, periods when I've sincerely questioned whether I could continue to lead the kind of life I lead.

But my Higher Power and the truth and wisdom of the AA way of life have given me the means to continue to grow as a person and a useful, sober member of society. I do my share of Twelfth Step work, with both heterosexual and homosexual people. I don't force my homosexuality on them. My interest is in their drinking problem. The Higher Power has enabled me to be, for me, extremely objective when working with a newcomer. I have hundreds of heterosexual friends in AA and many, many homosexual ones. Many, of both kinds, have no idea that I am a homosexual. Others know, understand, and aren't interested in my friendship for its sexual aspects.

In writing this, I am thinking that somewhere among the readership of this magazine there are other persons like me, as I once was—shakily sober, but still living in guilt and the indescribable fear that their homosexuality will prove to be an insurmountable obstacle in the path of sobriety and happiness. Have hope, my unknown friends! You *can* be happy and live a useful life. Two suggestions I might make: 1) Remember you're an alcoholic first and a homosexual second, and 2) ask *your* Higher Power for guidance and help. It's there, and it'll come to you if you sincerely want it!

S. B., San Francisco, Calif.

The Stranger
April 1952

I noticed him the first time he walked into a meeting. It was a Friday night closed gathering of the Cape Town fellowship and the presiding chairman had just started, when the door of the room opened jerkily and there he stood, strained and bewildered, as if wondering if he had done the right thing. Before he could change his mind, one of the fellows, sensing his awkwardness, jumped up from his chair and swiftly had the stranger seated.

Then a strange thing happened. No sooner were the two seated than the stranger sprang up to his full six-foot height, his face tense and working. He turned in a peculiar fashion toward the chandelier in the center of the room, as if trying to form a contact with an invisible presence. There were deep lines grooved across his tanned forehead; his thin cotton shirt, khaki trousers, and broken shoes told of dusty roads—of tramped miles. Suddenly he strode to an extreme corner of the huge room and sat down alone.

There was a slight ripple that ran through the meeting, not of laughter, but of bewilderment. The man was sober now. Glistening perspiration, twitching hands, tense muscles told us he had just pulled out. He remained motionless throughout the meeting, watching each speaker, and listening with intensity. As the prayer closed the meeting, I looked up. He was gone.

He never missed a meeting—open or closed. Always by himself, never talking to anyone and shouldering aside any contact by his usual swift exit. He always arrived immediately after the speaker had started talking, went always to an isolated place; and left before bowed heads had come up from the Lord's Prayer.

There were many questions asked as to who the stranger was, why he didn't take any literature, where he stayed. No one knew!

Six weeks after his first dramatic entrance, we were all, by now, watching the door just as the meeting began. Dead on time it opened to admit our stranger.

This time he had a brown suit and new shoes, and instead of picking his isolated chair, he sat next to me!

During the meeting, he watched, as usual, each speaker, his eyes never wavering from the talker's face. I offered him a cigarette. He ignored the proffered packet. Feeling rather foolish after holding it in front of his nose for a full minute, I pocketed my smokes. I was rather sore. This I repeated on three occasions, and each time I was completely ignored. Then came the closing of the meeting and he was still beside me. Before I could talk, he tugged my sleeve and motioned me to a quiet corner.

Then, with a charming smile, he spoke in a rich baritone: "Pat, my name is Morris. Could you tell me if they have the Big Book in Braille?"

"Why, I can make inquiries for you, Morris," I replied, "but who do you want it for?"

"For people who are handicapped, Pat."

I was puzzled as I looked at Morris, "But—I don't know of any bli–I mean handicapped alcoholics." I hesitated, stumbling, and then looking into Morris's brown eyes, a queer feeling ran through me as from what seemed a far distance I heard his voice:

"I am blind, Pat. But what you fellows have here has given me more vision and hope, plus inexpressible beauty, than human vision could ever give me. Booze was part cause of my handicap, and I was too full of pride to carry a white stick. The cops have jailed me repeatedly as a drunk, not suspecting a thing. I have hoboed every inch of this country like this. But now, thank God, at long last I'm home."

P. O., Cape Town, South Africa

I Want to Belong
January 1959

I am an alcoholic. I am an actress by profession. I am one of many in the fishbowl world who has the same deep need to belong, the same hunger for companionship, the relief from desperate loneliness that all alcoholics experience.

I have found sobriety and happiness and wonderful friends in AA. My work has improved by leaps and bounds, but I still live in the fishbowl, a finger-pointing world, and there is one place where I and many others like me should be able to find relaxation and the sense of belonging—and that is in AA.

Many of the speakers I have listened to have described the "reasons" for drinking as a desire to "be somebody" in this world, to be a "household word," to be pointed out as unique, etc. We learn in AA that the triggers for drinking are as varied as the individual and that it doesn't matter.

What of those who have achieved great "success"? Those who, because the spotlight was on them, found themselves front page items on a 502, whose marriages were spectacular failures, whose nightclub behavior was an item for every gossip column?

Being famous is no insurance against alcoholism. It is a heavy responsibility, and the alcoholic celebrity often dreams bitterly of being "like other people."

The very fact that I couldn't walk into a department store without people doing a double take, that when I dined in public there would be the thrust-out notebook for an autograph, made me, as an alcoholic, withdraw into a lonely shell, longing for friends who would accept me, who would love me and not the public figure.

All this is part of the business and can be accepted if one has a family and loved ones and friends. My drinking took the familiar pattern of self-centeredness. I suspected even those who loved me of "wanting something." I questioned every friendship suspiciously—until I had none. And I drank myself into anesthesia. Alone.

I would like to make some specific suggestions about the alcoholic celebrity and how to treat him (or her) as a result of my not too-happy experiences at AA meetings.

Treat him exactly as you do other fellow alcoholics. "Hi, Jane (or Joe)—how are you doin'?" *is music*!

Don't gush over him: "I've been an admirer of yours—I want a friend of mine to meet you—what kind of a person is Clark Gable?" etc. etc. Don't ask for autographs. (Would you ask someone in your family for one?) In asking him to speak or read the Steps, remember that one of the defects of character he is probably working on is "touchiness." He will be wondering if he is being asked *as an alcoholic* or maybe because the leader wants to bolster his own ego by capturing a celebrity. He may feel that he is expected to put on a show; to make them laugh, if he is a comedian; or to make a good speech simply because he is an actor and is "used to audiences."

Remember he has never talked about his alcoholism before an audience any more than the rest of the members. And what is more difficult—his training makes it almost impossible to be himself before an audience. He has always had the refuge of playing a character or a studied personality.

As an actor he feels very acutely "on the spot," because his refusal may seem like snobbishness. Make him welcome to speak—and free to refuse. Give him the feeling that he is safe in the bosom of a family. As an alcoholic he knows loneliness, and as a celebrity he is up to here with being singled out and made "special." He needs the same kind of encouragement and praise for his sobriety that we all do, but the last thing he needs to be told is that you have "recognized" him. He knows that.

In my own happiness, I want to be able to share it with those in my profession who are still desperately sick. I want to be able to still their fears of being stared at—even after they get sober; to help them know that in AA we are just as we are in God's eyes, individuals with a common problem. And that we can walk into an AA meeting and know the wonderful feeling: "I belong!"

Anonymous, Los Angeles, Calif.

The Great Equalizer
May 1980

The shrill ringing of the doorbell jabbed into my sleep. Another of those middle-of-the-night visitors. This one must be desperate or furious—or both. I groped for my robe and stumbled down the stairs. According to my watch, it was 2:00 AM. The porch light revealed my visitor, a man slumped against the doorjamb, his finger stuck to the bell.

"Come on in, friend," I told him, "before you wake my wife and kids." (Seven of our eight children still live at home.) I could see he had the shakes, so I guided him to a chair and went to turn on the coffee. I was sure it would be an all-night session.

He began his story the way most of us do—pretending. "Your name was given to me, Doctor. But I don't often go around disturbing my colleagues' sleep. I'm a physician, too, so I feel I can be candid with you. I believe I may have a slight problem."

I looked at him curiously. I recognized the struggle between his pride and his despair. He was still hanging on to his denial. But he was perspiring, and I knew his need for alcohol was blurring his mind.

As I watched him turn the hot coffee cup in his trembling hands, I recalled another room and another doctor, slumped in a chair with his coat collar turned up to hide his face. That physician—hostile and withdrawn—was myself, ten years ago. I can remember my surly explanation to the leader of the Alcoholics Anonymous meeting (where my wife had finally succeeded in dragging me): "My wife thinks I have a problem."

I can still hear the blunt reply of the AA, who had himself been evicted from medical school for booze addiction. He said, "Look, Buster, you may as well go home. We can use our valuable time helping somebody who really wants it." Well, nobody had ever talked to me, an important surgeon, like that. It was a revelation to me. And though I had gone into that meeting unreceptive, there was something that touched my heart and soul. That night, my renewal process began.

So now, ten years later, I put my hand on my visitor's shoulder and said, "Bill, it doesn't matter if you're a doctor, a corporation executive, or a garbage collector. You are an alcoholic seeking recovery. It's hard to admit you have this disease, but it is the first necessary step. Now, you have got to have two things: *a commitment to yourself and a program for sobriety.*"

Bill sat with his head in his hands. "Was it very hard for you to stay off?" he asked softly.

Hard? I was what they call a white-knuckled nondrinking drunk. For the first eleven months, I stayed sober by the hands of my watch. I was physically sick for seventeen months, chronically fatigued for the first three years, and mentally scattered for a long time. Then, one morning, I was in my backyard, and the sun was shining. I knew something was different. I was free. The craving was gone. I was in the world again, and it was beautiful.

"Yes," I answered. "It was painful. But the joy of being alive again is worth every second of the pain."

Would Bill make it? He was no more deeply submerged in his personal pit than I had been. In the process of my enslavement, I lost my dignity, my medical license, my practice (and with it the trappings of an expensive life-style—houses, cars, boats); also, I came near to losing all I held dear in life—my wife and the respect of my children. One can become so addicted that one's whole thought content changes. However, under the self-pity and hopelessness of my former life, a few shreds of my childhood religious faith still remained. And that proved to be the seed of my salvation.

"You're a surgeon—right, Bill? Well, I can tell you that a surgeon can cut, but only God can heal. The forces of man can help an alcoholic free himself from chemical dependence, but they are almost powerless unless they have the gift of knowledge from the source. I know for a fact, Bill, that God can heal the broken spirit and the blasted mind; he can eradicate the scars of alcoholism. He can reunite a family and bring back peace and harmony and joy."

Bill's defenses were finally broken down. I was pretty sure that he had made the *commitment* and was ready to start on the *program*.

What makes an alcoholic different from others who drink? That question haunts doctors like me as we treat those whose ruined lives bear witness to the tenacity of a disease afflicting millions. Could there be a metabolic abnormality? Perhaps. When I was a child, I couldn't tolerate honey. After I stopped drinking, I carried a honey jar around with me and also gorged myself with ginger ale or any carbohydrate that could keep me from shaking.

Is there a hereditary influence? Perhaps. My father, a Canadian judge, was a teetotaler. His father died drunk. I had my first drink, a glass of ale, when I was twenty-six, celebrating my graduation from medical school. Everyone else in my group had just one glass; I immediately ordered another.

But alcoholism is in a way like other diseases (cancer for one); it is not unique in the complexity of its cause, which is not really pertinent to recovery.

In the treatment facility where I work, we treat alcoholics who are extroverts and those deeply inhibited; those who are nervous, neurotic, calm, or passive. Women executives living alone in condominiums and imbibing secretly find their way to us. We treat loners and leaders, priests and potentates, and just plain folk from the mainstream of America.

For the alcoholic, there is no such thing as moderate drinking. I remember David, who walked hesitantly into our clinic one day, immaculately groomed, obviously a man with leadership skills. Shortly after David's retirement as head of a prestigious law firm, his wife died. In his bitter loneliness, he formed the habit of having a tumbler of wine before dinner. He told us, "I have just realized I don't get to eat my dinner anymore. I just drink it. And if I can't sleep, I have another glass, and then one during the night. I believe I have a problem."

Here was a brilliant, decent man whose dependence on alcohol had sneaked up on him. I told him, "David, I can assure you with absolute certainty, from my experience as a participant and spectator, that no problem will ever be alleviated with booze. None. The only approach to recovery for those of us whose primary passion is drinking is total abstinence. We are alcoholics, but we can always be sober."

A commitment and a program. I think of Amy, a bright and cooperative patient who had done well in her primary recovery stage. "What's your program, Amy?" I asked her as she prepared to leave.

"Oh, I'm fine, Doctor. I don't want to drink anymore." "Yes, but what defense have you set up?"

"Well, I plan to get busier."

"Amy," I said, "you've been here thirty days—and you don't have a program for the days ahead?" I asked her to memorize the Twelve Steps to recovery set up by Alcoholics Anonymous. Without support systems, a patient may delay progress.

There is still a low level of public awareness of the problems of alcoholism. Until recently, the stigma was akin to that attached to leprosy in biblical times. Many an alcoholic, confronted with the intervention process, will deny his addiction. Yet alcoholism *can* be treated; we constantly return patients to productive lives. It is a common misconception that an alcoholic needs to hit bottom before starting back up. Not so! The disease of alcoholism is progressive, and so is recovery. It can be accomplished in stages. An afflicted patient can be taught to take the first step up. The time to get sober is *right now*. The time to start improving is *today*. No alcoholic needs to suffer further degradation. Attaining a new life is like riding on an elevator: You push a button, and you can get off on any floor you wish. You can go up or down, but you certainly don't have to go all the way down.

Another cliche is equally true: We keep sobriety by giving it away. When I went, reluctantly, to my first AA meeting, I was on a desperate treadmill. But as a half hour passed, something penetrated my closed mind. I began to get a feeling of hope. There was something about those people; they seemed carefree, and there was a joy I hadn't experienced for a long time. Then there was total acceptance for that chap in the corner—me—who was ill and miserable. There was, in fact, love in that room.

This is not to say that all meetings are a panacea. Occasionally, a person will enter a meeting with the wrong attitude—irritation or depression, sometimes inevitable—and the meeting seems dull. But if alcoholics persevere, continue to attend, they find a mystical magic there, an indefinable spiritual quality that permeates them and helps them not to drink and to want to become completely well.

I can only emphasize that the trauma surrounding the lives of drinking alcoholics is unnecessary. We can abort the disease if it is recognized and if intervention is intelligent and loving.

The second of the Twelve Steps of Alcoholics Anonymous reads: "Came to believe that a Power greater than ourselves could restore us to sanity." To me, this clearly means a surrender to his will and a reliance on his grace. This Step provides us with a springboard to a new life. In my own family—perhaps because of our adversities—there is a new, joyful intimacy, an interaction and a communication among us. There is love.

J.R., San Diego, Calif.

TWO

Stay Sober and Help Other Alcoholics

———————— ♦ ————————

Unmanageable Lives
October 1978

In the first of AA's Twelve Steps of recovery, the dilemma seen by AA newcomers is set out: "Look what you people have done to us! You have convinced us that we are alcoholics and that our lives are unmanageable."

What separates the alcoholic's life from the nonalcoholic's life in this regard is that the alcoholic has a self-prescribed, temporary cure for the unmanageability of his life—booze. Aha, we say, but we're in AA and have found that it's possible to stay away from the first drink for twenty-four hours by asking for help and getting to meetings. Presto! We won't pick up that temporary cure. Right? Just maybe, very maybe.

There's an old story around law schools about how the law got started. A man moves to a new continent or a new island, builds a house, and plants his crops. He has no need for laws. It is only when a second man moves onto the island that there arises an immediate need for a third man. In the Old West, they called him the lawman. As soon as the second man arrives, some rules are needed as to how the two men will live with each other, and a neutral third man is needed to see that the first two follow their own rules.

The lesson of the story is that so long as there are more than one of us on this earth, our lives will be unmanageable to some extent. Other folks aren't always or even often going to do what we think they ought to do. People don't like having their lives manipulated by others, and alcoholics are among the world's great manipulators, or at least would-be manipulators.

Studies indicate that, by and large, alcoholics are a bright lot, regardless of the amount of formal education any one of us might have. Many of us managed to con our way through some parts of our lives, and most tended to do reasonably well at whatever it was that we did for a living, for so long as booze allowed us to. These same characteristics reinforced our impression that if only we could get sober, and stay sober, the world would be putty in our hands. Unfortunately, the world is made of firmer stuff.

To make matters worse, Mother Nature has a great deal to say about the manageability of our lives. She'll snow us in or rain us out, without even a smile. Somehow, the old gal can get her hands on our most modest plans—a cookout, a day at the beach, or a little golf with friends. Mother Nature is definitely not manageable, even less manageable than the people and objects around us.

Those objects bear mentioning, too, In addition to the laws of men and the laws of nature, there are also Murphy's laws. Nobody seems to know who Murphy was, but his first law is: if anything can go wrong, it will. So long as we own or want the things the world has to offer, Murphy's laws will apply—to our houses, cars, lawn mowers, electrical and water supplies, just about everything.

Some of Murphy's other laws are: A dropped tool will land where it can do the most damage (also known as the law of selective gravitation); all warranty and guarantee clauses will become void just before the last payment is made; the instruction manual will get thrown out about a week before the first time the thing breaks down; and finally, left to themselves, things usually go from bad to worse! Murphy may not have known about alcoholism, but he sure knew about unmanageability.

In the face of traffic officers, thunderstorms, and Murphy's laws, alcoholics still bound through life convinced that it's all manageable. There are no medals for their persistence, for, in truth, large chunks of everybody's life are unmanageable at best, drunk or sober, alcoholic or nonalcoholic.

Lest we think the unmanageability of life is all bad, it isn't. Sometimes unmanageability comes bearing gifts. We win a sweepstakes and are faced with the temptation of a spending spree. Alcoholics have been known to get promoted unexpectedly, sometimes when a boss is let go because of a drinking problem. And then there are the leftovers from our drinking days, some of which can suddenly turn our way—a criminal charge dropped, a wife who has a change of heart, a decent job opportunity when we have been convinced we were unemployable.

For the nonalcoholic, an unmanageable world and life may mean frustration, fear, anger, sometimes even mental illness, and sometimes great cause for celebration. For the alcoholic, unmanageability carries also the very real danger of death. That is why AA literature calls the high emotions that result from the unmanageability of life the "dubious luxuries" of nonalcoholics. Emotional sprees, high or low, lead us to believe we can or must fall back on our own resources.

In every day of every life, there can be a series of broken shoelaces or a winning ticket, an ankle-deep rainfall or a new car, a speeding ticket or a long-feared criminal charge that is favorably resolved. Perhaps the world should be posted: "Laws at Work—Natural, Manmade, Murphy's, and Pure Luck." For the alcoholic, there should be a second sign: "Danger—Obsession Ahead!"

The unmanageable aspect is part of day-to-day living and carries in it the trigger for the alcoholic's obsession with drink. All the laws that are at work in the world are going to make every life unmanageable to one degree or another from time to time. But for the alcoholic there is not only an additional danger, but also an additional opportunity. AA offers us a program of recovery from our past feelings about the unmanageability of life, a program that can put life's unmanageability into perspective. That's more than most of the rest of the people in the world have going for them when they find their lives have become unmanageable.

J. F., Wellesley, Mass.

Martian Report on the Curious Cult of "Alcohol" Drinkers
May 1961

Fellow members of the Martian Academy:
     My report on the first Mars expedition to planet Earth would not be complete without brief mention of the curious custom which centers around a substance which Earth-people call alcohol. Although alcohol is unknown here on Mars (our planet life and atmosphere do not contain the necessary elements to manufacture it), it is consumed in many forms on Earth.

Alcohol is a colorless, volatile liquid. Since it causes a burning sensation on the tongue and in the throat when imbibed, Earth-people combine it with water and flavoring agents to make it potable. Also, it is often given a pleasing amber color, for aesthetic effect.

The ritual of alcohol drinking is most difficult for a Martian to comprehend. We have nothing like it on our well-ordered planet. Earth-people of both sexes drink alcohol with intense fervor, gathering for the ceremony in dimly lit temples where they must raise their voices to be heard over the sound from automatic music machines.

The alcohol is dispensed by a Grand Mogul whose robe of authority consists of a white cloth tied about the waist and hanging freely to the knees. In larger halls he is assisted by handmaidens who wear similar white aprons.

The Mogul officiates at a mahogany altar backed with colored lights, ornaments and rows of glass containers of varying shapes, but all filled with the solution which he dispenses. An alcoholic potion is prepared in small glasses by the Mogul and handed to the slavish subjects over the barricade. This evidently symbolizes his exclusive and elevated role.

In exchange for his quantity of alcohol, the drinker hands the Mogul one of the tokens of metal or paper which are prized so highly by

Earth-people. The large number of these tokens which Earth-people exchange for drinks of alcohol is evidence of the importance which the drinking ritual plays in their lives.

One member of the MEF (Martian Expeditionary Force) sampled some of the alcohol and reported decidedly unpleasant effects: dizziness, difficulty in speech articulation, cloudy memory, a lethargy in the limbs.

The Earth-men who were acting as our hosts insisted that the volunteer try additional samples. There were remarks about a bird (a type of Earth-creature) flying on one wing. Our volunteer protested, but not wanting to be impolite, he allowed additional doses to be administered. What followed is outside the scope of this report; in brief, our poor companion had to be carried back to our spaceship to recover. He reported, upon regaining consciousness, that the experience was somewhat like the illness we often endure on Mars during the annual advance of the ice cap, when we have to resort to artificial foods.

We concluded that alcohol drinking is bound up in some way with the search for Truth and Happiness which is such an obsession with Earth-people. Some alcohol drinkers are more devout and persevering in this search than others, and their ecstasy often reaches a trance-like state, at which time they fall to the ground unconscious. Others make their way forth from the hall, uttering incoherent prayers and propelling themselves erratically in machines known as automobiles.

The alcohol persuasion leads a few to a monastic way of life. They renounce family and friends, their vocation, and all worldly pleasures, to carry out their devotionals. Some of these retire from human company for days at a time, to perform secret rites which, we are told, alternate between lengthy trances and disordered wakefulness.

A word must be said about a small but growing sect of comparatively recent origin, made up of those who have attained the rank of High Prophets of the alcohol cult. They evidently have found the answers which others are seeking in drinking alcohol. The knowledge was gained through such suffering and hardship that it is coveted and passed on only to those whose similar experience has led them to the threshold of understanding. These chosen ones meet surreptitiously, refer to each other by first names only, and their membership in the sect is known only to other members.

While each of them was at one time a dedicated practitioner of the alcohol-drinking ritual, they now joyfully shun alcohol on all occasions and devote much time to instructing novices in the secrets of the order.

They speak frequently of their search for Truth and Happiness, but under their new doctrine these treasures are found everywhere *except* in alcohol. This radical belief is regarded as subversive by many Earth-people, so members of the sect go about in anonymity. Their anonymity is not perfect; we noted they wore expressions of serenity seldom observed on the faces of other Earth-people, and they seemed to retain admirable composure at times when others were wringing their hands over the vexing problems of Earth-life.

It is our recommendation that the Martian Academy undertake further study of the alcohol cult on Earth to learn to what extent it may be responsible for the chaotic social conditions on that unfortunate planet. When our next expedition is dispatched—carrying colonists and missionaries to teach the Martian Way of Life—we must be equipped with as much knowledge as possible to help us get along peacefully with the Earth-people. If, indeed, it is possible to get along peacefully at all with people of such peculiar habits.

R. Z., Council Bluffs, Iowa

Eager Beaver
August 1975

I used to do all the things I was told to do in AA, no matter who told me to do them. "Never say 'No' in this program." "Make meetings, meetings, meetings." "Get active!"

When I came to AA eight years ago, I was destitute. I had lost two kids (for the fourth time). My husband had left me. My home was gone. My parents made it plain they didn't want me coming home to them (and Daddy was sober several years in AA).

I had tried many other avenues first. (AA? I wasn't that bad!) I had been hospitalized fifty-five times. (I know, because my husband used to wave the sheet of Blue Cross and Blue Shield receipts in my face, and count them to me one by one as proof of how he was trying.) I had been saved at the altar about three dozen times, had been healed at eight or ten healing services, and had spent approximately $18,000 on psychiatrists, not to mention the elaborate private violent ward where I lived for seven or eight weeks. I tried meditating on graves in the cemetery to make contact with God, and the police put me in jail, where I sang gospel songs. But I didn't stay sober or clean. The state hospital was a bit cheaper than the private wards, though living conditions were not so good. However, it was there that I was introduced to AA.

When they told me to get to meetings, I believed them. In my town, there was only one meeting a week, and I made it faithfully. I doubted that was enough, so I started a new group and attended its meetings. Many times, I drove sixty miles to another town and another meeting. I was grateful to have meetings. I had been around the program for three years (never making less than one meeting a week), and a couple of months' sobriety was all I had going for me. My children had been taken away again (while I was out doing ninety days' research with a super-AA guy who had been around the program for seventeen years—with several thirty-day periods of sobriety). I was still unemployable, and the state was paying me a meager $90 a month to stay off the labor market. I lived wherever anyone would let me shack up or room and board. I had no husband to take care of and no house to keep. I had all the time in the world to go to meetings, and I anxiously welcomed them. In the next few months, I became GSR of the group I had started and secretary of the other one.

After a year, I was possibly employable, so, on my analyst's and my sponsor's advice, I tried a full-time job. I worked forty hours a week in a rest home for the elderly and still made two meetings a week. Soon after that, I began Twelfth Step work and was put on a local AA conference committee. I attended about seven conferences that year. A year later, I got a better job and became editor of our AA newsletter.

Because of "my" splendid record (the grace of God, actually), I got a smashingly upsetting phone call one day, asking whether I would like to try to make a home for my two children. God knows, I did want to. I set about getting a house, looking for it when I wasn't at work or at meetings. I finally found it, scrounged some furniture together, and brought the two kids (seven and nine years old) home. I hardly knew them. They had been away from me a good part of four years. Now I had two kids, a forty-hour-a-week job, answering service duty, two meetings a week, the GSR job, the secretary job, and the conference committee.

Within the next few months, I met a wonderful man in the program. After a three-year courtship (which my sponsor helped me with), we were married on his third AA birthday. In the meantime, I had enrolled in college and was studying as well as working. Now we set up a real household. I was a wife, mother of two kids, college student, part-time employee, editor of the newsletter, GSR, secretary, housekeeper, and twelfth-stepper.

Three months later, to add to my many blessings, I found that the impossible had happened. The doctors had told me ten years before that I would never have any more children, but now I was pregnant. Nine months later, I had three children, a job, a husband, a home to maintain, still more meetings I was going to, the GSR job at another group, secretary at still another, trips to conferences, and the presidency of the conference committee I had been on all along. Oh yes—by now I was sponsoring three or four new babies (depending on how many were around at the time).

A month later, we made a major move halfway across the United States to live with my new mother and father-in-law for three months while my husband and I hunted for new jobs and got resettled in AA. Luckily for me, there were twenty-three meetings a week in our new location, and God knows I needed them. I began making approximately eight meetings a week. Of course, with a job (forty hours a week), a three-month-old baby, two teenagers, a husband, and a home, my life was somewhat chaotic. Kids went unfed; husband went uncared for; but I made my meetings. I not only made meetings, but immediately got *active*. Because I was a "worker," I was elected GSR of one group and secretary of another. Because of my experience, I was elected to a conference committee here, too, and my name went on the Twelfth Step and answering service lists right away. By my third AA birthday, I was sponsoring eight new people, plus all the other activities. And by my fourth AA birthday, after a year of keeping up the same pace, I stopped at the grocery store one afternoon and bought a quart of booze...

Someone had mentioned to me that perhaps I was too busy. Sure, but so what? I *had* to get to meetings. I had to be active. I *had* to be responsible. I had to never say "No." I *had* to do everything they told me to do, in order to get the benefits of the program.

"What do I do with my benefits?"

That's what I was asking myself. What had happened to "practice these principles in all our affairs"? There was only so much of me to spread around. What about the hostilities I created with my older children when I left them with a crying baby—because I *had* to get to meetings, because my sobriety came first? What about the piles of dirty laundry stacked in the bedroom, because I had three committee meetings and seven other meetings that week? I was losing my sanity and my serenity, and my sobriety wasn't so solid either...

When I took that bottle back to the store (thank God, I did not drink it), I made some new priorities.

I went to meetings (two to four a week) like a newcomer. I said "No." I gave all the activities I had to someone else. Surprisingly enough, there were others who could handle them. I let go of the eight people I was trying to sponsor. I took quiet moments by myself two or three times a day. I paused whenever I was agitated and confused (many times a day), and asked for the right thoughts and actions. I cooked meals. I fed the baby and rocked him to sleep. I talked to my husband. I did laundry. I sat in the bathtub for as long as an hour at a time and read the Big Book. I unwound inside. I *listened* to my Higher Power. I did my share of the load at work.

From some of the AA long-timers I had once thought boring, I learned the difference between *activity* and *action*. I took another personal inventory. I thanked God many times that I did not find it necessary to drink through this ordeal.

Today, exactly one year has passed since the day I almost got drunk, after four years of sobriety and seven years around AA. Tonight is my night at home with the family, to cook for them, to love them, to share with them. I went to a meeting last night. I am not GSR of any group right now, nor am I secretary, nor president of any committee, nor editor of any newsletter. I am learning my limitations. I give my telephone number to newcomers, and talk to them. Now, I *listen* in meetings. In over four sober years of attending a total of about 300 meetings I passed only once when I was called on to speak. My sponsor told me to be still and listen. Just recently, I have begun to *hear* what people say.

I am now getting acquainted with my thirteen-year-old son. Last week, a friend asked me what some of his likes and dislikes were, and I had to admit I didn't know him that well. I am finding out. I take him swimming once a week, and we are getting to know each other.

These benefits have been given to me as a result of doing what I have been told to do in this program, and I believe I am meant to take care of them. These benefits—children, job, husband, home, friends, Mama and Daddy—are mine to practice the principles with. Thank God and AA, now I am responsible.

J. Y., Sparks, Nev.

Divided I Stand
November 1968

That's right. One foot in AA and the other foot in the civilian world. Divided I stand, like thousands of other AAs who are married to nonalcoholics. I have heard glowing reports of Al-Anon, but my husband flatly refused to go to Al-Anon. Also, from the beginning of my AA life, he made it quite clear that he had no intention of sitting home nights with our three cats and the TV set while I gallivanted off to meetings. And he made it equally clear that I was to expect no coddling or pampering just because I was sober.

I am thankful that my husband had a fairly open mind. He comprehended the value of the Slogans, the Serenity Prayer, and the one-day-at-a-time approach. He even appropriated what he could use. So I had no skepticism to deal with, no denigration of the AA program.

We had been married for five years when I came into AA. I had already gone over the narrow line from heavy drinker to alcoholic before I was married, but no one seemed aware of it—probably because I was a weekend binge drinker, still able to exert some control on weekdays. The first two and a half years of marriage were one long, agonizing effort at control. Many times, I entertained guests, with no memory whatever of what I had served for dinner, nor of how I had conducted myself afterward. Of course, I always pushed drinks on everybody so they wouldn't notice my heavy consumption or (I hoped) my behavior.

The last two and a half years were ghastly. By then I was alternately confessing and denying to myself that I was an alcoholic. I don't think my husband knew what an alcoholic was except for the Bowery-bum type. To him, I was perverse, weak-willed, etc. He was baffled, miserable, resentful. Only an awful lot of love could have put up with the mess that I had become.

I joined AA with my husband's blessing, and after the first week or so he began attending open meetings with me. However, if I mentioned going to any meeting besides the two a week at my group, he grumbled that I was doing fine and why did I need to go. In all fairness, I realized that he had spent his evenings with a zombie for years, so I felt I ought to please him.

Reluctantly, I decided I could not go to several meetings a week, as other new members were doing. I ached to go. I was in love with AA. I yearned to throw myself into the program as a parched desert prospector wants to leap into a water hole. (I love that water hole bit.) Instead, I had to channel my enthusiasm into hospital visits to new members, daytime Twelfth Step work, a turn on the phones at our central office, and quite a bit of speaking. These things, plus my two group meetings a week, kept me sober and on the program: Also, I read all of our books and literature, and rationed myself to make each issue of the Grapevine last a whole month.

As I began feeling better physically; as well as clearing up mentally, I tried to live a "normal" life. But strange things began happening. When I entertained the same people I had known for years before AA, it just didn't work out very well. I had told a few of them I was in AA, but most did not know. A lot of them were heavy drinkers, and I began resenting their lushful emptying of my bottles of liquor during an evening, their boring, repetitive stories. So I cut out the heavy drinkers and hung on to the "light" imbibers, who did not bother me. In fact, I scarcely noticed whether they had one, two, or three, for I was drinking my one or two or more cups of coffee at the same time.

But again strange things happened. Although these friends didn't bother me (their drinking didn't, that is), my coffee began to bother them. I think they began to feel uncomfortable about drinking booze while I refrained. They began to make excuses not to come over so often, and when they did come they hurriedly explained they'd already had a drink, thank you. So I cut *them* out.

About this time, we were being invited now and then to AA parties. Sometimes there were other nonalcoholics like my husband, but more often there were not. Since he cares little or nothing for liquor, that aspect didn't bother him; but he just couldn't take all that coffee and all those hours of animated chatter about AA matters. He felt left out, a stranger in an alien land. He began making excuses not to go. I overheard him telling a friend of his, "They live in a different world. They understand each other; but you can't understand or join in. It's no use trying."

I could see his point of view; I wanted desperately to be fair and to make him happy. So we stopped going to AA parties. It seemed a dilemma. We had no social life at all except for visits with relatives.

Finally, I took up a hobby— after hearing a woman speaker state that all AAs should get a hobby as soon as they had been sober a few years. I began art classes in a small school. After a while, my husband decided to study sculpture at the same school. We began meeting interesting new people; we joined an art club. The school and the club provided some social life with people who knew nothing of my drinking problem. Occasionally, one or two noticed that I didn't drink; but made no comment on it. (A lot of people in this world don't drink, and they aren't all alcoholics, either!) The point is that I was at ease with them, and they with me. Since then, together, my husband and I have formed new friendships and found good friends. At parties, I hold a glass of ginger ale in my hand; no one seems to know or care what's in the glass.

Over a period of time, we have also made friends socially with AA couples, some of them half-and-half as we are, and some not. Most of the members have been in the program for a while, long enough to incorporate AA into their lives, not the other way round. Sobriety is the first concern with all of us who are alcoholics, but we are also interested in the world about us, in our jobs and children and hobbies.

It has taken a long time, and a lot of experiments in friend-making, to arrive where we are now. After many years, I still go to my two-a-week meetings at my own group. On the other five nights, I live as any normal person would live—with, of course, a few exceptions: no more big, horrendous cocktail parties; no more big evening bashes;

no more drink-swilling pals. I don't want them or need them, and my husband says he loathes them and always did. The fact is, our marriage now is workable, rewarding, and just about as happy as we care to make it—one day at a time.

F. C., New York, N.Y.

The Answers Will Come
December 1977

T he meeting had been over for two hours, but the warmth of it lingered. It was midnight on a Friday, and I lounged in bed feeling good about my sobriety, the lead of that evening, the words of advice from my sponsor, the horselaughs of an old-timer being kidded about his multicolored sport jacket.

The ring of the phone cut into my thoughts. It was a police detective. "We've picked up your son Christopher. He was caught smoking marijuana and drinking beer in the park. We'd like you to come get him."

This was the third time Chris had been nailed for the same offense, beer and grass. The other two times, the sheriff had brought him home. After several weeks of being confined to the house, no privileges but plenty of boredom, the incidents were forgotten. Now, the scab was being picked again. I saw myself in Chris. Was he headed toward the insane way of life that delivered me so much grief? What could I do to help him?

Because of that night's meeting and all the meetings before, I had no desire to take a drink. I prayed as I drove to the jailhouse. I thought of the promise the Big Book makes on page 84: "We will intuitively know how to handle situations which used to baffle us."

The three teenage boys were seated around a conference room table. Their backs were to me when I came into the room. They didn't see me enter. Several other parents were silently standing about. The arresting officer was seated across from the boys. At the end of the table was a plainclothes detective with a gun tucked in his belt, reading the riot act to the glazed-out kids.

One of the boys was crying. He couldn't remember his phone number or his mother's name. Obviously, it was his first clash with the law.

The other boy was red-faced and sullen. His mother threatened to "box his ears" when he got home. She'd need a ladder to reach them. The kid was over six feet tall.

Chris sat there like he was in geography class. Relaxed. No problem. Soon, it'd be all over and forgotten.

Exactly the way it was with me. Somebody was always lining my bottom with soft goose feathers. I was always forgiven for my drunks. Punishment was threatened, rarely delivered. Regardless of what I did or who I hurt, I would invariably hear: "You're not an alcoholic." Or "One more time and you'd better have your resume written. Now get back to your office." Or "Do it again and I'll go home to Mother. What do you want for supper?" I was always let off the hook as gently as possible.

The detective continued to chew on the kids. One of the fathers leaned against the wall. He was half in the bag. Fumes of bourbon began to drift over to me.

If that had been me during my drinking days, I wouldn't have been at home when the phone rang. Not on a Friday night. And if bad luck had put me near the phone, I'd have been more than slumping on the wall. I'd probably have been shouting advice to my son from the drunk tank.

Suddenly, I felt tremendously virtuous. For the first time in my life, I was looking at angry cops who weren't directing their wrath at me. I saw myself standing there like a statue, an angel with folded hands, eyes piously closed, dressed in a long white gown with sandals, with a halo shedding rays of goodwill upon everyone in the room.

I snapped back to reality when the detective looked up at the parents and asked if there were any questions. Silence. He dismissed the boys and told us to take them home. That's when I screwed up the courage to speak. Courage is the right word. When I see men wearing guns, I tend to clam up.

Chris, the two police officers, and I sat alone at the table. I mentioned that this wasn't Christopher's first offense. Then, words came to me that seemed to get through to my son.

"I can't change you, Chris. I can't make you stop drinking and smoking grass. There is no punishment I can offer that will keep you out of trouble. These officers can't change you, either. In spite of all the threats they made tonight, you'll be back here again and again until you change your attitude. You're the only one who can change you. Nobody else can do it. I learned that the hard way, and I hope you don't have to travel that path.

"So I'm asking the arresting officer to do you a big favor. I want him to write a note on your file that the next time you get in trouble, you'll be put behind bars. When they call me at home, I don't want to be told to come and get you. The only way you'll learn is by hitting your bottom as hard and as painfully as possible. Wake up in the drunk tank in the midst of vomit and urine. Face the judge with sweat rolling off your skin, with your head pounding and your body stinking and your soul filled with terror and remorse."

I can hear his grandmother saying, "How can you love your son and treat him that way?"

My answer is "Because I love him."

Chris values my sobriety. I believe he isn't copying my actions of the past. If he is, that's something else I can't change. Yet I'm convinced that if I got drunk, his heart would be broken. It may be he has the same disease I have. If so, thank God I have the tools he may eventually be using. They are available because I'm available.

One of the beautiful things about AA is the sharing of problems and insights. A member of the Fellowship told me of his son, who has a drug and booze problem, had a car accident last week, and was just released from the hospital with more than a hundred stitches in his body. Another dear friend told me of his son, who isn't walking around today. This young man received a stiff jail sentence for sticking up a filling station while under the two influences.

I grieve for them as I do for my son. But I can't change them. Only myself. My problems haven't gone away just because I'm sober. The truth is, they've increased. But it's a joy to fearlessly face the problems with serene confidence that the answers will intuitively come. Page 84 of the Big Book says so. It's the God's truth.

L. C., Fort Wayne, Ind.

Get a Fresh Start
June 1965

From personal experience and observation, I would say there are a number of us in AA who have almost more difficulty with jobs after we get sober than we did while drinking.

I know that before AA I was firmly established in the public relations and editorial field. I should qualify "firmly" to this extent: I had manufactured an aura of efficiency about my daily operations that fooled a lot of people. I was always being complimented by acquaintances who were not my bosses. And until the last year of my drinking, even the bosses felt fortunate to have me on their staff.

But came the shakes, long lunch hours, procrastination, and I resigned—before I was fired!

I became a "free-lancer" in public relations. I was really unemployed, but the former description sounded better on a resume. Through a process of elimination (I was the cheapest available), I became editor of two small trade magazines, which were already failing miserably. As I was little more than a zombie, their downward spiral continued. I never reached the office before 10:30 AM, left at 11:30 for "luncheon dates," came back tipsy at two, and worked feverishly until five.

There were, of course, many days when I skipped the office altogether. But I always managed to meet the magazine deadlines. Frequently, when the finished product was placed before me, I didn't recognize it. I would read parts I had written while drunk which I swear I had never seen before.

I was still with the magazines when I joined AA. I became beautifully sober, gloriously happy with the pink cloud of a newcomer and three weeks past deadline on the January 1959 issue.

I never caught up! I even combined two months into one issue (we had very tolerant or indifferent subscribers), and that still left me overdue on the current month's copy.

It wasn't only the magazines—I felt out of step with the whole atmosphere of my drinking world. I tried having lunch with close friends but their talk bored me. I was absorbed in a new life of AA, and the entire process of earning a living suddenly lost all its previous excitement and intrigue.

I quit the magazine, even left the city and found the dullest possible job in the suburbs. New faces surrounded me; I no longer had to make decisions, and I loved it—for three months.

I struggled for years to become established in a different field and today am happily engrossed in that career.

Before I found a foothold, however, there was much despair on my part because I had had to leave *everything* behind. There was, of course, no valid reason I could not have perhaps even saved those little magazines; no reason except my sobriety and my sanity. Regardless of what anyone else might have done under the same circumstances, I could not have wrestled with all the pressures of the old business and stayed sober.

I see people getting sober in AA every week who continue in the same job they've had for years. And they do such a bang-up *sober* job, they get promotions. This, to me, is fantastic and I envy them.

But there are persons who have had my experience: an accountant who became a contractor; a bank teller who opened a dress shop; a housewife who is now a barber; a trade association employee turned college professor.

I know of others who have left their former employment and are still floundering. I wish I had words to give them that would unlock the secret to successful reestablishment of their careers. All I can say is that, with me, the greatest factor was *time*. Time soothed the harshness of adjustment and somehow eased me into a comfortable new niche.

With the raise I have just received, I am now earning exactly what I was five years ago when I joined AA. That may not be the wildest kind of progress, but I've noticed an important reaction to the paycheck on my part. Today I really work for my money; I am no longer concerned that someone will call my bluff and fire me.

V. B., Falls Church, Va.

Did Anonymity Help Kill Jim?
February 1972

I have been led to believe that anonymity is a fact of my life that is only for me and perhaps a few close friends to know—a well-guarded spiritual enigma.

After all, the group I belong to still prints only my first name and last initial in the monthly group bulletin. I never questioned this. They have been doing it for years. I assumed it was to keep our egos in line, to keep us from getting too "famous." In retrospect, I realize that we all know one another's last names fairly well. *The New York Times* is not waiting with bated breath to publish our names.

I have been sober seven years—not only sober, but happy and productive in all areas of my life. You can't ask for much more than that. I work for a large organization. I began working for them after sobriety. They know me only as a sober man.

I had a co-worker named Jim. He drank to the point where it was obvious to all of us at work that he had a problem. I worked closely with Jim for two years. He had a part-time job as a bartender, and our company assumed that this was the reason for him coming to work late and smelling of whiskey.

I talked to Jim. I heard his resentments. I often knew what he was going to say before he did. I smiled. I kept my secret. I knew that eventually, when he asked, I would be able to help him.

I kept my anonymity. I felt he would appreciate this when he was ready. He would love us AAs for not being glory-seekers, though sober—simply sober people acting ordinary. I felt that he would really respond to this great humility. So I kept the secret that, I thought, gave sparkle to my eyes, the secret that, I felt, gave me the most marvelous advantage over the civilian world. Yes sir!

I have just come from Jim's funeral.

Something went wrong with my scheme. Jim drove through a red light on the way home from that night bartending job—the job he had held, not to make ends meet, but to be able to afford his habit. His widow is twenty-three. His two confused children were there, cute as buttons. I stared at them and wondered whether I could have helped. I certainly would not have hurt.

I know I did not kill Jim. But I did waste two whole years of chances. All I might have had to do was tell him I was an AA member. That's all. I realize now that the Eleventh Tradition asks us to keep our anonymity only in newspapers and on TV and radio. It does not prohibit us from telling friends.

Now I have started to tell people I am in AA. I see the zealous guarding of my secret was a reservation on my part. I was afraid I would drink again and they would all laugh at the Great Me. I lacked complete faith in our marvelous program. I lacked courage to speak up for the very thing I love most in life—AA.

No more. If a sadness like this ever happens again, it won't be because I did not love my fellowman enough to tell him about myself, to weather his temporary scorn, perhaps. And then...well, who knows?

There will never be another Jim in my life. I understand anonymity now.

E. S., Brooklyn, N.Y.

Boy Lying in the Grass
August 1962

When I was a boy, a summer vacation in the country always contained a good deal of fishing, not to mention hunting crawdads, shooting at crows with an air rifle, catching bullfrogs, collecting old birds' nests, and attempts to tattoo ourselves with ordinary pen and ink. But there were also hours of heavenly loafing, lying in tall grass, chewing a straw and listening to the insects making "a joyful noise unto the Lord."

It was heavenly just to be alive. Then, as the years wheeled by, the world seemed to fade. Things no longer glowed from inside with their own light, and the time came when a landscape had to be seen through a haze of whiskey before it spoke of peace. Even then it was only for a little while—a mirage that faded as the vision blurred and the booze conquered.

Summer then was a bitter mockery of the hints of heaven which had come to me in boyhood and I solaced myself with more drinks, as any alcoholic knows. I thought that the years of peace and wonder had gone forever; the years when little things—a butterfly poised on a porch rail, a scarlet tanager on a branch by the window, the taste of mocha cake with brown sugar filling —held so much excitement that the heart could stand no more.

When I was finally guided into our Fellowship, I thought it would be a dull routine at best, free from the tyranny of booze but lived under a constant sky of deadly grey. The surprise I got at finding the little delights of sheer living again was one of the treasures AA brought to me. But I know from conversations and from listening to speakers, that this happy innocence of a boy's view of life doesn't come back to all of us. And I've been wondering why.

I don't think the loss of it is confined to alcoholics. I think it is the spirit of the times which sweeps over us like a fog, obscuring the sun. For it is no news that this is the Age of Anxiety. One of the complaints of recovered alcoholics who have been in the Fellowship for some time is, "But what do you do with all your spare time?" It's a perfectly legitimate question. Not everyone likes to read. Not everybody enjoys or can go in for boating or gardening. Not everybody likes the movies. And if a man has spent every spare moment of twenty years in a saloon depending upon a chemically induced feeling of fellowship to keep him amused and feeling safe and comfortable, what is he going to put in its place?

Old-timers in the Fellowship have the answer all ready: "Pitch in and do more Twelfth Step work. Keep active in AA. Get to a lot of meetings. Get yourself a couple of pigeons to work with. Then you can't get bored."

All right—for them it works. But sometimes I think that even they are whistling to keep up their courage, especially when they give this advice in an extra-loud tone of voice.

I think that under the boredom, which is the curse of our jet age, lies concealed panic. Let's be honest about it. We're afraid the Russians are going to blow us to kingdom-come. We're afraid of death, quick death at the ground zero area or slow death from radiation. The thing we have to come to terms with in our hearts is death itself.

This fear wears a great many masks. I think it lurks behind the current cult of noise. My own boy spends precious little time lying in the grass and watching the clouds roll by. He will lie in the grass on rare occasions, but he has his transistor radio along. He doesn't know that he has a fear of silence. Nor do his friends. For in that silence, what whispers may come of guided missiles through the stratosphere arching above the Pole?

When I was his age, the world was at peace and we who were young knew that we would never die. But today even the young fear death. Man's tinkering with the bedrock of the planet has killed a part of childhood. Some find booze early, fearfully early. And in the darker corners of our cities (and even in the tree-shaded streets of our suburbs) others find the greatest horror of all, morphine.

The thirst for excitement grows in each of us. Cars are too powerful and are driven too fast by people who have had too many martinis, and so the tangled wrecks pile up on the superhighways.

The world is in the grip of fear, which comes out in a fear of silence, a fear of sitting still, a fear of the ordinary processes of consciousness, reporting God's world in little things.

Twelfth Step work is fine and necessary to keep our sobriety solid. But is it all we need? I don't think it is for all of us.

When we look about us in the Fellowship, we find people who have lost everything—homes, families, professions, jobs—yet some of these seem to be among our happiest members. And for them the hospital visit and the prison meeting are an outlet for their energies and a splendid antidote for loneliness. This is good and we love them for it. Some of them keep up an enormous correspondence with Loners in faraway places. Some have portable tape recorders and run their own tape exchanges with Loners and isolated groups. And this is great work. But it is not for everyone.

I know, for there was a time, after I had been sober for a few years, when such "good works" seemed to fail me, too. You will say that I failed them and I won't argue the point. But the day came when I felt that I had heard all anybody could possibly say about alcoholism. My pigeons seemed never to sober up: they just borrowed money and vanished. And boredom came stealthily in, as subtle a progression as alcoholism itself. Before I knew it I was screaming with boredom inside. So I got drunk. And I stayed drunk and away from AA for years.

When the desperation got bad enough, I was jolted awake and came back to AA, humbly and gratefully. Then, the speakers at the meetings seemed to be talking just for me. And the perfume of the coffee, drifting out on the night air when I was going down the stairs to the church basement to a meeting, had a heavenly aroma it had never held before. Something in me had changed, deeply and radically. I had tried everything else and I had at last given in and was able to "let God run it," because I was unable to "run" my own life anymore.

With this upset of pride and the beginning of a clear perception of the true role of the ego, the little things came back, one at a time.

When I step out under the stars at night, they no longer seem cold or far away. They are a part of me and I am a part of them, for we are all creatures of the Higher Power. Or, as it seems to me now, we are not solid, three-dimensional constructions that move only so long as the mechanism inside is wound up. We are not robots. We are dancing reflections of God on an ocean which is God. All we can lose at death is the ego, for life itself is God and everlasting.

With this view, a diamond necklace in a shop window is beautiful only because it is a work of God and throws back a reflection of God's sun from its man-made facets. The dew on a spider's web in early morning is even lovelier. And I always hated spiders until I came to know them as children of God.

I did not get this view of the world easily nor through my own efforts. Grace is not a do-it-yourself project. It comes through prayer, but prayer for only one thing—the ability to remain open to God. With my new world view has come the realization that what men of our age thirst for is the knowledge of God. Their attempt to satisfy this thirst with excitement—speed, danger, love affairs, travel, display of wealth—defeats them. Like drinking sea water, it carries its own thirst.

Church membership and conspicuous piety have nothing to do with satisfying this thirst of the soul for God. Philosophy, even if the product of a genius, takes us not a fraction of an inch nearer to real inner peace. There is nothing we can *do* to get it—except stop grabbing for it. We can "let go and let God" as the saying has it. But it isn't always easy.

Can nothing help us defeat boredom and achieve real peace, except prayer?

I think there are three things which can help, or at least they have helped me:

1) We can, possibly with some prayer to help us, stop chewing and worrying at the mysterious ways of God in apparently visiting tribulation on the righteous while allowing the wicked to flourish like the

green bay tree. It's God's world, made from the very essence of God, every dust mote, mountain, and mosquito. God will set your mind at peace if you can stop the squirrel-cage type of thinking. This again may call for prayer and patience. But it will happen—not by will-power, just by asking God for help with it.

2) We can cultivate the blessed silence in which divine guidance can come to us. And if we are afraid to trust our spontaneous impulses, to do something or to refrain from doing something, there is a simple test by which we can tell if the impulse comes from the divine self in us or from the ego—if there is fear or distrust buried in the impulse it is the ego speaking, not God.

3) We can allow the sweetness of little things to register in our minds again—one drop of mist against the face can convey as much as all the sermons ever preached, if the heart is open. We can try, with God's help, to regain our sense of wonder at the infinitely complex world. And once we do we can recover, late in life, the wordless delight of the boy lying in the grass and watching the great, piled, snowy mountains of cloud roll over him, drifting before the summer wind.

Boredom, I am now convinced, is a mask worn by panic, panic of the ego faced with its own ultimate destruction. With God's grace the blessing of wonder comes back again—the flash of water in a puddle, shining with the hues of heaven; a stray feather cast by a robin tells us, in the perfection and rhythm of its tiny veins, that God made us all and made us wonderfully. And there is no pleasure quite like the delight the fingers find in a pebble, worn smooth by tumbling waters.

At first we "made a decision to turn our will and our lives over to the care of God *as we understood Him.*" But as we progress in the God-oriented life, we come to know that "decision" has a special meaning. What we really gain is the knowledge—not the hope or the conclusion or the wish but the actual, intimate knowledge—that *we already are in the care of God* whether we have made a decision or not and whether we understand him or not.

Little children play a game which is always new to every generation. One child creeps softly up behind another, puts his hands over the other's eyes and whispers, "Guess who?" I think this is the kind of game God is playing with us. He temporarily blinds our inner eye with the perplexities and supposed terrors of the material world. And all the time he is whispering, "Guess who?"

When I realized this, it was the end of boredom—and of fear, which is boredom's big brother.

L.G., Ontario, Canada

The Shrivelage Principle
January 1976

D id the founders of AA give us the tools to cope with inflation, taxes, recession, unemployment, war, pollution, TV, energy shortages, and the new morality?

Did the authors of the Twelve Steps foresee that some of the cherished assumptions everybody once seemed to take for granted would today be under serious and responsible question? That the traditional roles of the sexes would be successfully challenged? That we would begin to ask whether intelligent life is necessarily good for this planet? That economic and technological "progress" would no longer seem automatically beneficial? That America would be neither invincible nor always right?

Did the founders foresee all this? Of course not. They never pretended to be oracular; they weren't even trying. Sobriety is what it's all about, remember? But did they, in spite of themselves, give us the tools to cope with a wildly uncertain world? Before leaping to a ready, loyal, and resounding "yes," let's look at those tools as a means of coping with exterior, not interior, problems.

1. The Steps—especially the Third, Eleventh, and Twelfth. These are personal; they bear on our relationships with our Higher Power, ourselves, and the suffering alcoholic. They gird us internally to meet outside assault. *Spiritual.*

2. The Big Book, the Serenity Prayer, the Grapevine, AA litera-

ture, the slogans, and all the other AA sayings that are capsules of truth. They help direct the active mind and keep it muscular. *Mental.*

3. The group, the meetings, the work, the activities, and events outside the meeting room. They keep us busy. *Physical.*

Spiritual, mental, physical—it's all there in the three-part AA way of life; a secure, solid, sober world to live in comfortably...unless the outside world comes crashing in and demands new answers.

When I put those three elements together, I get an impression of order, of perspective. Among them, there is an interrelationship which seems to lend scope, purpose, direction. In one enormous word, faith. It works when reason fails.

And faith fails only when we try to be bigger than faith. When this happens, as it does to me with annoying frequency, it is helpful to apply a new principle to meet this new situation. This principle, born of the contemporary scene, helps me to get back into the AA program where I belong. It is a way of coping with modern problems called the Shrivelage Principle.

Here is the Shrivelage Principle: All things are either Big Stuff or Little Stuff; of the two, only Little Stuff counts. Coping is a matter of ignoring Big Stuff, shriveling all medium or borderline stuff to Little Stuff, and letting the Little Stuff shrivel away to nothing by itself.

The only trick is recognizing the difference between Big Stuff and Little Stuff. A good clue is that man invented Big Stuff; nature is concerned exclusively with immediate, Little Stuff.

All things are joined together by Little Stuff—molecules, atoms, electrons. Even the mountains are assembled from small rocks; the rocks, from tiny grains. Nature does nothing suddenly; it moves step by step, working ever so slowly with Little Stuff. It took 50,000 years to stand us upright and another 10,000 to get us to the point of inventing the wheel.

People are separated by Big Stuff and united by Little Stuff. In the valleys of Appalachia, blood feuds raged for generations over long-forgotten principles; but the music and the fiddling and the dancing drew the people together—not concepts bigger than themselves, but experience small enough for all to share.

Notice how children never cry over Big Stuff—only stubbing toes or losing dolls. And Wordsworth said, "The child is father to the man." Kids know.

Even our common expressions testify to the importance of Little Stuff: what it *boils down to*; the *nub* of the matter. And things that *bug* us are all Little Stuff.

I remember when I was Big Stuff. Big trouble! Only when I stopped fooling around with Big Stuff and started concentrating on Little Stuff did my life become manageable.

Big Stuff is war and inflation and politics and ecclesiastical superstructures and My Future and foreign policy. Little Stuff is eating and sleeping and loving and listening to music and going to the ball game. Only the Little Stuff is important.

Coping with coping is Big Stuff; it is a man-made concept designed to produce worry. Apply Shrivelage to coping, and we're not coping at all; we're just taking care of the Little Stuff that happens to lie right in front of us, as nature does, as the animals do, as AA co-founder Dr. Bob did. He was the first to admonish us to "keep it simple," and thus summed up in three words the whole solution to coping.

Concentrating on the Little Stuff means that problems with which we cope are mere pebbles in the stream; they add interest, make the water bubble a little, but impede nothing seriously or permanently.

To cope, don't try. This is what I absolutely believe for all time—this week. I can hardly wait for next week's unshakable conviction. (The foregoing is Shrivelage in action, applied to my burgeoning "concepts" before they become Big Stuff.)

And as everyone knows, the real problem facing the universe is this: Why can't my wife put the car keys where they are supposed to be so I won't have to look all over the house for them? If I can get that problem solved, I shall be totally and infinitely happy for all eternity.

C.H., Fairfield, Conn.

Learning to Handle Sobriety
March 1975

The idea is not new. I first heard it a dozen years ago from a speaker who was then an old-timer in AA. But I've been giving it a lot of thought recently, because it is an important concept. I *know* it is not understood outside our Fellowship, and I suspect it is not well recognized inside, either.

The old-timer said, "AA does not teach us how to handle our drinking; it teaches us how to handle sobriety."

He went on to explain: "AA doesn't teach us how to handle our drinking. Most alcoholics know, long before they come through the doors of their first meeting, that the way to handle their drinking is to quit. People have told them so. And almost every alcoholic I know *has* stopped drinking at one time or another—maybe dozens of times!—when he went on the wagon, or took a pledge, or perhaps when he was hospitalized or jailed. So it's no trick to stop drinking; the trick is to *stay* stopped.

"No, AA doesn't teach us how to handle our drinking. It teaches us how to handle *sobriety*—which is what none of us could handle in the first place, and that's why we drank."

What a simple idea! But what a marvelous expression of the way AA works! It has so many advantages and clears up so much misunderstanding about our Society of recovered drunks.

First of all, it explains the need for a *continuing* program of recovery. One of the commonest questions we get from nonalcoholic friends is "You haven't had a drink in 'X' years, so why do you still have to go to meetings?" In my own case, it's true that I haven't had the slightest desire for a drink in many years. And the *reason* is that my continuing, regular attendance at AA meetings and my effort "to practice these principles" in all my affairs teach me how to live comfortably, productively, happily—without seeking these attributes in a bottle.

This concept also explains the puzzling and paradoxical fact that the halls of AA are crowded, not with shivering wrecks fighting off the craving for a belt of booze, but with healthy, clear-eyed, smiling people. On Twelfth Step calls, I've had prospects ask, "I've stopped drinking, so why should I go to AA?"

I reply, "I have also stopped drinking—long ago—and so have other members of AA. We find it essential to attend meetings to improve ourselves, to improve our relations with other people, and to learn to practice a better way of life. That's the only way we can be sure we won't slip into drinking again."

Indeed, this concept of learning how to handle sobriety is useful in explaining the need for what we in AA often refer to as our "way of life." To the newcomer, as well as to the outsider, this phrase often sounds pompous or supercilious. But a new way of life is what we *must* find if we are to handle sobriety successfully.

In our old way of life, even before we became active alcoholics, we were less successful than others in meeting the demands of everyday existence. We did not cope. When we encountered disappointments or frustrations, our solution was to drink. When we were reprimanded or criticized, the bottle was our refuge and our comfort. When we were faced with a special challenge or a special occasion—an important business presentation, for example, or a dinner party—we had to fortify ourselves with a couple of belts. (And too often, we had to overdo it and get drunk and make an ass of ourselves the *one* time we wanted to be at our best!) Above all, when our performance and our accomplishments failed to live up to our own expectations of ourselves (and the more we drank, the greater this gap became), then we *had* to anesthetize that inner pain with alcohol.

To quote an AA speaker I heard, "When we ran into disappointments and problems with people around us, we did the only logical and sensible thing: We picked up a hammer and beat our own brains out."

When I was in the "pink cloud" stage of my early months in the program, I tended to intellectualize and analyze what I heard (didn't we all?). My sponsor would jar me back to earth by rasping out, "The name of the game is 'Don't drink!'" At the time, I thought he was putting me down; now, I realize he was articulating an enormous idea! That is, the name of the AA game is not "Stop drinking," but rather "Don't drink." So worded, the advice assumed we are not drinking *now*, and everything we learn, everything we do, is aimed at living in such a way that we don't pick up that first drink. The Preamble doesn't say our primary purpose is to give up booze and make others do so. It states: "Our primary purpose is to *stay* sober and help other alcoholics to *achieve sobriety*."

If this idea was widely understood within our Fellowship, it would go far toward clarifying the role of Alcoholics Anonymous in the whole alcoholism picture. A drunk can sober up anywhere, and he can use all the help he can get in doing so. But the only place he can *stay* sober is in AA. Just as the meetings at the house in Akron and the brownstone in Brooklyn have grown to 22,500 groups in 92 countries [in 1986, more than 67,000 groups in 114 countries] throughout the world, so Towns Hospital (now defunct), where Bill W. sobered up, has grown to thousands of hospitals and rehab centers and other treatment facilities—and a vast profusion of federal, state, and municipal alcoholism programs. But AA should not feel threatened. The outside agencies are not in our business, nor we in theirs. Indeed, the stream of alcoholics who seek treatment through outside agencies and then are referred to AA to *stay* sober has become so large that, in some localities, it is taxing the ability of AA to absorb the newcomers.

Bill W. saw this with characteristic clarity. In the March 1958 Grapevine, he wrote, "Millions are still sick and other millions soon will be.... More and more we regard all who labor in the total field of alcoholism as our companions on a march from darkness into light. We see that we can accomplish together what we could never accomplish in...rivalry." On other occasions, he asked, "Could not still more friendly and widespread cooperation with outside agencies finally lead us to countless alcoholics who will otherwise be lost?"

God willing, we members of Alcoholics Anonymous will never again have to deal with drinking, but we do have to deal with sobriety every day.

How? By learning—through sharing at meetings—how to deal with those same problems that caused us to "pick up a hammer and beat our own brains out" in our drinking days. We are told we cannot afford resentments and self-pity, and we learn how to avoid these festering mental attitudes. We rid ourselves of guilt and remorse. We "clear out the garbage" from our minds and replace it with positive, spiritually uplifting thoughts. We learn how to level out the emotional swings that got us into trouble at *both* ends. We are taught to differentiate between our wants (which are never satisfied) and our needs (which are always provided for). We cast off the burdens of the past and the anxieties of the future and live in the present, one day at a time. We are granted "the serenity to accept the things we cannot change"—and lose our quickness to anger and our sensitivity to criticism. We reject fantasizing and accept reality. And we find it beautiful. For, at last, we are at peace with ourselves. And with others. And with God.

R.P., Conn.

THREE

Men and Women
Who Share

———————— ◆ ————————

Will We Squander Our Inheritance?
June 1978

Bill W. wrote to Dr. Bob in 1949: "The groups will eventually take over, and maybe they will squander their inheritance when they get it. It is probable, however, that they won't. Anyhow, they really have grown up; AA is theirs: let's give it to them."

As a sober member of AA for more than twenty-seven years, I see some disturbing differences between what I was taught in the beginning and what is happening now. What has happened to the pride we AAs have traditionally taken in saying, "I belong to the Guttersnipe Group"? To our feeling that each one of us takes part in the group's primary purpose—carrying the message? I see groups that regularly have thirty people at meetings, but only five active members. Who takes responsibility for the necessary jobs—group offices, sponsorship, coffee making? Is the AA group dying because of individual apathy?

The Responsibility Declaration is basic to AA thinking: "I am responsible. When anyone, anywhere, reaches out for help, I want the hand of AA always to be there. And for that: I am responsible." Yet central offices seem to be having more and more difficulty finding sober AAs to make Twelfth Step calls. One of the first things I learned is that I need the newcomer as much as he needs me, yet some members feel they are doing new people a favor by getting in touch with them. Are we trying to hold on to sobriety now by *not* giving it away?

I wonder how many are lost because we don't have the time—or won't make the time—to share or care. What about the still suffering drunk who calls AA and is told where the meeting is—and to go by himself? What of the newcomer who goes to a meeting and finds no one to talk to? Or is told to call other members but is given no names or numbers? When I was called in by an AA member, I joined a group and got a sponsor. The group gave me a list of members, with addresses and phone numbers, to use when needed. Today, there seems to be little follow-up, little caring, few phone calls.

How many alcoholics have we lost simply because they were never really accepted? Do sober members still say, "Hey, how are you doing? Call me if you get shook up, no matter what time it is. Remember, we need you"? Alcoholics may be getting sober, not because of us, but in spite of us.

I have talked to many older members who feel as I do. Remember, AA is not going to preserve itself automatically. What are we, each one of us, doing with the gift of sobriety, so freely and lovingly given? Will we soon squander our magnificent inheritance?

Perhaps each one of us should hold on to these thoughts: "Keep me mindful of the responsibilities that accompany the blessings of freedom. The only time that wrong can prevail is when good people do nothing."

G.G., Phoenix, Ariz.

Leaders in Sober Living
September 1975

On September 8, 1960, I came to my senses after a three-week binge. My wife realized that I probably needed hospitalization, and she called my doctor, who had hospitalized me in June of that year. He told her that no way would that hospital accept me as a patient. He referred to me as "a crazy man" and said that my stay at the hospital had caused the resignation of three staff members. For me, hospitalization was out. Later that day, I was told that I had two other choices: a high-priced sanitarium, which I could not afford, and the county asylum, which was a snake pit. Still later that day, thinking I had no option left, I was privileged to meet my sponsor in Alcoholics Anonymous.

In the 1960s in our area, it was customary for the Twelfth Step caller to work closely with the newcomer, and generally also to become the sponsor. So it was in my case. My sponsor literally lived with me during the first, crucial seven weeks. He practically did my thinking for me until I could begin to think for myself. After almost fifteen years, I am still in contact with him, probably once a month. I have since chosen another sponsor, who is also a member of my home group.

I don't think sponsorship is going out of existence, but I do think we are seeing radical changes. Most of the calls I receive today for help are from people who really want hospitalization or other professional treatment—and in most cases, they get it. The old type of sponsor, who carried a half-pint of whiskey and a box of chocolate bars in his glove compartment, has passed on. Today, the newcomer usually arrives at AA fresh from a treatment facility, dry, and in reasonably good physical condition. But this certainly does not lessen his or her need for sponsorship.

What is sponsorship? Sponsorship is guidance for the new person in the AA way of life. There is no special formula for sponsorship, but many different approaches. Here is what we do in my area to keep sponsorship alive.

At the close of each meeting, the following is read: "If any person here does not have a sponsor, please see the secretary after the meeting, and he will appoint a temporary sponsor." As a result of this statement, sponsorship becomes a subject mentioned every time a group meets. This leads the newcomer into discussion and contemplation on the subject. Likewise, it keeps before the older member his or her responsibility to become a sponsor. In this area the statement has been read for a number of years, and it works.

Temporary sponsors may or may not become permanent. As well as counseling newcomers on the rudiments of the program, they also talk about the things to look for in selecting a permanent sponsor. They stress that a newcomer need not actually like the person, but should simply respect his (or her) judgment, the manner in which he works the program, and the way he explains his own use of the program. Good rapport between the sponsor and newcomer is a wonderful thing, but it often comes only after a considerable time.

Another custom in our area is to hold discussions from time to time on the sponsor's responsibility and the qualities that go to make up a good sponsor. For instance, I have heard it said that a sponsor need not be a person who practices what he preaches, but rather should be one who preaches what he practices. Certainly, he (or she) should be exemplary in the conduct of his own life. A person who is a leader—and a sponsor is just that—should not only show the way and know the way, but also go the way. We have another saying in our area: Have a good program yourself, and learn to relay it to the person with whom you are working.

We emphasize the necessity of being honest with the newcomer, even though his or her feelings may be hurt. In growth, we feel, there is always pain.

Finally, sponsors are reminded that being a good listener is vital. This ability is what I value most in my own sponsor. After almost fifteen years, I still have problems and, from time to time, will go to my sponsor for answers. Almost invariably, after I have talked long enough, the answer becomes evident as a result of my self-explanation.

I do not feel that the wave of non-AA people coming into the alcoholism field decreases in any way the necessity of good sponsorship. But I do recognize that sponsorship will have to be of a different type. It will be sponsorship that explains the program, thrives on the Steps, and succeeds through the application of our Traditions. It will be, as it has been throughout our history, the combination of one person seeking and another person furnishing answers. Sponsorship, the one-to-one idea that started with Bill and Dr. Bob, is just as necessary and just as alive in our fortieth year as it was in Year One of AA.

J. M., Nashville, Tenn.

The Stranger
August 1965

I left my home in California the first of last June to travel around the United States. I planned to spend five months visiting friends and relatives here and there, but my primary purpose was to find landscapes to paint along the way.

My family was very concerned about my traveling alone; they feared that I would get lonesome. I assured them this wasn't possible. I could find an AA meeting wherever I went, and I would never be without friends.

And sure enough, as I started east, I found that I was received warmly. I was even asked to speak in many places. However, it seemed to me that the farther east I went, the less friendly the people became.

One night I went to a meeting on the East Coast and no one at all spoke to me. I smiled and said "Hi" to everyone. Although many of them smiled back and some even returned my "Hi," none left their own little conversation groups to ask me if I were a newcomer or a visitor.

I stood in line for coffee even though I didn't want any, thinking that would be a way to get acquainted. No luck. I took my coffee and roamed around, making it very obvious that I would like to get acquainted. No luck.

The meeting started. No one sat on either side of me. One of the speakers mentioned that AA was so warm and friendly—everyone extended a hand to the newcomer. Actually, I had been in the program five years and four months, but no one there knew that, and no one extended a hand to me!

After the meeting I went up to a woman who was one of the speakers and told her I had enjoyed her speech. She gave me a cold thank you and turned to friends.

Believe me, I have many friends, and I've never before been given reason to believe I was undesirable or untouchable. I was hurt.

I left with tears in my eyes and sat in my car for a few seconds and cried. I thought, I'm sober and I have a wonderful sister and brother-in-law to go home to, plus a background of many wonderful AA meetings. I wondered, though, what I would have done if I had been new and alone and had been seeking AA as my last resort.

It was hard to go to sleep that night. Among other things, I wondered if I had ever been as cold to a stranger in my home group. I do not think so. However, I know after this experience I will put forth even more effort.

I wrote a very bitter letter to the Grapevine that night, but, as I have been taught in AA, I tore it up and decided to go right back to the people who had hurt me and tell them about it.

At the next meeting, I went to the secretary and asked her if I could speak to the group for two minutes. She said they just did not do that at their meetings, and she asked if I couldn't talk to her. I told her what I wanted to tell the whole group: that they were the coldest, most unfriendly group I had ever met, and that I had been clear across the country and had met plenty; and that in comparison they did not even seem to me to be an AA group. She said that I had better talk to an older member, and so she called a very charming woman over, who, it turned out, had not been to the previous meeting. She said that she had heard my complaint many times. She always looked for newcomers herself, she told me, but knew that she was one of the few who did.

After the meeting, she introduced me to many of the women and told them all my story. They were all very apologetic and said it was because their group was so big. I told them I had been to much larger meetings and that my own home group was twice the size of theirs.

One woman said she had not seen me. I told her that I knew it, because I had seen her and she had talked only to her own little clique.

I must say they all took it beautifully, and they determined to do something about it. They had a meeting a few nights later and decided to make it their regular practice to shake hands with the persons on one's right and left at meetings, to get acquainted.

I am glad God sent me back to tell them of my hurt instead of allowing me to send the bitter letter to the Grapevine. These people are now my friends; I went home to California with love instead of resentment in my heart because I know they did not mean to hurt me. Above all, I know that they will always welcome a stranger in the future. And if the stranger is a newcomer, it may mean his very life.

Anonymous, Calif.

I Don't Go to Meetings Anymore
July 1960

First off, I'm a female alcoholic, and I owe a year and a half of happy sobriety to the desperate telephone call made to the AA telephone number. I still think that AA is a wonderful organization, although I no longer attend meetings.

Making the decision to call for help was the first step up out of the suicidal slime, and if there had been no AA to call I might never have made it. I'd already tried psychiatry with no success. Tranquilizers didn't seem the answer. Trying to stop drinking, with all one's friends and relatives still imbibing freely, though not as persistently, seemed impossible. Apparently, however, AA succeeds through group therapy—unfortunately the same group that I am now going to criticize very cruelly.

Most of my criticism has no doubt been voiced countless times, and probably there is no real solution. The trouble is mainly the people belonging to local AA groups—and who can do anything about people? My only aim in writing is to convey the thought that many hopeful alcoholics may be discouraged and drop out of AA—back into their private hells—when the first happy relief of not drinking passes and they take a cold sober look at their comrades. I was disillusioned and just stopped going to the meetings. I had received the message, however. Just the thought of that horrible other me kills any desire for drink. I pray God it will always be so.

The two charming ladies who called on me that portentous May afternoon (after I dialed the number I'd been debating for so long) were the best of friends—I supposed. This pretense was maintained for at least a week, when I found to my surprise that they hated each other's guts.

Then a concerted effort was made by one group to unseat one of my sponsors from her chairmanship. Failing this, the conspirators started a new meeting on the same night of the week, which caused considerable controversy in all other groups: "That's pretty good—fellows who haven't been dry six months starting new meetings." If I seemed confused by all this bickering within the supposed serenity, someone said, "You should have been here back in such-and-such a year—this is nothing."

Or someone would phone and say "So-and-So says you're not going to enough meetings" I have three preteen kids who need their new improved mother at home in the evening. "So-and-So said this and that and I'm so mad I could go get drunk." Children breaking their toys? "Well, everyone got through the holidays okay except for you-know-who, but then she welcomes any excuse." Is each holiday a fresh emergency to check the casualties? Almost every meeting produced some idiotic debate such as "Is it permissible to drink sweet cider?" Once a bunch of drunks came to the door of a meeting creating a disturbance. Everyone laughed. True, probably you can't help them in that condition—but laugh? Us?

I met women who were neglecting their children by attending meetings nightly—in town, out of town, anniversary, Al-Anon, speaking engagements, etc. Isn't that a substitution for the liquor that separated them from their obligations before? Another thing: I attended AA get-togethers off and on for nearly a year and saw only one colored person. Is there segregation in AA, or don't black people have any drinking problems?

In another vein, why is there so little actual anonymity? Someone might get up to speak, giving only his first name, but everyone appeared to know not only his last name, but how many times he'd been married and how much he still owed on his car.

And how some of them love to get up and talk. Disappointed thespians all, and how tiresome it gets! And how hideous when it's you standing up there, trying to avoid dredging up the waste products of your past and wishing you'd stayed home. I liked the round-table discussions best where coffee was served as the talk went on, but I suppose they can't do that all the time.

I know I met some fine, sincere people in AA, some I would have liked to know better. Perhaps I let the petty personalities blind me to the organization as a whole. I'd love to help someone else who needs it as I did, but would hesitate to introduce the quaking, fearful, but still hopeful creature to that assembly that met almost directly over the beer joint, whose lively jukebox was clearly audible throughout the uninspiring speeches and the after coffee-and-doughnut gossip. To quote my former pals, "It almost made you want to get drunk."

This won't do any good, but it's something I've wanted to say for a long time and I feel better.

Anonymous, Elmira, N.Y.

People Are Like People
January 1961

It had been several months since I had read "I Don't Go to Meetings Anymore" in the July Grapevine, but for some reason I couldn't forget the article, or the lady who'd written it. I found myself thinking of her as I drove along at night and in the morning as I started to work.

What was it that bothered me?

Was it the people in her group she found tiresome—the two women who had first called on her she discovered didn't like each other—the speakers she didn't care for, these "disappointed thespians dredging up their pasts"—the parents who were attending meetings and neglecting their children...?

Then I remembered.

I had been in that group. But the strange thing was, it wasn't in Elmira. It was in midtown Manhattan. I had seen these same people, made these same discoveries—and not only in my home group. I had gone to California for a few months and they were there, too. They followed me. Then, back in New York again, I had tried attending another, a smaller group and—yes, you've guessed it, the exact same thing: "Everywhere I go, I go, too, and spoil everything."

This had been my song, my story for ten years of drinking, and I had begun to wonder if it was to be a part of my AA life as well. At this point, I think I should say I had been sober eighteen months (the same length of time as the lady in Elmira), and there was one fact I was forced to face: Even though I was sober, *people were still acting like people.* And one other fact—not so easy to face—*I still wanted people to change. I wanted them to be more.* I think I was able to hide most of this—this desire to rewrite others and make them fit in with my notion of the way things should be. On the surface I'm sure I appeared calm, affable. I was grateful for my sobriety and genuinely pleased with many of the changes in my life. Yet inside, with some merciless inner eye, I still saw all the flaws in those around me.

Maybe there is a familiar ring to what I'm saying. "On the surface he was sober; inside nothing had changed." But for me the hell of those days—those months, really—was the fact that I knew all this. I knew all the old tensions, the old demands and fears—fears of losing what I had, or not getting what I demanded—all of these were still there and very much a part of me. Without booze I felt I had no escape. I was a battleground inside and I was trapped, imprisoned with the conflicts. Someone or something had to give, and from the looks of things it became pretty clear that it wasn't going to be the human race.

I don't want to sound flip about this. It was not a happy time.

I know now that my case was not unique. Many others have sobered up, learned to stay sober, and then been faced with themselves and this situation. All I'm trying to say to this lady, or anyone else who finds unhappiness in a group of people with too many human weaknesses and too wanting in those qualities we demand of others, is that I know. I was there—and it hurts.

I wish that I had some encouraging P.S. to add, some easy gimmick to suggest...but why? When did any of us ever choose an easy way? I can only tell how it was for me.

For me I had to realize, admit, accept that the only change I could make was inward. Living as I was, in a state of unfulfilled demands, there could be no peace, there would be only wild frustrations eating at me—and I knew it—until I found a way of coping with these demands.

My first glint of an answer came in reading and studying Chapter Seven in *Twelve Steps and Twelve Traditions*. Bill speaks here of reducing our demands and adds that "the difference between a demand and a simple request is plain to anyone." (Well, it was "plain" in my mind, but my problem was to accept it in my guts, and for me this was not unlike the road I had to travel before I could finally accept the fact that I was powerless over alcohol.)

The whole emphasis of Step Seven is on humility, and I found I was as unwilling to seek humility now as I had been to admit I was powerless months before. The word *powerless* repelled me then, and *humility* had no attraction now.

In a way, I had to hit another bottom, an emotional, spiritual one this time. I remember every bit of it, and it was rough. I wouldn't recommend my way to anyone, but finally one night, alone and lost, eaten up with old jealousies, old fears, I was fighting to hang on to the one thing I had, my sobriety. I was near an old panic that many of us know about. I couldn't, I wouldn't let myself take a drink, but I had to find a way to overcome the battle inside, to quiet the tensions. Then this happened: I knew that I had to admit I was powerless over other people. I had to admit this just as, in order to keep sober, I had to admit I was powerless over alcohol.

I cannot make anyone love me, or even like me.

Oh, I still have some of my active drunk's talent to create a scene and twist a conversation so someone may be forced into saying what I want to hear, but I have no power to make anyone feel anything.

All I can do is work to make myself worthy of love.

As these thoughts came to me—and they came almost in the words I've written out here—I felt a great relief. It was Armistice Day—after all these years.

After great pain, someone has said, a formal feeling comes, and maybe inside I still feel a little stuffy, a little pompous about this ancient truth I had to discover as if it were new, but a part of me has relaxed, one of my wars is over and I like the feeling.

I know I climbed that night all the way from pride up to humility. The journey was no fun, as I have said. It was terrible and lonely, but now I believe that it is a journey all of us must make alone. There was some comfort in knowing others had made it and a kind of hope in the feeling that for me it was a journey up to humility.

There's one more line from Step Seven I'd like to quote here for the lady from Elmira, or for anyone else who is focusing on all those faults other people have.

Bill is again speaking of humility and for me that's alright now, that word now means a goal of perspective, a sense of proportion about myself in relation to others, in relation to my God and the whole tremendous scene about me. Bill ends his Seventh Step by saying that if humility could enable us to find the grace to banish the deadly obsession of alcohol "then there must be hope of the same result respecting any other problem we could possibly have."

Anonymous, N.Y.

Passing the Basket...or Passing the Buck?
June 1983

When I was newly sober in AA, fourteen years ago, I seldom attended a meeting without taking a pamphlet to read. I always had at least two cups of coffee, and if there was anything to eat, I ate. When the basket was passed, I always put a quarter in it—for two people, my wife and me. If we could truly stretch a dollar as far as I must have thought we could, the financial world would be beating a path to our doorsteps to learn AA's remarkable brand of economics.

Most of us decry the fact that more than forty percent of the groups do not support the Fellowship. When it comes to AA's being self-supporting, many fail to recognize one important aspect: If we aren't even willing to pay our own way at a meeting, how can we expect the group to support the Fellowship? What we need to realize is that we are the groups, and we are Alcoholics Anonymous. I have seen AAs spend more money at a coffee shop than they would ever think of putting in the collection at a meeting.

Early in my sobriety, it was explained that it was imperative for me to get my priorities in order. Learning to become responsible was one of them. This financial buck-passing certainly seems to run counter to responsibility. If we want "the hand of AA always to be there," we each need to assume our own share of responsibility. If money and spirituality do mix in the basket, as the "Twelve and Twelve" says, then how much better they will blend when money is used to perpetuate AA by making more Twelfth Step work possible.

We, who have had so much given to us freely—in love, with no strings attached—sometimes forget that this also is an area where we have to give it away to keep it. One of the promises in the Big Book is freedom from "fear of economic insecurity." Long ago, one of my sponsors suggested that if I stayed sober and tried to live along spiritual lines, my needs would always be met. Today, I can honestly say that never has there been an instance where I have given of myself, financially or otherwise, and have not been compensated many times over. Our family has never lacked anything because we accepted our responsibility to help carry the message.

God has given each of us a share of the responsibility. He has given each of us the tools to work with and the ability to use them. Let's all of us assume our shares so that we may all reap ever increasingly the fruits of selflessness and love in service to our Fellowship.

C. C., West Palm Beach, Fla.

All This Reading at AA Meetings...?
July 1968

In a recent issue of the Grapevine, several articles mentioned new, exciting changes in AA meetings which were designed to foster greater in-depth communication for the participants. I was greatly impressed by the apparent similarity between these marathon meetings and a statement I heard repeatedly when I was a newcomer to the Fellowship: "When you get right down to it, Alcoholics Anonymous is one drunk talking to another."

Yet we have seen a significant trend in AA meetings in the past few years in a direction exactly opposite to "one drunk talking to another." And, as is so often the case with a potentially dangerous change, it has not come about through any direct attack on the basic communication so necessary to our meetings. It has simply eliminated a sizable portion of the time available for "talking" in an AA meeting by substituting a seemingly innocent and beneficial alternative—*reading.*

In an informal survey of meetings within one hundred miles of my home in Southern California, I have found that the following material has been officially incorporated into the format of various groups. The average number of such readings is four items per group. The minimum is two and the maximum is seven. The list includes most of the following format items:

1. An opening prayer (read by an individual member, who is joined by the group in reciting the Serenity Prayer as the final paragraph).
2. Preamble (which is usually the AA Preamble and which may or may not be followed by a formal statement of the particular group's avowed purpose).
3. A portion of chapter five of the Big Book.
4. A portion of chapter three.

5. A portion of chapter six.

6. The short form of the Twelve Traditions.

7. One or more pages from the book *Twenty-Four Hours a Day*.

8. The last three paragraphs from chapter eleven of the Big Book.

9. One or more excerpts on the Steps or Traditions from *Twelve Steps and Twelve Traditions*.

10. A formal explanation of group expenditures preparatory to taking up a collection.

11. A formal announcement urging participants to restrict their talks to five to seven minutes, occasionally accompanied by a warning bell or flashing light to indicate the passage of the allotted time.

12. Secretary's announcements, including a reference to available literature and the cost of books.

13. Miscellaneous closing announcements, formally requesting assistance in the handling and disposition of chairs, coffee cups, ashtrays, etc.

It is obvious that many of these items are well selected and worthy of repetition at any meeting. No one would suggest the arbitrary elimination of those readings which have become traditional in individual groups or geographical areas. Yet, because certain of these readings are so well loved, there is the temptation to add one or two more items each year or so. The temptation is abetted by the fact that most of them can be read in a relatively short period of time.

Yet, in a ninety-minute meeting, if you were to read everything on this list of material, approximately eighteen to twenty minutes would remain for the substance of the meeting! In one group with which I am familiar, the three items in its format of five years ago have now expanded to seven. As a result, some members celebrating AA birthdays must forgo the opportunity of speaking on the anniversaries of their sobriety whenever a guest speaker is scheduled for the meeting. There simply wouldn't be time to read all the required material and still listen to a guest if each birthday participant were so acknowledged. The group averages twenty-five minutes of reading at the opening of the meeting and another five to seven minutes of ritual at the end. This is, of course, an isolated example and does not reflect the situation as a whole.

It would be presumptuous of anyone to condemn the practice of reading *any* material at meetings. No such condemnation is intended. However, it would be less than honest if we did not ask: Is this initially good approach to an AA meeting format being carried to an occasional extreme?

It is an acknowledged fact in educational theory that reading requires (and receives) less attention from an audience than does extemporaneous speaking. There is a strong tendency in the school pupil to gradually "blot out" that which is simply read to him on a repetitive basis. He comes to know it so well that he ceases, for all practical purposes, to listen at all. Even a conscious effort to listen will result in only a few minutes of active attention before the mind again begins to wander. While a short amount of reading material can be given full attention, any extended amount will result in a virtual auditory "blackout." (To test this, stop reading this article right now and recite every word of "The Star-Spangled Banner." If you cannot recite every word correctly, despite the thousands of times you've heard it, take heart! You're in the same category as the great majority of American adults. Your chances of knowing it are almost twice as good if you are a naturalized rather than a native-born citizen.)

Any lengthy period of reading in an AA meeting produces the same sort of auditory "blackout." Try as you will, it is almost impossible to give full attention to much more than chapter five and the Twelve Traditions. Yet the addition of more reading material seems almost as progressive as the disease we share in common. And the number of groups who have reduced their formal reading is extremely small.

The obvious answer to this is, "Yes, but I don't always listen completely to all the talks I hear, either!" And you would be right. But we come closer to giving our full attention to an AA talk—even a disagreeable one—almost all the time. If we are psychologically tuned in on anything, it is the basic and free communication that comes from the spontaneous talk. The very fact that a speaker is unpredictable will cause us to keep a sharper ear than would be the case if we knew his every word.

There is an added warning flag that hides behind this increase in reading at meetings. The more formalized we become, the more likely we are to give way to ritualized meetings—and thereby lose that very spontaneity which gives excitement to any AA meeting. The dangers of becoming dogmatic are exclusively given to the successful. And because of our very success, and our desire to keep that spiritual contact which has been its foundation, we sometimes seek the security of a ritual rather than preserve that very freedom of expression upon which AA is built.

Alcoholics Anonymous is two years younger than I am. And I find that as I grow older—and, I hope, more mature—the temptation to become conservative in personal attitude grows. There is personal security in "shifting into neutral" in one's daily life, in not fighting the battles nor suffering the resulting anxieties that I would have taken on without thinking when I was younger. There is an accumulation of material goods, with an accompanying desire to conserve them while adding to them, which was foreign to me when younger and poorer. But I have come to believe that any such "shifting into neutral" is fundamentally dangerous. The fact that the battle is not easily won does not excuse us from taking part in it when we know it is right to do so. And the temporary security of material things is a hollow shelter if built at the expense of spiritual growth, particularly in times of emotional storms.

So, too, the temptation to preserve AA by "shifting into neutral" in our meetings, through extensive reading at the expense of talks or discussion by the members, seems questionable. Are we preserving the Fellowship better by lengthy readings from its literature than by filtering its principles through our lives and sharing that experience, strength, and hope which inevitably come about? Are we giving too much attention to the formalities out of fear of change or innovation? It is well to remember that a hardening of the opinions is just as fatal to the spirit as a hardening of the arteries is to the heart.

My six years' sobriety in AA has not given me enough perspective to see the long-range view of this trend, but it has given me enough understanding to realize that there are no quick and easy answers. Therefore, I ask the questions contained in this article, in the hope that together we can find answers which indicate whether a real problem is in the making, and, if so, how best to deal with it.

It is of concern to me that the old saying "one drunk talking to another" seems to be in danger of becoming "one drunk *reading* to another." I should be pleased if time showed that this problem is an illusion resulting from my anxiousness, rather than a genuine trend in our program. But if the problem is real, let's consider it now, before the emotional cement hardens into a liturgical prison of our own making.

P. P., Stanton, Calif.

Of Cakes and Ale
December 1968

Involvement. Participation. Service. These are important to our continued sobriety in AA, the winners tell us. These concepts would have been Greek to me when I first dabbled with the program—and yet my own early experience bears out the wisdom of this advice. For I can say quite honestly that I owe my sobriety to a cake.

Not a birthday cake or an anniversary cake, but a run-of-the-meeting, refreshment-type cake that turned out to be the most important cake of my life.

It all began because there were no doughnuts. I had been going to meetings only a few weeks, but I knew there should be doughnuts for refreshments at the meetings, along with the coffee. When someone failed to provide them this particular night, my sensibilities as a good hostess were offended. Mind you, I hadn't entertained for perhaps eight years, because I was too occupied with the bottle; but by golly I knew what was right for that AA meeting, and I was vociferous about it.

"Okay," they replied. "You do it."

So I did. I bought a luscious mix and put loving care into it, too, and decorated it nicely and brought it proudly to the next Tuesday's meeting.

It was a hit. The other members admired it and said it was delicious and showered me with compliments. My ego fed itself eagerly. This was exciting and flattering. It gave me *recognition* —something that had long been lacking in my life. And I loved it. In fact, I said I'd continue to bake cakes every week.

And I did. The people continued to say nice things. I continued to glow. But you can't expect people to rave about a cake every week, ad infinitum, can you?

About a month later, on a Tuesday, things had gone wrong at home. Either I didn't like the color of the necktie my husband wore that morning, or some equally world-shaking crisis had occurred. And suddenly all the effort I had been putting into my sobriety was *just not worth it!* I wasn't getting the appreciation I deserved, nobody loved me, and there was no solution but to get drunk!

The trouble was, there was no liquor in the house. So I was about to go out and buy a bottle. As I headed for the door, a nagging thought hit me. Darn! It was Tuesday. I was committed to furnish one of my incomparable cakes again that night—committed not so much to the group as to myself. I was convinced that the group would fall apart—or, at the very least, its carefully nurtured reputation for hospitality and delicious refreshments would be tarnished— if I didn't produce a cake.

And it would never do to deliver the cake with my breath reeking of liquor. Bad for my image as Hostess. So, reluctantly, I *had* to postpone getting drunk until tomorrow. Then I would, for sure, just to show the ungrateful world. But meanwhile I commenced work on the cake.

When I arrived at the meeting that night, sulkily sober and with cake in hand, an older member introduced me to a new girl. She explained that she was going to be unable to take the newcomer, whom she was sponsoring, to a meeting the following night in an adjoining community. "I know you usually go to that Wednesday meeting," she said, "so could you take this girl?"

I was thrilled. This was real responsibility. This was real appreciation of my sobriety. Here was an older member, whom I respected, actually trusting me to take care of a precious newcomer, whom she was helping. I accepted the assignment eagerly.

Not until I got home that night did I think: Ye gods, that means I can't get drunk tomorrow either! And from that moment until today I haven't had another desire to take a drink.

Oh yes, the upshot was that I continued to bake a cake for every Tuesday-night meeting for fifty-two weeks! But it was that one silly cake, that magic cake, that introduced me to involvement, participation, service—and to my first subconscious application of the twenty-four-hour plan. Surely my Higher Power had a hand in that batter!

M. M., Millburn, N.J.

No Price Tag on Benefits
July 1980

T he group is asked by the chairman to please stand, and he says, "We will open this meeting with the Serenity Prayer." Sounds like the opening of an AA meeting anywhere, right? It could be, but this is the way the Recovery Group starts its AA meeting every week at Jackson Prison. How do I know? Well, I happen to be there each Thursday for the meetings.

I have been asked why I go every week to these meetings, 262 miles round trip. The answer is simply, "Why not?"

The main thing that is lacking about AA in prisons is understanding. Ask most people, "Who are the people in prisons?" and they most likely will answer: murderers, rapists, robbers, extortionists, con men. While in prison, they are called convicts, inmates, residents, even numbers. But not many outside know that many of these people are alcoholics. They could probably never have done the crimes if they had been sober. In a few cases, some are there because of an accident under the influence of alcohol, such as vehicular manslaughter. Some crimes were committed in blackouts. They don't even remember what they did, yet they are serving time for their crimes.

Some on the outside question why AA is needed in prisons. They have the false impression that people can't get alcohol there. Alcohol is very plentiful in any prison. Inmates can make their own, or they can buy it. Last year, some men stole wood alcohol from one of the offices and sold it to the prisoners. Four men died, after a great number got deathly sick. Some are blind today.

The main reason I feel that AA is needed in prisons is that most of these people will be getting out of prison in time. With AA to take out with them, they stand a chance of not having to return, simply because they found someone who does love them and understand them. They found people just like themselves: alcoholics.

It really is surprising, the number of people who find their Higher Power through AA. They come to believe, and they gain faith. This is so important to people in prison. They need both, just to serve one day at a time in a place like prison.

I think the thing they gain the most from outside speakers at their meetings is moral support. They get the feeling that some do care and that they are not alone, even if they are in prison.

If you have never attended an AA meeting in a prison somewhere, I beg you to attend one. If you will, I promise you this: You will want to go back.

Sometime this month, I will be bringing in to the Recovery Group nine more Big Books. This will make 700 Big Books that I have brought to these guys since I started bringing them, about four years ago. We decided that every AA man in the group who wanted a Big Book would get one, if possible. We have a drawing, using the men's prison numbers, and if they don't already have a Big Book, they win one. We have been able to start a Big Book study group, with each man having his own book. The reason we need to keep bringing books is simple: Men keep getting out of prison, and they take their Big Books home with them; some get transferred to other prisons or honor camps or farms, and they take their books with them. We also feel that if all these books help one man there, it is worth every book we have taken in there. This is a small price for one's sobriety.

In the years I have been going to AA meetings at Jackson Prison, I have received thousands of letters from these men. I write twenty to twenty-five letters a week in response. I couldn't put a price tag on all the benefit I have received from attending AA meetings in prison.

In these years, I have seen a lot of men get out of Jackson. Most are making it on the outside, I am happy to say. It is rewarding to get letters from these people telling how they got a good job or got married or some other good things that have happened to them. In a little over seven years, I have been best man four times, and I have become godparent to a child five times.

Sure, there are men that get out and have to go back in. But when they get back to prison, we try a little harder. Sometimes, people see one guy go back to prison and draw the conclusion that they all go back. Well, for every one that has to go back to prison, I can name at least ten that are making it outside.

I heard from an old-timer a while back, "The benefits of the AA program are beyond your wildest dreams." To me, it is a benefit to be able to go to an AA meeting in prison. If you are from Michigan, I just may see you at the meeting. God bless all my AA brothers and sisters incarcerated.

R. M., Bay City, Mich.

What AA Meetings Taught a Non-AA Counselor

by Lee A. Crutchfield, M.Ed.

December 1977

I n late 1971, while I was working in the Air Force's drug abuse program, it became apparent that I needed to learn more about our number one drug of abuse, alcohol, and dependency on it, alcoholism. A friend suggested open AA meetings as a source of education. I attended my first meeting shortly thereafter and have continued to go ever since. These are some measurable benefits I have derived:

Discovering our common humanity: From the first meeting I felt a sense of identity with many of the speakers I heard. I began to say then, and have said many times thereafter, "I've never had any serious problems related to alcohol, but there's a lot of alcoholic in me." I said that because the alcoholics' concerns with ego, anger, frustration, manipulation, and fears of inadequacy sounded a lot like mine. Hearing how they dealt with them became more than an academic interest.

An AA friend in Colorado put it in perspective for me when he said, "Lee, what you have discovered is your common humanity with the alcoholic. There's probably no more alcoholic in you than in anyone else; but you've learned that between you and the alcoholic, there are more similarities than differences." Discovering and exploring our common characteristics, strong and weak, have been good for me and for my relationships with clients.

The vicarious experiencing of alcoholism: I've never experienced alcoholism. Is my best bet to try to experience it intellectually through books, workshops, and seminars? I think not! I have found that the best way I can approximate the visceral experience, the despair, jubilation, madness, and agony, is to be with people who relive their experience verbally—and with real feeling. Sure, the intellectual grasp is important, but how much more real and meaningful it becomes when vicariously experienced at the emotional level. It's the next "best" thing to having been there myself.

It helps my credibility, too, with those people who are inclined to say, "How can you help me? You've never been there." Willingness to vicariously share and to respect the validity of their experiences has helped earn me the title of "honorary alcoholic" from my AA friends—a title I am proud to have.

Free education: I have attended alcoholism schools at universities in Utah, Colorado, and Oklahoma and several others with National Council on Alcoholism groups, and have heard therapists espouse the application of transactional analysis, Gestalt therapy, behavior modification, reality therapy, rational emotive therapy, and other techniques. I swear to God, after that kind of exposure (which has certainly been good and worthwhile), I have learned more about alcoholism—its treatment and mistreatment and the ways it affects people and families—at open meetings of AA and Al-Anon. And it's free! And it's in my own community, wherever I am.

Experience love and fellowship: To me, an ongoing relationship with AA is an ongoing exposure to love and warm fellowship. Now I guess I can grasp that intellectually and have it in mind when I refer someone to AA. But that sure ain't no substitute for walking in the door of the Saturday night open meeting of the East Side Group in Panama City, Fla., and having Dot S., a loving Al-Anon, hug me and make me feel welcome, or to have Curly D., an AA, take my hand in his burly paw and say, "Good to see you," and mean it. There's a feeling there that transcends learning. And I believe that if you don't know the feeling, you don't know the program.

Professional sustenance: Working with alcoholics in the depths of their illness is a discouraging business, and if all I ever saw were sick alcoholics, it would be devastating. (Note the dropout rate among professionals in the field.) By attending AA meetings, I can associate with well alcoholics, and that sustains me in dealing with the sick alcoholic. Hearing their stories, knowing how it was for them, enables me to see the potential for recovery in others. As I have often said, "Seeing you sober and envisioning your sickness enables me to see the sickness in the drinking alcoholic and envision his sobriety." That gives me strength.

Increased exposure: Many of the clients of our agencies are the poorly paid, the powerless, and the poorly educated. If those were the only alcoholics I saw, I'd get a distorted view of the cross section of humanity that is affected by this disease. By attending open AA meetings, I become exposed to the case histories of the business person, the society matron, the professional person, the top-level military officer, the rich as well as the poor, the highly educated as well as the illiterate, and I experience a more realistic sampling. If not for open AA meetings, I wouldn't have met the pilots, the dentists, the clergy, the lawyers, the working women, the housewives, who have experienced the devastation of alcoholism just as deeply as have our agency clients.

Source of material: As a public educator, I'm always on the alert for entertaining jokes and stories. At AA meetings, I have heard enough stories to fill a large book. Unfortunately, I wasn't taking notes. However, I can remember enough material to include anecdotes and jokes in my presentations, to liven them up. Nearly all have been "borrowed" from AA speakers who were introducing some levity into their stories. Finding humor at AA meetings surprised me initially. Now, I find it an ongoing delight.

Twelfth Step referrals: A major benefit of being closely in contact with AA people is personally knowing the stories of well alcoholics. By knowing what it was like, what happened, and what it's like now with them, I can better decide whom to call when a client wants to talk with someone "who's been there." What a joy (and relief) it is to discover where my client is at and to say, "Would you like to talk to someone who's been where you are now and was able to do something about it?"—and to have a specific someone in mind. "Selective referral," I call it, and it beats the hell out of guesswork.

First-name friendships: Ongoing contact with AA brings me a degree of acceptance in the community of recovered alcoholics. I buy my gas from one AA member and have my dental work done by another, and I have numerous contacts with AAs and Al-Anons outside of meetings. We know each other because of our common interest in attending meetings. We are on a first-name basis and do a great deal of cross referring. I receive much more than I give, but I sometimes have an opportunity to be helpful. I may be asked to cite a source of help for a youngster who's into drugs, or offer budget counseling for the indebted, or provide the name of a good therapist for someone sober but troubled. Similarly, I get recommendations and guidance from my AA and Al-Anon friends.

Avoid stereotyping: I don't know about others, but I tend to generalize when I deal with large numbers. When I do that with people, that's stereotyping. When I stereotype, I lose sight of the dignity and individuality of the person I'm dealing with. By frequently attending AA and Al-Anon meetings, I am reminded of the many faces of alcoholism and the many ways it is experienced by alcoholics and their families. With that reminder, I am more able to be human with my client and to deal with the person, not the label.

If ever I had the point driven home that there's no such thing as a "typical" alcoholic, it was in observing the milling throng of approximately 20,000 at the AA International Convention in Denver, in 1975. I saw men and women of every racial and ethnic group, of every occupational and economic classification, and of all ages. God, what a blessing to be exposed to that reality!

Uncover my real feelings: By attending AA meetings, I am able to get in touch with my real feelings about alcoholics. If, for example, I avoid AA and alcoholics because I'm afraid I might be considered one of them, am I not revealing my belief that alcoholism is a shameful condition? By refusing or avoiding contact with those who call themselves recovering alcoholics, am I not conveying my doubts about prospects for recovery? By avoiding alcoholics outside the treatment situation, am I not transmitting the message "I'm okay, and you're not okay"? And what does that say about my attitudes?

I hasten to say it's no great sin to have such attitudes; they come with the society in which we live. But for heaven's sake, if I'm going to work with alcoholics and their families, I must recognize them and work on changing them. To work in the field and not do so breeds depression, discouragement, ulcers, resentments, and a short, unhappy career marked by little success. I just get in touch with all my negative feelings and deal with them, for my sake as well as my clients'.

Personal growth: Since I invest my time in attending open meetings of AA and Al-Anon, I may as well get something for myself. I have discovered there's a lot to be gained by trying to incorporate the Twelve Steps of those programs into my life. The soundness of the Steps is demonstrated by the growth of the Fellowship over the past forty-two years and also by the adoption of the Steps by other self-help groups such as Gamblers Anonymous, Parents Anonymous, and Neurotics Anonymous.

I have discovered that by working the Twelve Steps in my life and by taking what I want from the meetings I attend, I grow personally as well as professionally. Also, I have been able to make contact with my spiritual self, something that had eluded me prior to my AA relationship.

Common bond: By bringing the Twelve Steps, the Serenity Prayer, and other AA tools into my life, I have reached a common ground with the recovering alcoholic. We don't have the commonality of the alcoholic experience, but we can have a common bond in working the Steps. If I allow myself to try to find a God of my own understanding, or to make a searching and fearless moral inventory, or to admit to God, to myself, and to another human being the exact nature of my wrongs, or to become ready to have God remove all my defects of character, am I not on common ground with the recovering alcoholic? By bringing my experience closer to his, am I not sharing my humanity as well as my professional capabilities? And does that not contribute to the growth of both of us? I think so.

Source of ideas and speakers: In my job, I run group counseling sessions. I find AA open meetings to be a rich source of ideas, topics, and guest speakers for my groups and classes. By attending many meetings at many different groups, I get stimulating ideas from people who share their experiences as they carry the message.

My hope is that others in the field of alcoholism education or rehabilitation enjoy the same closeness to AA. It has helped me. I've always been made welcome. Attending has contributed to my knowledge and growth. I'm confident that if others in the professions caring for alcoholics allow themselves the experience, the same will happen. For those who don't, may I recommend the Serenity Prayer? It will help!

FOUR

Experience, Strength, and Hope

———————— ♦ ————————

Those Twelve Steps as I Understand Them
by the Rev. Samuel M. Shoemaker
January 1964

One of my most treasured possessions is a pair of gold discs which I carry daily in my pocket, attached to my watch chain. One is engraved "From the Manhattan Group of AA" and was given me by Bill when I left New York in 1952; the other is engraved "Honorary Member in Perpetuity of Pittsburgh AA," given me when I left that city in 1962. They mark one of the happiest and most privileged relationships I have ever enjoyed. I watched the first beginnings of AA always with interest, sometimes with misgivings proven false by all that has happened. I thank God for AA and pray daily for all its leaders and members. One of my cherished memories is of one of the girls at St. Louis, who said to me, "Dr. Sam, you may not be an alcoholic, but by God you certainly do talk like one!"

I have always been interested, not alone in what AA is doing for the alcoholic, but in what this program can mean to anyone who wrestles with a real problem. And who does not? A pile of wisdom and experience is packed into the Twelve Steps. I have even compared the inspired forty minutes during which those Steps were given to AA's co-founder to the time in which the Ten Tablets of the Law were given to Moses on Mt. Sinai.

Many skeptical folk are inclined to say, concerning Moses' inspiration, "Oh, this is a gathering together of previous experience; it didn't come all at once like that." I have no doubt about the previous experience entering in; but I know that there are inspired hours when people have been able to gather and put down compendia of truth in a fashion that can only be called "inspiration." It is an hour when men's powers are at high pitch and tension and when the Spirit of God hovers near, making suggestions. I doubt if the Twelve Steps that have changed the course of existence for so many thousands of lives could have been the product of mere human insight and observation. And they can and will bless anyone, alcoholic or not, who will follow them through and be obedient to them. They are morally and spiritually and psychologically and practically as sound as can be.

1. *We admitted we were powerless over alcohol—that our lives had become unmanageable.*

The reason so many people in AA give thanks that they are alcoholics is that the problems of living and of failure to meet life successfully are singled down for them to the problem of alcohol. It is definite and specific. This is exactly what Christianity has taught from the beginning, not only about a problem like alcoholism, but about the whole range of human defeat; that the old cliches like "exerting more willpower" are utterly impractical. We are just as powerless by ourselves over temper, or a bad tongue, or a moody disposition, or a habit of lust, or a hard and critical spirit. It is only pride and lack of insight into ourselves that would keep anyone from saying, no matter what their problems or lack of them, "Our lives have become unmanageable." This is the first step, not only toward sobriety, but toward self-understanding and the knowledge of life.

2. *Came to believe that a Power greater than ourselves could restore us to sanity.*

"Came" how? By standing in the middle of a field calling out to some nameless power? By reading long books of philosophy or theology? No! By seeing scores, and maybe hundreds and then thousands, of individual men and women whose lives had been defeated and wretched (making thousands more wretched also) transformed into new men and women. Each one of these lives is a kind of miracle—

not to be explained in purely human terms. Doctors and psychiatrists and clergy, helpful as they have been to some alcoholics, have no opportunity to report such a high percentage of victories as AA. How wise AA was not to attempt too specific a theological definition! Too finespun words were bound to offend some and put off others; nobody can fight against the rather vague term "Power greater than ourselves," forged in the crucible of laymen working it out among themselves, sharing experience with one another.

    3. *Made a decision to turn our will and our lives over to the care of God as we understood Him.*

William James, in a classic passage of *The Varieties of Religious Experience*, said that the crisis of self-surrender has always been and must always be regarded as the vital turning point of the religious life. Look through the life of any saint, almost any great servant of mankind, and you will find a moment, an hour, a day when the crisis took place. You can gather materials for a decision over months and years, and you can carry out the effects of a decision over long periods of time, but a decision is sudden. It is a crisis.

This is a vivid way of saying that all spiritual experience must begin decisively if it is going to begin at all. This is the great, open, spiritual secret which so many have missed. They tried to ooze into it. You can ooze into booze, but you can't ooze out of it. You can't ooze into God. Everybody in the world needs to learn this truth. I had been a nominal Christian for ten years before anybody challenged me to surrender myself to God. This has to be done more than once, as we shall find; but it has to begin somewhere. This decision puts us in touch with God, so that he can work. It is like screwing the bulb in tight enough to touch the place where the current comes out; but this decision of the will is not the current itself. The current is the spiritual power that flows when we cry out our need to God and he answers.

    4. *Made a searching and fearless moral inventory of ourselves.*

There is no more difficult thing in the world than to face yourself as you really are. We flee from one sin after another as they catch up with us, making excuses all the time, and pleading that our virtues in another direction more than make up for them. What most people need, what all must have if they are to find an answer, is just the willingness to make "a searching and fearless moral inventory" of themselves.

Some sins are obvious. But when it comes to the spiritual sins —like pride, and unforgivingness, and resentment, and touchiness, and inflexibility about having our own way—they are *not* so obvious, because their damage is less easy to see quickly. The Ten Commandments will form a good guide. So will the Sermon on the Mount. We may need to sit down with someone who knows us and will be honest with us, and ask him to give us a good going over, for most of us are terribly blind and terribly self-deceived. One can even make a "formal confession" to a priest in the church and not really get wise to oneself. Deepest of all, greatest of all, and subtlest of all will be *pride* in some form, usually masquerading under the guise of some virtue. Alcoholism may force such an honesty about oneself; would that all the other and more respectable sins did the same thing!

5. *Admitted to God, to ourselves, and to another human being the exact nature of our wrongs.*

The practice of confession is, of course, an old one and in some churches a constant one. I suspect that its efficacy depends in part on the sincerity with which the confession is made, and on whether the person confessing really means to get out on new ground and be different thereafter. True confession not only cleans up the past with God's forgiveness, it looks to a new kind of future, else it is bogus.

Confession to other lay people has generally been discouraged by the church as being risky, but AA has proved its efficacy in the case of alcoholics, it being possible to take for granted some degree of maturity in the one who hears the story, and some discretion in the keeping of confidences. Let's face it—a certain desperation underlies this. Every minister wishes he could induce the same kind of desperation in the general run of his people, so that they would face their overall spiritual ineffectiveness and their need to make the same kind of "admission" as alcoholics find necessary. This is always a costly and painful process. I suspect that one reason why it is so effective is that what happens is not only the opening to another human being of "the exact nature of our wrongs," but the laying of pride in the dust by letting someone else know the depth and desperation of our need. Shams go off when you do this. You can't keep on faking. This, and not only the detail of misdoings, is what gets us where we can begin to be different.

6. *Were entirely ready to have God remove all these defects of character.*

It's not hard to feel like that on a morning after, but we know this may be remorse and not repentance, superinduced more by a heavy head than by a contrite heart. The further away we get from the last binge of alcohol (or of temper, or whatever), the better the wrongdoing looks—more innocent, more attractive. Are we ready *then* to "have God remove all these defects of character"?

It is one thing to want to put behind us the inconveniences of wrongdoing, but another to leave behind the wrongdoing itself. This requires two things, I think: 1) a real vision of how much better the new life really is than the old, fortified by what we have heard from people living in it; 2) real help from the Higher Power, for the will alone is not capable of sustaining this attitude. It is good to be pushed by the danger and hell of the old life, but we must also be pulled by the constant vision of life integrated under God, living in and for and by him and in and for other people. This is why fellowship is so essential, why it is so dangerous for anyone to think he can take a little spiritual inspiration or power and go off and enjoy it all by himself. Soon or late, he is back in the old groove. We need God and we need each other. God alone can give us this new mind and keep us in it. All people need it, so-called good people as well as so-called bad ones. We need to pray for this fundamental willingness to have God change us.

7. *Humbly asked Him to remove our shortcomings.*

How often have we prayed for "things," or favoring circumstances, or a hundred and one things that were really selfish in nature! Here

is where real prayer begins—not ends—in asking God to *change me.*
"Lord, I'm not much. You aren't getting much of a prize. It's mostly
broken pieces I'm giving you. But I ask you to mend them. You can
take the pride and the lust and the anxiousness and the fear and the
resentment. Please do take them, and me with them." Something
like that.

We may say it in the quiet of our own rooms or we may say it kneel-
ing in our church, or we may say it as we pray with another person.
There must be an intended finality as we make such a prayer. We
can't do it with tongue in cheek. So far as it is possible, we mean to be
done with the offending thing. We find again that "willpower" only
goes far enough to secure our intention; the actual praying of such
a prayer already implies help from him to whom we pray. Sins get
entangled deep within us, as some roots of a tree, and do not easily
come loose. We need help, grace, the lift of a kind of divine derrick.
The amazing thing is that such a prayer is answered if we truly want
it to be. Our own wills are so much a needed part of this that it almost looks as if we had done it. But the help from God is still more a
needed part of it; we are sure that without him we could not possibly
have done it. We learn great truths, long known and often discovered,
as we begin a genuine spiritual awakening.

8. *Made a list of all persons we had harmed, and became willing to
make amends to them all.*

In some ways, it is easier to straighten things out with God than
with other people. He fully understands everything; we can count
on his forgiveness; we talk to him, as it were, in private. But it is
not enough to be right with him; we must also be right with other
people. How well do I remember that, from my first moment of fresh
conviction. There was a letter I had to write to someone in the family,
toward whom I held a long-standing resentment. It was one of the
first things I had to do after my decision.

You see, we want to get *clear,* to begin anew, to start life all over
again. This Step calls for *definiteness,* and it calls for willingness:
"Made a list" and "became willing." How many strained and broken

human relationships drag on through years, unresolved, unhealed, unmended. Nobody will make the break and say the two great words of renewal, "I'm sorry." We are willing to tell God of our repentance and desire for new life; we are not willing to tell others. This can hold us back at the first, and it can trip us way down the line.

The laws governing human relations are as ironclad as those that uphold the stars. Individualize the persons whom we have wronged and those who have wronged us. Don't forget the wise adage that "It is harder to forgive those whom we have wronged than those who have wronged us." Get willing to go to them in honesty and humility. It may be the hardest thing you ever did in your life but it will be one of the most rewarding. We shall need to do it in the beginning of our new life; we shall have to do it, perhaps often, in the after-stages of it.

9. *Made direct amends to such people wherever possible, except when to do so would injure them or others.*

We must be willing to be absolutely honest, but indiscriminate "absolute honesty" would blow the roof off many a house and destroy entirely some human relations. We must hold nothing back through deceit or pride; we may need to hold something back by discretion and consideration of others. Take a thing like infidelity in marriage. Sometimes, this must be disclosed to wife or husband in all candor. Sometimes, as in the case of someone with a bad heart, or terribly sensitive or innocent of nature, "telling all" may be almost a self-indulgence for us. The people we have hurt may be dead, in which case prayer to God to let them know our repentance may be all we can do. Or there may be facts in the situation which would help clear the relation, but they involve telling what we know about someone else's sins. This is allowable under only the rarest circumstances; usually, it spreads the evil and does more harm than good. If, in order to clear our own souls, we must damage the reputation of another, it is an extremely dubious practice.

Those who deal much with human souls—priests, psychiatrists, lay folk like AAs—must learn the secret of a tight lip, or we shall do damage and gain the name of gossips, which will shut off people's confidence from us. Such actions are usually those of the Pharisee type, the good and righteous type. But they are sometimes those of the changed Prodigal also—and nothing is worse than the fury of a Prodigal turned Pharisee. What is made known in confidence should be kept in confidence until or unless the person involved gives us permission to speak of it.

10. *Continued to take personal inventory and when we were wrong promptly admitted it.*

This is one of the hardest Steps in the Twelve. Many of us get steamed up to be completely honest with God, ourselves, and some other person at the outset; this points up the wisdom of continuing the attitude all the rest of the way. We like to think we have grown past this stage and are well on the road, but none of us ever get finally past it. We shall find that when we seek God's help and guidance on some problem, we may need to be open first to conviction of sin— then to direction. This is part of what keeps the whole thing fresh and contemporary and alive.

I am convinced that pride is the root-sin. It is not only, in moral theology, the first of the seven deadly sins, it is by so much the most serious of them that it is as if it stood apart from the rest as being of a different quality. Pride gets right into our spiritual victories. It insinuates itself into all our achievements, all our successes, even when we attribute them to God, unless we keep open to facing ourselves afresh and making things right where they have gone wrong.

11. *Sought through prayer and meditation to improve our conscious contact with God as we understood Him, praying only for knowledge of His will for us and the power to carry that out.*

After we see daylight on the conquest of such a clear-cut problem as alcohol—or fear, or resentment, or pride—and feel we are at least making progress, we need a great, overall purpose and motivation upon which to center our growth. Prayer, we shall increasingly find, is not asking God for something we want; it is really asking him for something he wants. The best of all prayers is "Lord, what wilt thou have me do?" (Acts 22:10). Prayer does not seek to change God's will but to find it.

> 12. *Having had a spiritual awakening as the result of these Steps, we tried to carry this message to alcoholics, and to practice these principles in all our affairs.*

This principle applies to all who have known a great before-and-after experience of spiritual rebirth. Two things are involved in the Twelfth Step: the spread of the awakening to others, and the deepening and continuation of the awakening in ourselves. This was surely the secret of the Twelve Apostles and all the early Christian disciples. J. B. Phillips says they kept to their main purpose of bringing people to God through Christ, and "were not permitted to enjoy any fascinating sidetracks." I should say unhesitatingly that the success of AA lies in the readiness of its members to go to any trouble to help other alcoholics, and that when this readiness cools it is a danger signal.

There was an old saying that used to be current and still contains a great germ of spiritual truth: "Out of self into God into others." Herein are spiritual wisdom and health. We have had to look deep within, probe, burrow, struggle, and in a sense this never stops. But now we must begin to look wide without, concern ourselves with individuals, causes, communities, and the wider world. Here is the secret of growth and of spread—not for alcoholics only, but for all.

I often say and shall always say that the Twelve Steps are one of the very great summaries and organic collections of spiritual truth known to history. They have an almost universal relevance (not a relevance for alcoholics alone). They will offer a way out for many a person who knows nothing personally of alcoholism. They will point up the way for those who have known it and lost it. Thank God for the Twelve Steps and for a man wise enough and open enough to God and to the observation of human experience to receive these truths, and transmit them to the world!

First Step

We admitted we were powerless over alcohol—that our lives
had become unmanageable.
January 1970

B efore I came to AA, I took Step One slowly, over a period of
years. It was not AA people who helped me with it. Instead,
it was all the nonalcoholics who misunderstood and mis-
treated both me and my disease. In retrospect, I am grateful for their
harshness. It forced me to AA, twenty-five years ago this month.

That first faltering step I took to AA recovery was not placed exactly in the first of the twelve footprints left us as a guide by the earliest AA members. But before I came to AA I had begun to realize that
my drinking was causing me trouble. This, of course, was hard to believe; so many other people who drank did not get into trouble. My
life presented a tough sequence of problems, yes; but I argued (with
myself) that drinking surely was not the cause. Fate had just handed
me unfair breaks: my family, my love life, my bosses and jobs, my
unsteady finances, my friends, my insomnia, my nervousness.

So I desperately kept trying to prove that drinking was not one of
my problems. If I was a failure at drinking, rather than a success, it
wasn't for lack of trying! Looking back, it is not so hard to understand
now why it was difficult for me, as it has been for others, to accept
this inability to drink (for which pharmacological addiction provides
a simple explanation). The rewards, pleasures, and gratifications of
drinking were so overpoweringly great. Drinking was easy to do, and
it worked almost instantaneously, anesthetizing any discomfort as if
by magic. It was socially acceptable; my whole social life, all the activities I considered fun, were accompanied by drinking.

The idea of *not* drinking was so unfamiliar to me that it was
frightening. If I thought of a nondrinking life at all, I thought of

it as a cheerless existence devoid of grace and charm. To give up drinking would mean turning into the bluenosed, narrow-minded, Puritan type.

It is important now for me to remember that my entire style of life was at stake, not just the apparent benefits of alcohol. Lying to people and sinking into gloomy self-pity were habits neither unfamiliar to me nor frightening. I was thoroughly comfortable with them—even, in a way, found them enjoyable. Besides, "I was drunk at the time" was a marvelous excuse to have when I did shameful things.

Giving up drinking, then, looked like an unpleasant, unendurably long-term proposition. Anyhow, it wouldn't be necessary, would it, *if* other people would just change?

But they didn't. They got worse. My family, in their displeasure with me, pointed clearly to drinking as the source of my troubles. Friends who expressed concern and bosses who fired me helped drive home that truth. Kind strangers and bartenders who shook their heads while being helpful all said in effect, "You should not drink." A cop who jailed me for being drunk and disorderly, a doctor who scolded me for drinking too much, a grocer who wanted his money, and a bouncer who shoved me out a tavern door all reinforced the lesson.

My repeated solo failures to "do better" kept building an interior despair which finally crushed my false reasoning and false pride. Hung there at the edge of madness, I read a newspaper story about AA.

And so, on the day I first telephoned AA, I was not struggling too hard against the mountains of undeniable proof that my life was one awful mess because of my drinking. I had also already admitted, unwillingly, that I could not handle alcohol.

Those admissions of mine are not necessarily identical to scientific diagnosis of the disease of alcoholism, of course. Any well-trained physician, alcoholism counselor, or other professional familiar with the symptoms of alcoholism can correctly determine whether or not a given drinker has the symptoms.

But such diagnosis by another person is not a step toward recovery for the drinker—until he himself takes the First Step. I took it blindly at the start, and that was not the best way for me, although any beginning is better than none. In subsequent AA years, through conscious, systematic efforts to understand and practice all the Steps, I have found that they repeatedly come to have new and surprising values.

For me, the hardest part of that First Step has been in the implications of the statement that my life had become unmanageable. With the effects of booze a bit behind me, I could see more plainly than ever what a mess my life was, what a job lay before me. And it became clearer than ever that, in order to stay sober, I had to undertake a mammoth overhaul of myself in many aspects which, at first, seemed unrelated to drinking.

In short, stepping into the first footprint that led from the dismal swamp of alcoholism toward the sunlight of sobriety would not take me far enough. Would I muddle along on some little trail of my own in the weeds, vaguely paralleling the clearly marked AA road? Or would I choose to follow in the exact footsteps of the AAs who had preceded? The choice was up to me. I could do either, but I had to cover the whole trail if I wanted to get where the others were. Since I had already taken Step One, I could decide to stop right there. I could just dry up, period. I could survive like a raisin the rest of my life.

Going the whole route looked too hard—until someone said to me, "One step at a time." So I looked ahead, along the path marked by the footprints of hope, commitment, and action. All around me were many happy, sober people who had walked that path. Listening intently to their stories, I heard some more horrifying than mine, others less so. But it was plain that all these alcoholics had once *felt* the same hopelessness, fear, pain, and anger I had experienced. It was also obvious that people with drinking troubles like mine could come out of them and—unbelievable as it seemed at first—laugh at them! It was evident, too, that these people had much knowledge of alcoholism that I did not have. They knew that it was an illness, that it could deceive its victims, that the danger lay in the first drink.

They had some magic or information, secrets or power which I lacked, but which might get me out of the fix I was in. I had to believe what I saw: that some power wiser, stronger, or greater than mine could restore me to health. Next came a decision I did not even notice making at the time: to try this AA plan of theirs, even though I did not understand it. Some said it was God doing the good work, but I saw unbelievers like me being helped, too. So what had I to lose by going along?

Beginning with the First Step, I have found the following Steps out of alcoholism to be true and benevolent. I still know of no other suggestions more effective as a program of recovery.

B. L., New York, N.Y.

Second Step

Came to believe that a Power greater than ourselves
could restore us to sanity.
February 1970

I f the First Step is a measure of our despair, the Second is a measure of our hope. The First Step is the admission and acceptance of our defeat—total, absolute defeat. With all our resources, we can't stay sober; with the best intentions and with the utmost determination, we still find our lives crashing down around our heads. Indeed, we are powerless over alcohol, and our lives are unmanageable.

But if we are powerless over alcohol, then who or what will keep us sober? And if we cannot manage our own lives, then who or what will guide us, help us return to some sort of rational existence?

In answer to both questions, the Second Step says: A power greater than ourselves can restore us to sanity.

With that single, simple statement, the Second Step lays the spiritual cornerstone of AA: If we are to recover from the physical, mental, and spiritual disease called alcoholism, we must come to believe in and rely on a force *outside* ourselves.

This is not easy for most of us to do, and for many it takes time. Fortunately, the Step is very careful to use the wording "Came to believe." Some of us come to believe almost instantly; others take weeks or months; still others take years. There is no set timetable, and there is no reason to feel guilt over inability to accept the Second Step immediately, with all its ramifications. On the other hand, though, if we do not work toward an acceptance of the Step, if we ignore it or kick it under the rug and hope it goes away, we cut the spiritual heart out of the program.

So, by hook or by crook, we come to believe. But believe in what?

In three things: the existence of a force outside—and greater than—ourselves; the fact of our own insanity; the ability of the greater power to take care of that insanity.

For reasons which someday someone may explain far better than I can, many or even most alcoholics seem to have trouble with the word "insanity," though the track record of any practicing alcoholic—even the part we remember—should be proof enough that we are at this stage somewhat different from the normal. To many, the word conjures up visions of men in white coats, or patients chasing butterflies across Happydale, or any one of a dozen forms of psychotic behavior. But a word is only a word, and "insanity" can refer to any kind of behavior that is at variance with what is generally accepted as normal.

Our obsessive, compulsive behavior in relation to alcohol can hardly be termed normal. Nor can the things we do while drinking. Nor can many of the habit patterns, mental processes, or just plain hang-ups we have after we stop drinking.

Any discussion of the Second Step will show that the word "insanity" means, to different people, that we were insane while we drank, or before we started drinking, or after we stopped, or at all three stages. These differences of opinion become unimportant in the light of this statement: If we were insane while we drank, the craving to return to that life must be equally insane, and if there was or is some problem that adds fuel to the craving, then the problem must be eliminated.

But the solution offered by that statement is not as easy as it looks.

To put it crudely: A truly sick mind cannot repair itself; in fact, many times it can't even see what's wrong.

The human mind has a marvelous ability to protect itself from outside influences. Although the conscious portion of the mind may have a sincere desire to find out what's wrong and to fix it, the subconscious part will block any such effort by putting up a bewildering variety of misleading motivations, misinformation, and misdirections. The more important—the deeper—the particular hang-up is, the higher and thicker this wall will be. If the problem is big enough, the conscious, thinking mind will not even be aware of its existence, and the mind that does become aware will still be powerless to do much about it.

The knowledge of that helplessness in trying to cope with our own problems by ourselves is an integral part of the First and Second Steps. The Second Step states very clearly that our insanity can be taken care of, our sanity can be restored, by a power greater than ourselves. Once we have become aware of our own irrationality and our inability to cope with it singlehanded, it then becomes a question of searching out a solution that is outside—and greater than—ourselves.

It would be hard to overemphasize the importance of this search for an acceptance of a power, a force, an influence that is outside ourselves. The Step refers to a power greater than ourselves. Obviously, if we are unable to solve our problems alone, the power *must* be greater than we are in order to bring about anything much worthwhile. However, babies have to creep before they can walk, and walk before they can run. It is tough merely to begin to look outside ourselves for any kind of force or power, let alone a greater power. In fact, it is hard for some of us to accept the idea that there is anything outside ourselves.

That last statement deserves some explanation. A rational, thinking, conscious mind has no trouble with the idea that each person, thing, and force has a separate and distinct existence. We can say (and believe), "I am. You are. He is."

However, the subconscious or unconscious mind often rejects this idea. It says, "I am, but you exist only as I think about you." Extreme? Hardly. One of the most powerful tools in AA is the process by which one alcoholic identifies with another. First, this identification consists merely of recognizing that there are other people who exist independently of our own minds. Then the process goes further: It identifies another alcoholic as a *similar* human being. But the basic identification is with another human being as a separate entity.

Once that log jam has been broken up, the rest of the process is relatively easy. Once we become aware that there are other people and things—and forces—outside ourselves, it becomes a matter of searching until a power that does some good is found. Eventually, through any one of a wide variety of spiritual experiences, the power is recognized as the basic driving force of the universe.

Disposing of the whole concept of acquiring a greater power in one or two sentences may seem abrupt, but is anything else worth saying? Those who have had a spiritual experience already know all about it, while for those who have not yet had one, an outpouring of words would have no real meaning.

The search for a higher power and the nature of that power, when found, are very personal matters. Many of us have no trouble in accepting God as our Higher Power; many others shy away from the word "God," but have no trouble in accepting the presence of some sort of universal force; still others look upon our AA group or all of AA as a power greater than ourselves.

In all these cases, though, we have acquired a belief in some force that is external, more powerful than we are, and capable of helping us return to sanity. This implies that the external, more powerful force is a force for good, an orderly force capable of making sense out of the chaos of reality, and bringing order to our own chaotic lives.

The final stage in a full acceptance of the Second Step is to come to believe that this greater power—a good and orderly greater power—will indeed actually help us. We have already accepted the idea that this force can do the job. Now we must become convinced, completely convinced, that the power *will* do it.

Once again, words are hardly an adequate method of trying to express belief. Those who have thrown themselves on the mercy of the court, so to speak, know that the higher power will do exactly as the Step says. But that statement is no help at all to those who haven't.

What may help is a very brief description of one member's struggles with the Second Step.

I came into AA as an agnostic—or, rather, I didn't believe in anything much, but I wanted to. Although I couldn't begin to accept the concept of God, I certainly liked the serenity and obvious peace of mind I saw in those who did believe.

As my time in the program grew, this desire grew. Also increasing day by day was pain—pure, unrelieved pain—not physical pain, but a longing inside my brain and my heart for something above and, most important, beyond me.

My group and the whole AA program helped, and as time went by I began to perceive some sort of order where there had been only confusion, some sense of guidance where there had been only a labyrinth of blind alleys.

Then, one day (on the Garden State Parkway, unlikely as that sounds) all the pieces fell into place. Whatever barrier had blinded my vision, preventing me from seeing the true nature of things, was gone. For the first time in my life, I became aware of the all-pervading presence of an incomprehensibly vast power.

Then, too, I became aware that I was only one infinitely small—but vitally important—part of the universe. Infinitely small because I was one tiny soul on one planet going around one sun in one galaxy of countless billions, but vitally important because the entire, immense universe would be very, very, very slightly different without me, as it would be different without any one of us.

The vision, if I may call it that, was momentarily staggering, but only momentarily. The essential rightness of my vision sustained me, and still sustains me. If I am part of the whole—even a tiny part—I *belong* here.

And if I belong here, all I have to do is find out exactly what I am supposed to be and do. For me as an alcoholic, part of this answer is obvious. The universe has the ability—in fact, makes it a rule—to

THE BEST OF THE GRAPEVINE

eliminate the bad and the sick, and since an alcoholic is indeed a sick person, the universe—or society—will eliminate him. Therefore, to drink is for me to deny my higher power.

But that is only part of the problem, although perhaps the most important part. I personally conceive of the universe as a very orderly place; to achieve a serene and happy existence, all that is necessary is to be aware of this order and fit myself into it. This is a lot easier said than done, of course. So, in AA, after the Second Step there are ten more designed to help accomplish this.

But once we have accepted, as ineluctable fact, our powerlessness over alcohol, and once we have come to believe that a greater power will give us all the help we need, we have made two giant steps along the road to recovery.

P. S., Greenwich, Conn.

Third Step

Made a decision to turn our will and our lives over to the care of God as we understood Him.
March 1970

Willfulness was the name of the game, and I was the dealer. I shuffled the deck, cut the cards, dealt the hand, called for the openers, and played the game by my own rules. As the chips piled up in front of me, the other players pulled out of the game, one by one, and I was left alone, master of a deck of blank cards and banker of a worthless cache of poker chips. I had become an alcoholic, and I couldn't even see what game I was playing.

I came into AA at thirty, emotionally about half that age, stumbling down the steps into the old intergroup office on 39th Street in New York, knowing I couldn't go on drinking as I had been, knowing that the walls of my life had come tumbling down and that I needed help.

How easily the First Step came: "We admitted we were powerless over alcohol—that our lives had become unmanageable." I had been on a vodka and wine binge for days and was in a state of physical exhaustion and emotional near-hysteria.

Step Two, "Came to believe that a Power greater than ourselves could restore us to sanity," took its course over the next few months, as I actually experienced the beginning of recovery and then came to believe that *something* was taking me over, bringing me back, restoring me.

But oh, that Third Step! "Made a decision to turn our will and our lives over to the care of God..." *What* God? For years I had been doing battle with the whole concept of God. Now I was sober, and still battling. I was sober, and grateful to be sober, but the God hang-up was still there. It has taken nearly nine years for me to begin to apply Step Three, and I have had to turn it around and look at it in reverse to do so.

"...God *as we understood Him.*" As a timid, obedient little girl, I had understood that the God to whom I prayed in Sunday school every Sunday loved me and was watching over me. But at the age of sixteen, my understanding of God underwent a metamorphosis. Under the influence of a course in biology, I began to see God, not as a grand old man peering through the heavens, but as a nonhuman power behind the orderliness of human life, the source of the clean, beautiful creativity inherent in protoplasm, and the energy behind the development of cellular structure from the amoeba to mankind. Suddenly, my former personal concept of God turned me off, with a force so violent I surprised even myself. When the headmistress of the girls' school I attended asked God to "watch over us here in school," I wanted to scream out, "Why *should* he, with a whole universe to run?"

After I left school, my drinking started. At eighteen, I was hanging out in bars, drinking with older men, trying to match them drink for drink, blacking out, and having hallucinations. I was already reputed to be a hopeless drunk. I turned away from all of the values that had been taught me in Sunday school and, believing myself to be terribly evil, gave up on the idea that any God could care for me, anyway. He, she, or it certainly seemed to have no use for me. But at the height of my drinking, slumped over a bottle of port in my apartment two blocks from the Bowery, I wrote a poem to God that began: "Dear God, if you exist at all, a sparrow is about to fall." The prayer came from my despair. My intellectual rejection of a conventional God had not removed my emotional need for a God of comfort and caring.

Then I hit my alcoholic bottom and found hope in AA. Three months after my entrance into the program, I spoke for the first time. Again I surprised myself as, completely without preparation, I heard myself say: "'The Lord is my shepherd. I shall not want. He maketh me to lie down in green pastures. He leadeth me beside the still waters. He restoreth my soul.' AA has restored my soul to me," I said.

It was the beginning of an understanding of what God was to me. It was the recognition of a Higher Power and the role of that Power in bringing about my recovery from alcoholism. But that was as far as it went. Beyond this, I was not letting a Higher Power or any other kind of power into *my* life.

"...The care of God..." I was sober for the first time in my adult life. Through the power of AA, I could stay away from the first drink. I was feeling healthy again, and my self-respect was returning, and morning was a beautiful time of day. But I still ran the show. I had no faith that a God could or did care, or would take care of me. Nor had I the humility to permit a power other than myself to manifest such caring. Although sober, I continued to make my decisions in the same way as before—haphazardly, hastily, without thought. When AA friends told me to "turn a decision over," I thought they meant "turn it upside down" —look at the other side! So I did, or thought I did; but looking at the other side (of the issue at hand) only seemed to confirm the decision I wanted to make. I had no understanding whatsoever of the process of turning anything over *to* a Higher Power. Talk of "the care of God" offended the intellect I thought I had. I considered such advice evangelical and would have no part of it.

"...Our lives over to the care..." My life had to be cared for by someone, and despite my newfound sobriety, willfulness still abided. I spent the next eight years holding on tight to the reins and doing the things I wanted to do, rather than the things that greater wisdom seemed to indicate. I charged into a marriage with an active alcoholic against even my own sense of intelligence (I certainly would never have recommended such a move to anyone else), believing blindly that somewhere along the way AA would get him, even though he made little effort to get AA. My own sobriety was tested again and again as one of his periodic binges followed another and I was forced to hospitalize, institutionalize, and even jail my husband. After every binge, I briefly considered bringing my marriage to an end, but each time fear of loneliness and fear of admitting failure motivated me to give it another try.

In another calamity of willfulness, I embarked upon a publishing venture in a field that was considered risky, against the advice of all acquaintances with any business sense whatsoever. But the image of myself as the head of a successful publishing enterprise was attractive; the need to be considered "successful" after the multiple failures of my past life was great. I invested all my worldly goods in the dream—and lost.

I had *not* turned my life over to the care of any power. There had been no intelligence, no order in my decisions. The only criterion upon which I had based my moves was the satisfaction of my emotional needs—to be loved and to be respected. And I lost the ballgame. Eight years sober, I still hadn't been able to come to grips with that unbelievably elusive Third Step.

"...To turn our will..." I *had* to turn my will over in order to turn my life over to the care of a God. As I had hit bottom and admitted my powerlessness over alcohol, so I now hit another kind of bottom and admitted powerlessness over willfulness. Just as my alcoholic bottom had been accompanied by mental, physical, and spiritual pain, so also was this new bottom steeped in a suffering of its own: the loneliness of a broken marriage, the humiliation of financial collapse, the pressure of resentments against the people who had warned me

(I was ready to clobber the first rat who said, " I told you so"), and the inconvenience of going it alone. I took a close look at myself.

It wasn't hard to trace the suffering to its source. My whole way of life followed decisions predicated on convenience and expedience, as well as willfulness. If I continued to bungle my decisions, there would be more suffering, and perhaps one of these days I might even forget and pick up the first drink, not caring anymore, because everything was so lousy anyway. Well, I didn't want to pick up that drink. I didn't want to go back to the binges, the blackouts, the hallucinations, the awful hangovers, and the guilt of past days. The only thing left to do was to try for the first time to turn my will over to some Intelligence, to become "willing to grow along spiritual lines." I had to accept the fact that the way would be paved with inconvenience, loneliness, discomfort, and financial hardship, but that it was the only way if I was going to survive.

And so I "made a decision" to turn my will and my life over to the care of God as I understood him. *How* I made it is not easy to put in to words. It wasn't a matter of taking conscious steps, like blending the ingredients of a cake. It was an unconscious blending of thoughts, attitudes, and actions.

First, I evaluated myself and the current status of my life. What was right about it? What was wrong? Then I divided the "wrong" things into those I couldn't do anything about and therefore must accept, and those I could do something about and could change. The next step was an act of faith. For the first time in my adult life, I came to believe that I was doing "God's will"—or, in words I feel more comfortable with, doing the intelligent thing, the thing that makes sense. This belief gave me the courage to start making the necessary changes in my life. The courage has not been consistent; there have been peaks and low points in its intensity. I take advantage of the peaks of courage by taking the more difficult steps while I am feeling strong. During the low points, I am gentle with myself—even indulge myself!—and don't require of myself anything more than staying sober and doing only what is required to get by. I live a day at a time, believing that all is going according to plan, and that there is no need for me to waste valuable energy worrying about the future.

I have to maintain absolute, unwavering faith in the validity of the steps I am taking. Without this faith, there would be no Step Three for me. The faith is continually tested by my overriding human frailties—the need for love, the desire for easy living—but so far the strength of this Higher Power has sustained my (or should I say "God's"?) will.

And I have known loneliness and hardship, while living alone, holding down three jobs, and waiting for what will be my second divorce. But, having come to believe in a Power that can and will be responsible for my life, and even in a Power that cares, I believe the strength will be there. Having seen for myself that my own navigation served only to slam my boat up against shoals, I have at last become willing to turn the steering over to a more adept helmsman. The decision is clear.

Tomorrow I may be drunk. But today I have the tired peace that comes from doing the things you have to do when you turn the wheel over to a mariner who knows the way across, but makes you work with him through every inch of the crossing. I am not saying that for me the Third Step has been completed. My willfulness is still very much a part of me and may always be a stumbling block to progress in my life. So I will have to stay very close to AA, where my strength lies. I am so full of human frailty that I think it is a miracle I am here today at all. It's only through AA.

And it's only through AA that I can now appreciate and understand a passage from Romans (5:3-5) which I once scoffed at: "We rejoice in our sufferings, knowing that suffering produces endurance, and endurance produces character, and character produces hope, and hope does not disappoint us." Perhaps "hope" is the real name of the game.

Anonymous, N.H.

Fourth Step

Made a searching and fearless moral inventory of ourselves.
May 1970

The idea of "morals" scared hell out of me for years—the years before my drinking became unmanageable, then the alcoholic years, and even the first three or four years after I had found the shelter of Alcoholics Anonymous.

Nothing could dull the edge of what I realize now was simply cold fear. I was frightened at the very mention of "morality" because it posed too big a problem for me—big because it was simple. If I accepted the challenge that the consideration of morality hurled at me, I would have to begin dividing my life—and the things I did every day—into two long columns headed "right" and "wrong."

Try this simple experiment, and you'll discover exactly why I was scared. Pop into your neighborhood gin mill or a local cocktail party. Find the drunkest lush around and start a discussion about "right and wrong" with him (or her). What you will hear will be roughly equivalent to the confusion in which I lived for nearly a quarter of a century. Or turn back your own psychic clock to those boozy meditations, crazy distortions, and amoeboid transformations of "rights" and "wrongs" by which you lived—or tried to live—while you were on the sauce.

Like most enlightened moderns, I had come under the wing of Uncle Sigmund Freud. (My analyst's analyst had been analyzed by Freud in person, so I drunkenly thought of myself as a legitimate great-grandson of the great man himself.) Years of probing into the sexual enigmas of individual and collective living left me, like many of my generation, believing the vague dictum that bore the imprimatur of the Vienna school of psychology: *"Everything* has to do with sex." I knew, therefore, that I was somehow liberated from the repellent, antique morality of Queen Victoria. I was free, morally speaking, to pursue the truth of my own nature and to rise above the tyrannies of repressed (and therefore "wrong") sex.

Accordingly, again like many of my generation, I was literally *obsessed* by sex, an obsession (but not, thank God, a compulsion) second in importance only to alcohol in my life. Drinking, for at least a dozen alcoholic years, was not a moral matter at all; that is, it seemed to have nothing to do with right or wrong. Alcohol meant survival; anything that kept me alive, I assumed, was necessary and hence, in the philosopher's words, "beyond good and evil." So I did not see alcohol as a problem, except at the moments when I dimly noticed (with frequent amusement) that the stuff was killing me. But this subtle observation appeared almost totally irrelevant to the clear truth that booze was also keeping me alive. Such a state of affairs is too much of a puzzle (a moral puzzle, when you get right down to it) for any man's gin-soaked brain, including mine.

What I am getting to (slowly) is that morality for me centered, I thought, on matters having to do mostly with sex. Drinking unleashed a panorama of sexual fantasies within me. (These fantasies, let me add, were rarely implemented in life. The business of living was just too jammed up with wide-screen and stereophonic hangovers, the logistics of getting the next drink while battling for social survival, and the exhausting labor of achieving the maximum possible intoxication. There was just no time or energy left to turn those sex dreams into reality.)

Imagine, then, how I felt after a dry year in our Fellowship when I first bruised my sensitivities upon Step Four. A *moral* inventory! "Rights" and "wrongs"! Sex! More than this, it was suggested that I commit my inventory (one way or another) to writing. I made a few scratches on a yellow pad, thought a bit about the antipornography legislation being proposed in those days, and retired in a sulk to a closed AA meeting where questions could be submitted anonymously on slips of paper.

Before the meeting even began, I wrote, "Why does the Fourth Step ask us to take a *moral* inventory? Why not just an inventory?" I folded the paper discreetly and slid it under an ashtray on the speaker's table at the front of the room.

I had never seen the leader of that meeting before, and I have not run into him since. In his qualification, he explained that he was a professional gambler, whose usual beat was in Nevada, and that "business" (having to do, I gather, with the sport of kings) had brought him to the East for the current season. His story was nothing short of inspirational. His ten years of sobriety—in the midst of the uncertainty of his particular occupation—were clearly a triumph of living a day at a time. He seemed to have absolute confidence that his Higher Power cared as much about decks of cards, dice, roulette wheels, and parimutuel machines as it did about more sacred and cultural artifacts. To me, that was both astounding and comforting.

Eventually, he unfolded my question and looked at it as if it were a hopeless poker hand. He read it aloud and repeated, "Why do we take a *moral* inventory?" He paused and examined the ceiling. Then a weary look overcame him, a look indicating that he had indeed thought about this before. His voice was so low I could hardly hear it, as if he were reluctantly sharing a sure thing on tomorrow's daily double.

"The reason we take a *moral* inventory," he said carefully, "is because the word 'moral' forces us to divide into rights and wrongs the things we do—and have done—to ourselves and others. This forces us to make decisions— personal decisions—and asks us, in effect, where we stand as human beings, what we hold to be right and wrong, whether we're alone in the dark of night or with other people."

Quite suddenly, I realized that I was in the company of an extremely wise man, and I listened closely to the ensuing discussion. Nobody even brought up the topic of sex! Our gambling man had set the tone for the discussion; it centered mostly upon the maintenance of sobriety and upon the clear thinking and strength required to stand up as a man or a woman, ready to be counted, ready to affirm, "This I believe to be right—this I believe to be wrong," and ready to try to live just that way.

I spent the rest of that evening with my copy of *Twelve Steps and Twelve Traditions*. I came to see, first, that on the analyst's couch I was able to do a lot of things, but never to take (even with the help of a skilled therapist) a true moral inventory; then, that until I did I would be adrift in the contemporary relativism of wishy-washy, vaguely "scientific" amorality. I thought of the words "right" and "wrong" as they applied to the brilliant men who invented bacteriological warfare and nuclear warheads. I thought of Ernest Hemingway's "emancipated" notion that what was moral was what felt good, and I tried to think about, not only what felt good now, but what could be counted upon to feel good tomorrow and the day after.

I thought about sex. Certainly, the wake of joy and sorrow we leave behind us in our pursuit of instinctual pleasure is a moral matter (and a measure of character), as Bill wrote. So are the numerous choices that the pursuit forces us to make in daily life. We must consider, not only whether we are adhering to a certain social concept of what is "right," but how we feel if we do not adhere to it, when (as sometimes happens) the spirit is willing, but the flesh commands otherwise. Certainly, I thought then (and still do), the implication of a willingness to "stand up and be counted," the real moral imperative of life, takes us far beyond the simple roster of "rights" and "wrongs" concerning "genital commotion" (as psychologists often call it) and into the entire realm of human relationships.

In my solitude, I asked myself, "What *do* I believe in? What *would* I stand up and be counted for? What do I *really* consider right and, wrong?" And immediately I understood that I had now begun to take a meaningful "searching and fearless moral inventory"!

That evening passed nearly five years ago. I am still trying to answer, to my own satisfaction, those three simple questions. How sorry I am to say that I do not yet know the final answers, even for myself—and certainly not for you. But I think I am on the track in pursuing them within our AA program and I think I am pursuing them well, because I am sober. I think the answers have something to do with love, a word I don't use freely. And they cleave close to Bill's observation that, when we were drinking, "Of true brotherhood we had small comprehension." Without love and brotherhood, I think, we might each turn into the sort of walking moral disaster area that I was before I first met the Fourth Step.

G. G., Queens, N.Y.

The Twelve Steps Revisited—Step Five

Admitted to God, to ourselves, and to another human being the exact nature of our wrongs.
December 1961

Ordinarily you go along the street or drop in at a meeting and somebody says, "How are you?" and without thinking you say "Fine." Things may be terrible, your whole world may have just fallen apart, but you say "Fine."

I suppose on the whole it's a good custom. It cuts off random complaining and acknowledges that nine times out of ten the greeter doesn't really care how you are but is only making a conventional inquiry.

It comes as a kind of surprise, when we encounter the Fifth Step in AA, to discover that there are people on earth who really take an interest in how we are, and wouldn't mind being filled in with quite a bit of detail.

It comes as a surprise and, once we get used to the idea, a relief, because somehow human beings need this honest exchange now and then in order to go on living. Commenting on this, the poet Edwin Arlington Robinson once did a bit of verse about a man everybody thought was on top of the world all the time, "he glittered as he walked"; then one day went out and shot himself. There are times when we have to tell somebody how we *really* are. Step Five takes care of this need better than anything else I know.

How important this action is to getting sober, and *staying* sober,

and growing into a cheerful and useful sobriety, is attested by the
position given it in the Big Book. Step Five, you recall, leads off the
chapter headed, "Into Action." All the Steps before this are regarded
as preparation. But when you get to Step Five, brothers and sisters,
you're in action. You're "building an arch through which we shall
walk free at last."

When I first came into AA I carried a load of resentment I could
hardly walk with. A business associate I had befriended and given a
splendid opportunity had just given me the good old double-hex, gone
over to my opposition and helped heave me out of a firm I had myself
founded. I was so mad that at times I think I could almost have killed
him. My wife had taken up with another man and successfully sued
me for divorce, cleaning me out, and I didn't take that kindly either.

But I was trying to follow the tradition of the stiff upper lip, keep
the old chin up. *Illegitimati non carborundum*—don't let the so-and-
sos grind you down, as the Latin scholars say. And, though by some
miracle I was staying sober, I was getting nowhere with the quality
and enjoyment of my sobriety.

Gradually, however, the friendliness of AA began to make me feel
that I might be able to open up about what was really wrong with
me and not lose friends but possibly actually gain some. After a few
months I took Step Five—first having written my inventory down on
paper as suggested in the Big Book in Step Four.

Step Five was not easy for me. Seven years later, in the Grapevine,
I described my feelings. I can do nothing today to improve on that
description:

"For me," I wrote, "a terror goes with a sense of having been in error. I am almost physically allergic to the word 'wrong' as applied to
myself. I tense up and shorten my breath and feel scared at the mere
mention of it. I go on the defensive at all points, fairly bristling like a
mental porcupine, yet with an underlying deeply panicked sense that
my defense is not going to be successful. The word 'wrong,' directed
personally to me, means shouting, scolding voices, threats of beat-
ings and incarceration and ostracism and disgrace—an eternity of

unfriendliness. It means ultimatums impossible to meet, standards that cannot be attained."

But somehow I took the Step. It happened in this way (I further wrote):

"One night after a meeting, at an hour when most good AAs are sound asleep in their beds, I called up a member I scarcely knew and told him I had my list ready, as directed by the Big Book, and wanted to take the Fifth Step, could I please come over? I don't know how I can ever express my gratitude for the kindness and understanding that man and his wife showed me that night. Obviously a thoroughly mixed-up pigeon, tense and nervous, I descended on them and began my painful recitation of wrongs. They gave me coffee and cake, they were patient and understanding and good, and he heard me out.

"When it was over I found I had learned something. I had learned that the Power called God was a *kind* power, before whom one who had done wrong need not stand in fear. And I had learned that there are kind human beings, to whom one could admit error without fear of attack or denunciation. This made it possible for me to *admit* wrong; thereafter I was spared some of the exhausting effort of trying to maintain a facade of phony bluster intended to *conceal* wrong."

Seven years after these events I presumptuously set down for the Grapevine some advice about taking Step Five: "Follow carefully the directions of the Big Book, and don't be scared if you're scared. Don't press on too rashly; if the going gets too tough, retreat to Step Two—the Higher Power is kind and can restore us to sanity. But don't procrastinate too long. We cannot continue in the maintenance and growth of a spiritual experience until we can live with God, ourselves, and man without fear of being found, from time to time, to be somewhat in the wrong, along with the rest of day-to-day humanity."

Another seven years have passed since this was written. Meanwhile I have applied Step Five many times, seeking out a "close-mouthed, understanding friend," as the Big Book puts it, and going over what's been wrong with me lately. It is easier than it was the first time, and less formal, but I still use written notes sometimes.

Nothing could be more important, in this one AA's opinion, than keeping open these channels of candid, constructive self-discussion. If you don't, as I wrote seven years ago and have seen no need to retract, "the old alcoholic phoniness begins to reconstruct itself back of a new front of unctuous and respectable sobriety. People are less inclined to 'go into all that' in their talks, and more inclined to pontificate. It becomes harder and harder for friends to get through the shell and reach a real person."

Have I, as the Big Book predicted, finished building that arch through which I shall walk a free man? Frankly, no. I'm still not entirely free of fear of admitting I'm wrong. But I'm better than I was, I have improved, I'm *freer*. Perhaps the quality of my sobriety is not all it should be. But my lowest quality sobriety is better than my highest quality drunk. And the Steps have given me uninterrupted sobriety, to my daily and, I hope, continual gratitude. I came into AA still a youngish man. Now I am in my mid-fifties, and some things have changed. Older people, you know, do not take kindly to correction, hate to admit when they're wrong. If, as an old duffer, I'm to be fit to live with and able to make any kind of contribution to AA or to anything else, I'm going to have to watch this. I foresee no chance to ease up on Step Five, but will have to lean on it more heavily than ever as time goes on.

I've remarried since coming into AA, and would like to say something about marriage in the later years. AA has helped me discover that the later years of marriage can be even more exciting than the romantic years. Oh, my courtship of my second and most wonderful bride was a heady business, and I wouldn't have missed it. Our child-rearing years were full of surprises and had some tough going, but the kids' responses showed us we were getting somewhere. Now the kids, one by one, are going off to school and getting married. More and more the word "family," to my wife and me, will mean each other. What we make of the rest of the trip depends pretty much on how we treat each other. So sometimes the "close-mouthed, understanding friend" for my wife (who, though not an alcoholic, works the Steps) is me. And every so often she serves as a fifth-stepper for me.

As I now see the Fifth Step, it's a kind of way of living. Sure, you have to take it formally, by arrangement complete with your written inventory, the first time. But at some point after that, it seems to me, it ought to begin to be second nature.

J. E., Guilford, Conn.

Sixth Step

Were entirely ready to have God remove all these defects of character.
September 1970

I have attacked Step Six many times. It has attacked me in return. We have had open warfare, and we have had moratoriums. For periods of time, I have purposely ignored this Step. Often, I have stated that it did not make sense to me.

The battle began some years back, when I regularly attended Step discussion meetings. I had done my best on the first five Steps, I thought. I had even made a written list of all my defects. They counted up to twenty-seven.

Following the example of an old-timer friend of mine, whose quality of sobriety I admired, I printed, in ink, each one of my separate defects on a white poker chip. Then all twenty-seven chips went into a small, fat, yellow pitcher. Every morning on awaking, I plunged my hand into it (like picking a number from a goldfish bowl) and came up with the "chip for today." The defect might be anger, fear, pride, resentment, gossip, snobbery, self-pity, and so on, but whichever one it was had to be concentrated upon for the next twenty-four hours, and either reduced to a minimum or cast away.

It was a kind of game. I enjoyed wrestling with one "defect" a day. I felt I was making progress, really working the AA program. It hadn't yet occurred to me that I had gone overboard on this "defect" business. Twenty-seven indeed! How is that for the "pride" defect! Of course, most of them were not serious flaws of character, such as the inability to be honest with oneself. Most were bad habits possessed, in some degree, by most humans.

Nevertheless, I kept up this game for two or three years, telling many AA friends about it and urging them to go and do likewise. I explained that, although the Step suggested that God would remove these defects when and if I became ready to let go of them, I was of the school that believed in the saying "Pray for potatoes, but reach for the hoe." I did ask my Higher Power to lend a hand on the day's defect I happened to confront, but I felt that he expected me to use energy on rooting it out of my character.

Still these dozens of defects I had laid claim to kept cropping up again and again, over and over. It seemed that the harder I fought them, the harder they fought back. I became quite discouraged. I decided I had been willing, I had tried, and I would now let Number Six, and myself, have a vacation. I put the little yellow pitcher on a shelf behind some books and only now and then dipped into it. I kept busy and active in AA; I felt comfortable being sober; I was trying to practice the AA principles in all my affairs. Then, out of nowhere, came a deep resentment toward an AA friend. I agonized over it, prayed over it, but discussed it with no one. I had insomnia, indigestion, and fatigue. (Any good doctor can tell you that negative emotions make people physically ill.)

Fortunately, just about that time our group was slated for discussion of Step Six. I opened my copy of *Twelve Steps and Twelve Traditions* and read the Step all the way through. Although I had read it many times before, it seemed as if I saw its meaning for the first time. I gathered that, instead of fighting mightily against a defect, I had to let go of it. Just simply open up my hands, my heart, and my mind and say to my Higher Power, "Here it is, this defect. I give it to you. Please remove it from me." In this case, it was the bitter and destructive resentment that I wished to be rid of. And so it happened. It faded away and never returned.

Since then, I have followed the same procedure on other serious emotional problems, with the same result. I just have to keep in mind that if I am not 100 percent sincere in my willingness to be rid of the problem, the procedure won't work. I have come to realize that Step Six means exactly what it says. No more, no less. When, and if, I become ready to have painful, inhibiting, or long-standing flaws removed, they will be. Not always permanently, not all of them. But if and when they return, they will be weaker and much easier to let go of. As for all those bad habits I once listed as defects, I am trying to arrest them a day at a time, as I do my alcoholism.

A little progress has been made on pride. I can now admit that most of my troubles stem from one large and glaring defect: self-centeredness. For how can I wallow in self-pity, weep over resentments, be sick with righteous anger, ache with envy, tense up with fears and anxieties unless all my thoughts are exclusively on poor me?

A long time ago a very wise man, Marcus Aurelius, wrote: "A man's life is what his thoughts make it." Through Step Six, I have learned how true this is. I may never comprehend it fully, yet I know its value to me. It calls forth the most precious asset any recovering alcoholic can have: the willingness to get out of the driver's seat, to stop trying to run the show. I need to keep the Sixth Step message of letting go and letting God in my own thoughts at all times.

F. C., New York, N.Y.

Seventh Step

Humbly asked Him to remove our shortcomings.
November 1970

For me, at first glance Step Seven seemed a cinch, especially in comparison to some of the preceding Steps. As is often the case, on closer examination the seemingly simple proved to be anything but! I thought this Step was only a kind of mopping-up maneuver or an interlude where I could rest on my laurels. (I was wearing them in the wrong place at the time.) Steps One through Six had shown me how inadequate my own powers and resources were—as far as my alcoholism was concerned. Besides, I had to be entirely ready to part with my defects (Step Six), and I wasn't at all ready.

The earlier Steps, however, had removed some of the careful padding from my ego, and a remark made by an old-timer and dear friend had helped. I had heard one member complimented by another for a wonderful talk. The speaker said, "Don't thank me or give me credit. Give God the credit." I was determined that if ever anyone thanked me for my talk, I would say the same thing (humbly, of course).

Finally, my old-timer friend did compliment me on my talk one night, and I did say "Don't thank me. God did it."

The old-timer smiled, put his arm about me, and said, "Honey, it wasn't *that* good!" Up until that time I had thought "humble" was some kind of pie.

I knew from the beginning that my vices were way ahead of my virtues. That was bad. Worse, some of my vices were being classed as virtues. But since other members seemed to be gaining on their vices, I could hope for myself. By this time, introspection had become somewhat habitual, and I realized that I would have as many hangups in working these Steps, as I'd had hangovers during the wet years (or should I say the monsoons?).

In Step Seven, the word "humbly" threw a monkey wrench into my sensitive emotional gears. Oh, what it did to my poor id! It seemed I was forever searching feverishly through all the dictionaries I could lay hands on for a definition of "humble" that I could accept. Even the excellent coverage of this aspect in the "Twelve and Twelve" availed me nothing. Humble? Humbug! Hadn't I always been the one put upon? The doormat type? Was I now to wear sackcloth and ashes or a hair shirt?

All my life, I'd been taught that I alone was responsible for my character, including my shortcomings—responsible for self-discipline and self-reliance also. That reminds me of the fellow who claimed that he was a self-made man, whereupon his friend remarked that this belief certainly relieved God of an embarrassing responsibility!

Still, I could plainly see the golden thread of true humility running through all the Steps, and I knew how very important humility was to my continued sobriety. I became reconciled to the definition I found in a new, revised dictionary: "Humble indicates a personal realization of smallness, without loss of respect, and differs from humiliation, which implies public shame in front of others or being made to seem foolish or inferior," and "to be neither inordinately proud of our talents and assets, nor ashamed of our defects or failures, nor unduly on the defensive over them." Also: "free from vanity."

In other words (I quote Tryon Edwards): "True humility is not an abject, despising spirit; it is but a right estimate of ourselves as God sees us."

My willingness to have my defects of character removed was bolstered by the realization that little, if any, spiritual growth was possible as long as I held on to my old ideas and defects. The words in our Big Book keep appearing before me: "Burn the idea into the consciousness of every man that he can get well, regardless of anyone. The only condition is that he trust in God and clean house." This is what Step Seven is to me; it means I am going to clean house and I will have all the help I need. By taking this Step, I am not *giving up* anything; I am getting rid of whatever might lead me to drink again and whatever might prevent achieving real serenity. Now, with God's help and my own cooperation, via Step Seven, I can become on the individual level a first-rate power, instead of the second-rate power that I was before AA. (I was truly suffering from an immense power failure—or bad wiring.)

I have a favorite reminder which helps me keep Step Seven in view: "At moments she discovered she was grotesquely wrong, and then she treated herself to a week of passionate humility." This quote from the works of Henry James has become part of my inventory.

I believe that through the first six Steps I have gained some knowledge of my character defects and that I know (at least in part and at times) what I need to get rid of! It is certainly no problem for me to humbly ask my Higher Power to remove them, either. I never *did* know what to do with them before. Besides, my pride is the only thing I can swallow anymore that is nonfattening. In fact, this diet tends to reduce the ego and eliminate fatheads—mine, anyhow.

Step Seven simple? Not on your ego!

M. U., Brighton, Colo.

8½

Made a list of all persons we had harmed, and became willing to make amends to them all.
October 1986

As I continue to live each twenty-four hours in the Fellowship of Alcoholics Anonymous and attempt to practice its principles in all my affairs, one Step seems to play an increasingly important role in my life and in my relationships with others. This quiet but potent Step is Step Eight: "Made a list of all persons we had harmed, and became willing to make amends to them all."

Many people, myself included, tend to lump Steps Eight and Nine together. By doing this, I never really achieved even a glimmer of the humility and love that Step Eight has to offer. Being a person of impatient actions, I was off and running on Step Nine, with a simple list of names tightly grasped in my sweaty hand and a bad case of false humility to go along with it. Needless to say, I came home each evening with a battered sense of justice and my tail tucked underneath me.

As usual, I did not read all the words contained in the Step, and, just as I had done in Step One, I read only the first half before jumping to the next Step. The resulting self-induced pain has, however, taught me much about myself and the principles of this simple program.

Going back to Step Eight, I read the words at last, "...became willing to make amends to them all." As I began to absorb what was being said to me, and as I reviewed the first seven Steps leading up to this one, it suddenly became clear what the message was for me and what the hasty mistake of impatient interpretation had cost me in serenity. The word "identify" held the key to my success with this Step. To become willing means to become willing to identify myself in others. I had been using Step Eight not as preparation for Step Nine, which is the carrying out of that willingness, but as a hiding place for my own real fear of my true shortcomings. The purpose of Step Eight for me is not to hide but to identify. In order not to identify, I either condemned or forgave as if I were some kind of standard for comparison. In this Step I receive the humility to "identify," to see myself in others and to share their burdens and difficulties by sharing myself. In this Step I truly join the human race. My identification becomes my freedom—freedom from fear and anger. When I can identify my own shortcomings in another, the battleground between us is removed.

I cannot make an amends when I am still condemning or forgiving myself or the one I am making amends to, because of the judgment this implies. I have always found condemnation to be a lonely road and have always found forgiveness to be a confusing and impossible task. When I forgive someone I guess what I really mean to say is that I admit I judge others. Forgiving and condemning are God's business, not mine. Only he has the mercy to judge and to accept at the same time. My job is to achieve enough humility to see myself in others and to accept both myself and others, by identifying. The willingness to make amends will grow from this act of love. When I become "willing to make amends to them all" I am saying to them, "Your pain is my pain; when I hurt you, I hurt myself; I will try not to hurt you anymore."

When I have achieved this kind of willingness to identify, my Higher Power has always set up my amends and allowed both of us to grow from the love involved in such an act.

                                                        E. C., Bowling Green, Ky.

Editorial: on the Ninth Step

Made direct amends to such people wherever possible, except when to do so would injure them or others.
July 1945

L ike others of the Steps, Number Nine is closely related to Number Three—"to turn our will and our lives over to God *as we understood Him.*" If we have accomplished this Step to any measurable degree, we have attained at least a small measure of humility and a realization of our dependence on him.

Having prepared a list of all people we have harmed and brought ourselves to the point where we are *willing* to make amends to them, our Ninth Step is one calling for positive *action*. There is a world of difference between being willing to do a thing and actually *doing* it. How many times in the pre-AA state have we said "I am sorry, I won't do it again" and felt that that constituted complete amends.

A sincere apology, with a true explanation to the person harmed, of what we believe to be the reason for our past actions can quite frequently readjust personal relations—but the AA realizes that this cannot take care of the ones we have really hurt, and invariably these are the ones we should and do love most.

Most of us had at least a few years of real pathological drinking behind us when we first learned of the Twelve Steps. Those terrible years are the ones that become repulsive to us as we progress in our newfound life program for order and happiness—years in which our every action was influenced by alcoholic thinking, with all its implications. It naturally follows that whatever our state in life may be, those close to us bore the brunt of our outrageous behavior. How can one make amends to a dear wife, son or daughter, or parent who through no fault of their own truly suffered physically and financially, and more important, mentally; the humiliation and embarrassment of going through life with a drunkard? A simple "I am sorry; it won't happen again" is not enough. It is not enough for us, and it is not enough for the aggrieved person.

Direct amends, by all means, is a must, in restoring physical property to the rightful owner, paying debts willingly within our ability to do so, and retracting the lie that hurt a reputation; but the real amends are made in scrutinizing our day-in and day-out conduct and keeping that conduct "on the beam." The loved ones whom we have hurt don't want their "pound of flesh." Whether they are still in daily contact with us or not, amends are best made to them by restoring the love and confidence and respect they once had for us by the *action* of right living. With that thought clearly in our minds that "first drink" is an improbability, even an impossibility, and the well-rounded, good life we all yearn for becomes readily visible to us.

B. H., Forest Hills, N.Y.

"When We Were Wrong"

Continued to take personal inventory and when we were wrong promptly admitted it.
January 1983

Other people's being mistaken, or saying or doing dumb things, I can stand. It is a bit upsetting and off-putting sometimes, but I can go right on loving them and admiring their other, excellent qualities.

What I couldn't do, before AA and for quite a while in AA, was extend a similar tolerance to myself. All the rest of you could indulge your normal human foibles and frailties as much as necessary, with my blessing. But not me. From myself, I demanded a standard of perfection unattainable by any human being. I never got perfection or anything resembling it, but I never stopped demanding it. From me, there should be no mistakes; no half-witted remarks, no errors of fact or judgment.

What made this especially frustrating was that I, more than average, was just not cut out for perfection. While it is not literally true that I have five thumbs on each of my left hands, that is the impression I create. If you doubt it, look at my handwriting or my pitiful dabs at artwork or needlecraft. On second thought, don't. Too depressing.

You shouldn't believe the story that my feet are on backward, either. They aren't. It's only that the amount of tripping and stumbling I do makes it seem that way. As I say to startled AA friends I have just clutched in a death grip to save myself from a header down the stairs, "If I'm this awkward sober, think what I was drunk." They turn pale.

There must have been some kind of slip-up when the link between my tongue and my brain was put in. I have stood in red-faced horror at hearing what came out of my mouth when I had intended to utter the most innocent remark.

It was from this general mess that I demanded perfection! In the course of the struggle for it, my alcoholism developed. You are welcome to any opinion that appeals to you about whether my insistence on impossible standards had anything to do with the onset of alcoholism. My own opinion is that it didn't, but I could be wrong. I'm frequently wrong, and I can live with that thought quite comfortably—now.

It took the AA program, hundreds of AA meetings, and a startling discovery about the Twelve Steps to get me to that point. Making the transition from obsessive, compulsive drinking to total sobriety was not easy for me. Trying at the same time to extract error-free performance from myself was such an exercise in futility, I wonder the sobriety survived. Perhaps a Higher Power was involved.

My first years in AA brought on massive upheavals in my thinking. I had to discard old values and discover new ones. I had to reexamine everything I believed and everything I thought I knew.

In trying to bring my unrealistic expectations of myself into line with the other changes taking place, I was whipsawed between "I can't do anything right!" and "I have to do everything right!" Trying to have it both ways, I went through a period of starting every observation with: "I may be wrong, but..." and going on from there.

At this time, a dogmatic AA member joined my group. She was very positive in her approach to AA, extremely sure her position was correct about everything. She promptly took me to task for my "negative" attitude. "You shouldn't say you may be wrong," she admonished me. "Be positive! Be sure of yourself! Know you are right!"

For a few seconds, I said nothing, while wondering what in blazes this dame did about Step Ten. Then, I produced my favorite way of getting myself off the hook when I think I've been handed a hunk of baloney but it would be impolite and unkind to say so. "A very interesting idea. I'll certainly give it some thought."

In this case, I gave "it" a lot of thought—not her idea, but Step Ten: "Continued to take personal inventory and when we were wrong promptly admitted it." It didn't say, "*if* we were wrong"; it said, "*when* we were wrong," as though we were certain to be wrong sometimes. I hadn't noticed that before. Step Ten expected me to be wrong occasionally, and was perfectly calm about it. Unlike me.

As many times as I had read and studied the Steps, examining them in reference to my passion for perfection had not occurred to me. Now, with Step Ten so plainly telling me something about myself, it was time to submit my problem to all twelve.

What do the Steps that led me into sobriety and a much improved life have to say about my being wrong, mistaken, awkward, tactless, and generally imperfect? Which of them mention it?

The first three Steps do not. It might be said that an admission I was "powerless" includes "powerless to achieve perfection." However, as worded, these Steps do not refer to mistakes or wrongdoing.

Step Four? Yes. A moral inventory certainly must include wrongs and errors, past and present.

Step Five? Yes. "The exact nature of our wrongs" assumes there are bound to be wrongs. It doesn't add, "in case there are any."

Step Six? Again yes. "Defects of character" were just what I could never tolerate in myself. AA placidly expects them.

Step Seven? Yes. If we asked to have "shortcomings" removed, they could hardly have been nonexistent.

Step Eight? Most definitely yes. This Step says that every one of us, including me, has wronged others and should become willing to make amends.

Step Nine? Yes. If wrongs have been done—and they have!—amends should be made.

Step Ten? Yes. Oh, yes! Not only have I been wrong in the past, I must expect to be wrong occasionally for the rest of my life.

Steps Eleven and Twelve? No. Since it has been established in earlier Steps that perfection is forever impossible, these last two address larger issues.

Seven of our Twelve Steps state unequivocally that I have been, am, and will be wrong. I have shortcomings and defects of character. I never have been and never can be perfect.

As that realization became a part of me—and it took time—it brought me one of the greatest of the many blessings that have come to me from AA. I learned to accept myself as a fallible human being.

I do not have to strive for perfection. Mistakes are permissible. I have the right to be wrong.

And what a comfort that thought is to me, as I make my bemused way through life, one foot in a bucket, pushing on doors marked "Pull."

E. E., Tulsa, Okla.

Eleventh Step

Sought through prayer and meditation to improve our conscious contact with God <u>as we understood Him</u>, praying only for knowledge of His will for us and the power to carry that out.
August 1971

When I was small, my parents sent me to several different Sunday schools, but I don't think they ever went to church themselves. My aunts and uncles were members of different sects, and when they came to visit, they took me with them to their churches. My parents made no objection, and, in fact, I believe they thought it would be good for me. As it turned out, it wasn't.

Before World War I, religious intolerance was much stronger, more prevalent, and more open than it is today. I heard hellfire-and-brimstone sermons, and usually the damned were those people who did not attend that particular church. Since I attended a number of different churches, I heard them all ripped up and down at one time or another. To a youngster, it was very confusing.

By the time I was in high school, I had come to the conclusion that all religion was a lot of baloney. I had tried to find out more for myself and had actually read most of the Bible. I'm sure now that I understood very little, but I found enough nonsense in it to prove my case to my own satisfaction.

When I took my first drink (and got drunk) at the age of seventeen, I was already an all-out atheist. As my alcoholism developed, my atheism got nastier. I was absolutely certain that I was right, and after a few drinks I enjoyed imparting my wisdom to anyone who would listen or, preferably, argue. I ridiculed anyone who was so stupid, ignorant, or superstitious as to believe in any sort of God or religion—or who was so hypocritical as to act as though he believed such nonsense.

Twenty years after my first drink, alcohol had me licked. I heard that a friend of mine had been sober for four months. Since I knew that he absolutely couldn't stay sober, anymore than I could, I drank enough to get my courage up and went to see him to find out how he did it. I had read a newspaper article about Alcoholics Anonymous, had sent for the Big Book (for a friend, not for me), and had read part of it; so the thought had already been in my mind that maybe that was how he had gotten sober. Sure enough, it was. He gave me a drink and talked with me from mid-afternoon until after midnight.

The next day, I remembered just two things he had said. 1) "Can you stay sober twenty-four hours?" I had answered "Yes," because I had. 2) "AA has a spiritual part to it." (My heart sank.) "But I know you, and I advise you not to pay any attention to it. Just skip the whole subject, and try to keep an open mind." (Heart went back up.)

"There is no religion in AA, but there is a belief in a power greater than ourselves, and your higher power can be AA."

My sponsor kept me with him overnight and all the next day and took me to my first meeting the next night, at the Old 24th Street Clubhouse in New York City. For the first time in my life, I felt at home. People were kind and welcomed me uncritically. I didn't know it then, but I had had my last drink.

From then on, my higher power *was* AA. I lived it, breathed it, became immersed in it. There was no doubt that I was powerless over alcohol and that AA had enabled me to do that which I had been unable to do myself. I took my inventory repeatedly, tried to make amends, did Twelfth Step work, went to numerous meetings, spoke, worked in the group jobs and at the intergroup office, admitted my shortcomings, and wanted them removed by God...as I understood him? I didn't understand him at all, because he wasn't.

In group discussions, my good AA friends said things to me like "You have faith in a dollar bill, don't you? Yet it's nothing but paper." Many who had gained some faith themselves tried to pass it on to me—but it didn't work.

Then I went to a small closed meeting and listened to a real old-timer, who had preceded me in AA by six or seven years. He said that when a new member comes into AA, he naturally leans on his sponsor. After a while, he transfers his leaning to the group to which he belongs, and later on he transfers his leaning to AA as a whole. He leans on, depends on, gets his help from AA philosophy, rather than from any particular individual or group. And then, finally, if he is to stay sober for the long, long pull, he makes the final transfer and leans on God. Then he puts his reliance and dependence on God and lives by his will—and if he doesn't do this to some extent, he will not stay sober indefinitely. You have seen AA members, after some years of sobriety, get drunk. They didn't make the final transfer.

That was the gist of what he said, and it scared hell out of me, because I didn't want to get drunk, ever, and I didn't see how I could make the final transfer. So I doubled and redoubled my efforts to get some kind of faith, whatever that was. I think my mind finally may have opened, not only to the *necessity* of getting faith in God, but to the *possibility*, because I did begin to remember a few things.

Not long before coming into AA, when I was down so low that I was thinking about what a relief it would be to be dead, I remember saying out loud to myself something to the effect that I knew there was no God, but I wished there were, so I could ask him, as other people did, to get me out of the horrible mess I was in. I began to wonder if this wish had been a prayer that had been heard and answered. But, of course, it couldn't have been. It was just a coincidence that I had come into AA shortly thereafter.

When the Lord's Prayer was said at the end of meetings, I didn't say it because I didn't know it. But I thought I should say it, so I looked it up and memorized it. Then I read Emmet Fox's analysis of that prayer, and the empty words began to make sense for the first time.

The old-timer had convinced me that I had better start doing something constructive about acquiring some kind of faith; so I started a ten-year stretch of reading books—probably a couple hundred of them—and have read more since then.

One of them, Aldous Huxley's *Perennial Philosophy*, taught me that men, almost all of them, had always believed in God (or gods) and in life after death. It seemed to have been an instinctive belief, going back at least 25,000 years. Could it be that I was wrong? It occurred to me that I had judged churches by the people who were in them, rather than by their teachings. Maybe I had been unable to accept religion merely because people didn't live up to its teachings. Could I judge AA by some drunks I knew who occasionally came to meetings, but never made any real attempt to get sober? That thought set me off on a good many years of experimental churchgoing to find out what the various religions taught, rather than what their members did.

I was beginning, I think, to have the first glimmerings of faith, of belief in some sort of Power that created the universe—but not in a personal God. About that time, the thought came to me that I had been personally created; that each and every individual had been personally created—no two alike. We are not part of some mysterious cosmos as a drop of water is part of the sea; each of us is an individual, separate entity, each created individually—and, what's more, each of us is of the most supercolossal, amazing complexity. With all our knowledge of DNA and heart transplants, we haven't the faintest idea how life comes to be. One thing is certain—*we* didn't invent it. Some intelligence, ten thousand trillion times more talented than we are, did. And that intelligence invented us, not as a general class of undifferentiated creatures, but each specifically. I could now see that whatever Power could do this could be called God. Since God could, and did, invent each of us individually, why could he not look after us individually? It began to seem illogical that he wouldn't.

I read a book by LeComte deNouy called *Human Destiny*, which reinforced and solidified my growing belief. DeNouy was a biologist, whose science had convinced him of God. One of his arguments was this:

There are various kinds of protein molecules, and in any particular protein there are billions of identical molecules. Each molecule contains several million atoms of oxygen, hydrogen, nitrogen, carbon, etc. The thing that makes them proteins, rather than some other kind of substance, is the structure of the molecule. The position of each atom has to be the same in every one. Since there are several million atoms in each molecule, the probability of even two identical protein molecules occurring by chance is about as close to zero as you can get. Then, of course, the probability of a thousand or a million or a billion identical protein molecules being generated by chance becomes infinite nonsense. They must be generated, not only by intelligence, but by infinite intelligence.

DeNouy's book has much more than this example. Its general thesis is that man's brain is getting to the point where he will more and more control his own destiny. It is in this sense, I take it, that man is created in God's image and likeness. Man can think, and, through

God's evolution, he gets better at it as eons pass. Thought (I reasoned) must be the basis of all life.

What I was trying to do, as you no doubt have observed by now, was to work the Eleventh Step: "Sought through prayer and meditation to improve our conscious contact with God *as we understood Him...*" That means we think about it, consciously. *Thought.* Everything springs from thought. Action must be preceded by thought. Maybe thought is the ultimate power, the final energy of creation. We know that matter isn't really what it seems to our senses—it is a form of energy. We know from elementary physics that chemical energy can be turned into electrical energy, which can be converted into heat, which can be converted into motion, which can be converted back into electrical energy, which can be converted into light, etc. So what is energy?

Rhine's experiments proved to my satisfaction that *thought* can be transmitted through space from one person to another (ESP, extrasensory perception). Something must be going on that we know very little about. One thing seems certain: Energy is transmitted by waves—light, heat, electrical, sound. The living brain produces waves which medical men and researchers record on machines. Or is the brain a receiving station, like a radio? Does it receive waves that bring information from some cosmic source?

Pick out any particular point in space, the size of a pinhead. Through that point pass thousands of light waves, radio waves, TV waves, electrical waves, and all the waves from the distant stars and suns, and undoubtedly billions of thought waves, and all the kinds of waves we know nothing about—all at the same time. They are passing through us right now, and all the time. Ten thousand telephone conversations could be put on one high-frequency wavelength. Then could not all the information, data, processes, remembrances, thoughts of the entire universe be put on *all* the wavelengths? That would mean that all the infinite knowledge of the universe could be available at any one point, anywhere in space. Could that be how an infinite being would know everything about everything, everywhere? Is that how he would know every thought of every one of his creatures? Wouldn't he know every one of *my* thoughts, just as religion says he would?

Some of my thoughts were good and some were bad; most were in between. If, as religion teaches, God is all good, he would "hear" the good thoughts and aspirations. Would he ignore the bad ones? Or would he set events in motion to teach me better? The latter seemed more logical, if God is love and if God is our Father. A loving parent would teach his children so that they would live happy, productive lives. At any rate, this speculation satisfied me, so that I didn't have to believe in a God of wrath and punishment and vengeance.

How about guidance? How do we get knowledge of his will for us? I remember, when I was in college, one of my fraternity brothers was a premed student nicknamed "Judge," who was interested in hypnotism and could sometimes be prevailed upon to hypnotize volunteers, usually freshmen. Before he awakened them, he would give them posthypnotic suggestions. He would say, for instance, "When you wake up you are going to be very, very thirsty. You are going to get hot under the collar and itch, until you go and get a glass of water and bring it in here and drink it." After coming to, the subject would stand in the group talking nervously, running his finger around the back of his collar, and shortly he would excuse himself and bring back a glass of water and drink it before the gathering. He hadn't the faintest idea why he had done it.

So thoughts *can* be put into people's minds without their being aware of it. Certainly, the Creator of my mind could easily insert in it thoughts that would lead to my growth, without in any way interfering with the free will that he apparently wished to build into humans. My pea-sized intelligence can only speculate that he wanted to create a race of free-thinking beings, rather than a race of automatons—and, within limits, he has given us the ability to be just that. God could control human events by controlling thoughts. When I pray and do not "pray amiss," the prayer could be answered by putting the proper thoughts into my mind, or into the minds of others who would act as agents to carry out any necessary actions. I have never been aware of receiving any guidance, but I now believe it is entirely unnecessary for me to be aware of it. I can receive it just the same.

People do get original thoughts. From where? There is such a thing as inspiration, and most of the time it cannot be traced to any source. Two people often get the same idea at the same time. Thought is prayer, and thought is power. But there are two kinds, good and bad. Energy is divided into two kinds: for instance, positive and negative electricity. If thought is the basic energy of creation, is it surprising that there are positive and negative thoughts? We know that we have to learn to use energy wisely and carefully. Wrongly used, electricity can kill, fire can burn, sound can shatter, light can blind. Wrong thoughts either are full of negative energy or are negative energy—and they can kill and cause destruction and misery. Right thoughts can soothe and heal, bring knowledge and happiness. "As a man thinketh, so is he" is literally true, because a person's whole life is lived in his mind and nowhere else. His thoughts make up his identity. Paul said a man's whole life is a prayer.

Speculations and meditations like these have done something to me, I'm very glad to say. Thanks to the Eleventh Step, I have had to discard from my mind all the thoughts and beliefs that were once there. I gave them up reluctantly. I liked my old thoughts, even was proud of them. I didn't want to believe in God, but through AA I got to a point where I had to. I didn't want to believe in prayer, but finally I had to. Now I believe it to be the strongest force on earth—if the quietest. You don't have to be aware of power. It doesn't have to be loud, like a hurricane. In one day, sunshine delivers to the earth's surface more energy, more horsepower than the total amount delivered by all the power we have ever developed artificially. And we are not aware that the force of the sun is power at all. Gravity acts on every cell of our body, every second, and we are not conscious of it.

Before AA, I wanted more than anything else to get sober. That was a positive thought, and it was a prayer that was answered. Once my closed mind was pried open, once I consciously tried to meditate and increase my conscious contact with God, my life started to straighten out, and it has continued to improve ever since. I can look back and see where I received guidance and where I made right decisions without ever knowing that I was doing so, or why.

When I came into AA, if anyone had told me that I would some day believe what I now believe, I think I would have shot him. How did the change happen? After joining AA, I had complete faith in everything AA said or stood for. I could see the results all around me, and, as time went on, I could see what AA was doing for me. Now, as I look back, I realize that AA was teaching me spiritual values without using religious words. For example:

AA tells us to try to help other people, and the people it tells us to help—other alcoholics—can be anything but lovely. AA tradition tells us to go to the most inconvenient lengths to help others. Religion tells us, "Love thy neighbor," and illustrates it with the parable of the good Samaritan.

AA teaches us tolerance, as we learn not to be irritated by the ideas and idiosyncrasies of others. Religion says, "Judge not...."

AA teaches us to get rid of resentments and to replace them with a feeling of goodwill toward everyone. Religion tells us to love our enemies.

AA says that we must be absolutely honest with ourselves. Religion says that to know the truth will set us free.

AA suggests to us the advisability of getting rid of pride and replacing it with humility. Religion says that pride is the deadliest of sins and that it "goeth before a fall."

AA says it is necessary to get rid of our irrational fears, to live the kind of life that makes fears largely unnecessary. Religion says that "perfect love casteth out fear." If we could reach such an unearthly state of perfection, it would mean that our minds would be 100 percent concerned for the welfare of others, and then since we would have no concern for ourselves, we would have no fear. Couldn't we say that the concern and fellowship existing among so many AA members, much deeper than friendship, can be called love? Not perfect, perhaps, but love just the same. The more of our minds we fill with concern for others, the less room is left to be concerned for ourselves. Thus, in AA, we slowly learn to stop stewing in our own juice and to start loving other people. (Certainly, we are not talking about romantic love, any more than Jesus was when he talked about loving your enemies, or your neighbor as yourself.)

In spite of my original bias, AA *was* teaching me spiritual values—love and kindness and consideration and humility, attitudes opposite to the resentments, pride, self-centeredness, and fear that had previously all but consumed my mind. And it was not until AA had taught me these values, to some extent at least, that my mind was ready for faith to enter.

How much faith? I don't know how to measure it. But now I have faith in the teachings of both AA and religion, because I find them much the same, though expressed in different words. Faith is a matter of degree. I am grateful for whatever faith I have now, even though it is little more than a seedling—far, so very far, from the kind of faith that moves mountains. There is so much more to know, and no limit to the growth of faith. So I shall continue trying to work the Eleventh Step, trying to improve my conscious contact with God as I understand him.

As I look back, I am aware that I now live in a comparatively happy and serene world, entirely different from the world of self-centered misery of not too long ago. Yet, whatever progress and happiness God has given me through AA, they are only a beginning. I feel sure that, if I keep trying to practice these principles in all my affairs, I will slowly but surely reach an even more splendid world some day.

R. S., *Tucson, Ariz.*

Twelfth Step

Having had a spiritual awakening as the result of these steps,
we tried to carry this message to alcoholics, and to practice these
principles in all our affairs.
October 1971

For this article, my AA library remains untouched. It would be an easy matter to refresh my mind with the writings of other members, to freshly assimilate their thoughts and present a rich pudding packed with stolen plums. That's called research. But the Twelfth Step is too important a part of my life for me to let this article contain any thoughts except my own. That means, of course, that it will carry the thoughts of others, but only those thoughts and ideas that have become a part of me and my way of sobriety.

The Twelfth Step is the capstone of the AA program. It announces itself as being such with its opening phrases, "Having had a spiritual awakening *as the result of these steps...*" Whatever is to follow those words is the result of all that went before. But first let's examine the opening words.

Few of us experience the "wind...of spirit" described by Bill W. Indeed, very few of us experience a sudden, startling spiritual experience of any kind. Usually, the change is gradual. Yet it is no less a spiritual awakening. Whether we awaken with a bound or after much stretching, we awaken. When there is a spiritual awakening, self-centeredness, fear, and frustration are supplanted by helpful friendliness, happiness (perhaps even a touch of serenity), and fulfillment.

I joined AA a few weeks before Vinny F. did, and it was remarkable to me to watch the changes that transformed him within a few months. Why couldn't it be happening to me? I said as much to an old-timer. "Oh, you've changed just as much as Vinny," he told me with a broad smile. I couldn't believe it!

But indeed I had changed, and if my search for spiritual guidance was unsuccessful in its church-oriented aspect, the search itself continued. It went on and on, at regular meetings and at one-to-one meetings with individual members.

Incidentally, during those first, wonder-filled months, I concocted a description of my feeling about most open and closed meetings. I said that the total effect was greater than the sum of its individual parts. To put it another way, a list of the people at a given meeting and a recap of everything said were not enough to account for the height of my elation. The human element alone could not have lifted me so high. There was a mysterious, indefinable "x" factor, which I choose to call spiritual.

That there was nothing sudden about this, no bolt of lightning, no rumble of thunder, is evident from the fact that for several years I could not bring myself to go and speak in a prison. One day, as though a veil were torn away, I realized that I *could* speak in jails and prisons. I would not be going beyond the locked gates in order to identify with the men as prisoners. Perhaps some of them would consider me an amateur for not having lost my liberty, but that would be their hang-up, not mine. Since then, I've had good AA conversations with a number of prisoners—as fellow alcoholics.

That leads right into the next phase of the capstone Step: "we tried to carry this message to alcoholics." What message? Hope. Example. The way out. The way back. A handful of simple principles to unravel most of our snarled-up problems. A touch of humor—not taking ourselves so damned seriously. Meetings. Availability. Talk, talk, talk. The willingness to listen with understanding as the still-suffering alcoholic thrashes his way out of his mental mire. Tolerance. Guilelessness. The honesty to face situations and people, not go around them by the old, familiar route of sneakiness and subverted honesty. "Carrying the message" is all these things.

And the list could go on and on. There are the specifics of babysitting, housecleaning, and other chores that so many AAs have performed for shaky newcomers. There are the specifics of slogging through a snowstorm to answer a call for help, or driving a guy to a state hospital to keep him from winding up in jail. Practicing the Twelfth Step does not allow for questioning the merits of, or probable "returns" on, these actions. They are the philosophy of the Twelfth Step made manifest. When we do these things, we are carrying the message with a sense of responsibility.

It is precisely at this point in the AA program that a member's depth of understanding is plumbed. "We tried to carry the message" is a saying so battered out of shape by steady use that the deep humility of its intent is frequently lost from sight. This single saying is the basis for calling a visit to an active alcoholic a "Twelfth Step call." We know that speaking at meetings is a form of Twelfth Step work. Occasionally, we learn that we have fortuitously performed a Twelfth Step activity—helped someone without being aware of it at the time. It is the Twelfth Step in action which, to a large degree, keeps AA self-regenerative. Every meeting is an experience in sharing, but Twelfth Step activity is a more personal—and can therefore be a more deeply felt—form of sharing.

Being more personal, Twelfth Step work can become ego-oriented. Like the missionary who believes he is saving the pagans rather than himself, the egocentric member believes he is saving the other person rather than fortifying his own sobriety. Nonsense! The member is merely being given an opportunity to exercise his grasp of the program. Anyone who would take the credit for sobering up another person must also take the blame for failing to salvage those who don't sober up promptly, by the numbers and according to the book. Bunk! Let's remember that a Twelfth Step call is a visit, not a visitation.

Speaking of calling on the suffering alcoholic, it is frequently stated that "When a person wants sobriety badly enough, he'll come to AA." (The statement is often fortified with the remark "That's what I did," which makes it the word of God, of course.) *That* is carrying the message? I don't believe it. I didn't know enough to look for AA. Someone brought the message to me. Over seventeen years ago.

You and I know members who, having "caught" the program themselves, find the repeating drunk someone to avoid. I have heard from more than one repeater that some member has told him he cannot return to AA. Imagine one lush excommunicating another! *That* is carrying the message?

You and I have called on drunks whose remorse and frustration were founded principally on their not having done what the self-righteous member had told them to do. They felt beyond the pale.

The last two examples are spoiled fruit of the ego tree. The poor drunk who can't immediately catch fire from Ardent Member's magic words is discarded as unworthy. "He isn't *trying*" says Ardent Member. On what profound knowledge does he base his opinion? So far as I know, there is only one with the power to say, "Go and sin no more."

We have seen old-timers founder. And we have seen old experimenters finally succeed—because someone held the door open. When we close the door, we are really saying, "You have tested my tolerance and won. Your ability to go on drinking and living threatens my sobriety." So, if we can't give someone the hope implicit in the capstone Step, let's not blame the sick alcoholic. Let's admit that the case is beyond our personal ability to translate the message of AA into terms he can understand. Trying to find new translations is a great way to strengthen our own sobriety. Closing the door to the constant repeater, on the other hand, is an admission of our own lack of tolerance or self-belief. The last clause of the last Step advises us "to practice these principles in all our affairs." What "these principles" are is contained in eleven Step articles that preceded this one and in numerous other AA sources.

To me, the last four words have shed one of the most penetrating lights of all AA's illuminating suggestions and ideas for living. I interpret "in all our affairs" to mean that we can have a sane, sober, rewarding life outside our AA meetings. We do not have to be introverted AAs, safe from the lurking horrors only when among fellow alcoholics.

AA is our serum, our antitoxin. The last part of our last suggested Step tells us that AA will guard us through meetingless days. It even tells us that sobriety, like all good news, is communicable.

W. R., South Norwalk, Conn.

FIVE

Not Allied With Any Sect Or Denomination

————————— ♦ —————————

Paradox of Power
April 1982

For several years before I began my new life in AA, I taught American literature in a university. One of the writers whose work I enjoyed reading and discussing with students was Emily Dickinson. She captured in a few words the peculiar definitions of experience that I had felt but could not articulate.

One of her poems had a special appeal that brought me back to it over and over. It begins: "I can wade Grief / Whole Pools of it / I'm used to that / But the least push of Joy / Breaks up my feet / And I tip—drunken."

Those brief lines describe clearly what kept my drinking habits active. I could wade whole pools of grief and depression; over the years, I had psychiatrists to help me through them. I was used to that. But the least push of joy broke up my feet and tipped me, drunken, every time: a vacation, a raise or a promotion, an anniversary, Millard Fillmore's birthday. Those were occasions to drink. Soon, I was finding a reason to turn every day of the year into a festival. When that happens, none of them is special or very festive.

After being around AA for a while, I went back to the poem one day and found an entirely new way of reading it. I had never realized that all my drinking had begun with the carefree moments of celebration and joy, only to end in those desperate years when I had tried to keep up the pleasure and the fun. The program was giving me an understanding of my dependence upon alcohol, and as a fringe benefit, a new reading of a favorite poem.

But that wasn't all. Several lines further on, Dickinson comments that we must guard against those unprotected times of cheer when we are open to hurt and anguish. I then began to grasp the full meaning of two crucial lines: "Power is only Pain — / Stranded, through Discipline..."

I had often used that definition of power to start classroom discussions of its possible meaning for students. But now I seemed to be reading it for the first time. It expressed what I was beginning to understand about Alcoholics Anonymous.

Power is a key word in this program, and its importance is underlined repeatedly in the Twelve Steps. We admitted in the beginning that "we were *powerless* over alcohol—that our lives had become unmanageable." Then we "came to believe that a *Power* greater than ourselves could restore us to sanity." And in the Eleventh Step, we pray "for knowledge of His will for us and the *power* to carry that out."

I began to see the emphasis this program places upon force and drive. I realized that anyone who regards AA as only the passive giving up of alcohol has not carefully read the Steps. Our continual dependence upon a Higher Power demonstrates further the importance we place upon action and accomplishment.

The source of power, Dickinson adds, is pain. In my AA experience, I have never met a member who has not experienced some degree of pain. I have never met anyone who decided to come into the program on a beautiful morning in spring when everything was going well. Most of us entered on our knees, and the sharing of this mutual pain is a large part of what brings us back to meetings.

"Strand" means to form by twisting together, as in the strands of a rope. So it is implied that the achievement of power comes by way of mixing pain with discipline. And discipline, the word that all of us dread from our years in school, was the part of AA that frightened me most.

In those early days, I hoped that with harsh discipline and self-will, I might be able to stop drinking. I was prepared to sit through meetings holding on to my chair with the grim determination to see this thing through, no matter what. As a child, I had been taught that if I worked hard enough and disciplined myself, I could accomplish whatever goal I set. Maybe that principle would hold true for my desire to stop drinking.

But the members of AA surprised me with a new definition of the term. Instead of holding on, I was told to let go. Instead of using self-control, I was encouraged to turn my will and my life over to God. And at the end of Chapter Six in the Big Book, I read that "we alcoholics are undisciplined. So we let God discipline us in the simple way we have just outlined."

That was a definition I had never heard before. "Letting go" had always meant self-indulgence: polishing off the rest of the bottle, eating the whole cake, sleeping until noon. Now, I heard that letting go meant acquiring discipline. I had to redefine the term in light of what AA members were telling me.

"Power is only Pain — / Stranded, through Discipline."

I have been around the program for a few twenty-four hours now, and I'm beginning to understand the meaning of those lines. The renewal of discipline is a process that I must set in motion every day. But I'm learning to wade each pool of grief, to take each painless step of joy, with the power given me through the discipline of Alcoholics Anonymous.

D. H., Delmar, N.Y.

No Trumpets Blew
February 1953

Many and many a week and month had passed for me in AA and I was still troubled about that "spiritual awakening" deal. In fact I was about five or six years old on the program before I understood that I really had *had* a spiritual awakening a long time before I realized it, and just didn't recognize it.

You see it was like this.

I was born and brought up in a strictly religious family, and I mean religious in the sense it was used fifty or more years ago. I had the Bible, Sunday school, prayer meetings, choir practice and all the rest of it shot at me from every angle *all* the time.

By the time I got out of high school I had a mess of ideas about religion and God and so on in my head, and none of these ideas was good or particularly attractive.

God, to me, was a large man with flowing white whiskers who alternated between being a fatherly, gentle sort of a guy and a vicious tyrant who condemned people to fry in hell for eternity. And I didn't like him.

When anyone talked about things spiritual, I could imagine nothing but something connected with this God and his heaven which, it seemed, was populated with hosts of angels clad in white robes who spent their time soaring through the air playing harps.

It never occurred to me that there might be a meaning to the word "spiritual" besides the one I gave it.

Of course, to be strictly honest about this thing, I must admit that I gave very little thought to such matters anyway. I started my drinking career when I was just past seventeen and, as I remember it, I had very little time, wish, or opportunity to meditate deeply on any of the abstract facets of life while I was drinking.

What with trying to make a living for myself and the distillers and saloon keepers, I was pretty busy without getting all tangled up in a lot of meditation about "spiritual" matters.

Whenever I did give such things a little thought, I assumed that if a guy had a spiritual awakening he could only have it by a flock of angels descending from the skies playing harps and trumpets and shouting loudly enough to penetrate his thick skull: "We have a spiritual message for you." This is probably a slight exaggeration but it conveys the general idea.

Well, of course, I never did have that sort of a spiritual awakening and, in fact, have never had it yet after all these months of sobriety. Furthermore, I never expect to have it nor do I want it.

I *do* know now that I *did* have a spiritual awakening and, as a matter of fact, I had that spiritual awakening at least a month before my original AA sponsors found me in the county jail where I was doing four months.

Here's what happened.

I had started doing the four months on August 15. You can figure that four months put me on the bricks again on December 15.

When I entered the jailhouse I was nattily clad in a pair of white (but dirty) pants, a white (and dirtier) shirt, no coat, no hat, and nothing else except a pair of socks and a pair of badly worn shoes.

Not bad costuming (except for the dirt) for August, but how about that December 15 exit date? And in Iowa, yet, where the December breezes are distinctly not on the balmy side.

It wasn't the first time I had been in such a fix, nor the second nor the fifth nor the tenth. (It was, thank God, the last.)

However, I was stretched out on my bunk in my cell one afternoon in November figuring out ways and means. It was snowing outside, and brother, it was cold.

I had talked to the sheriff a day or so previously and he had fixed it for me to do a "pearl diving" stunt at a greasy spoon joint about two blocks from the jail. The job was to pay $8 a week, cakes, and a flop upstairs.

Alright, so far, but I was wondering if I could run fast enough to keep from freezing to death in that two blocks between the jail and the job. I decided it was a risk that would have to be taken.

And I went on from there. I had it all calculated just how many weeks I would have to wash dishes and pots and pans in that joint before I would have dough enough to get together some sort of an outfit of clothing and also accumulate getaway money.

My wife and kids were in a nearby city, but I was about as welcome there as a skunk would be at a May party, and anyway the law in that city was hostile and I knew it was no place for yours truly.

So I had picked out Kansas City as my objective when the wardrobe and financial status indicated the move was in order. I had even found out what the bus fare was to Kansas City.

And so I mused on to myself.

"So, on or about April 1, I will shake the dust of this town and state from my feet and get a fresh start in Kansas City. I will get into town with about $15 or $20 over and above expenses. I will rent myself a nice room and pay a week's rent in advance and wash up and go out and hunt a job."

All of a sudden something clicked in my head. Where had I heard that song before?

And then it came to me in one big, blinding flash.

"Why," I said to myself softly, "you damn fool, you have done just that same thing before. Work like a dog, get halfway cleaned up and presentable, and go to some new spot. You'll do it all, too, *except* for one thing. After you get the room and take the wash you'll go out to the first tavern you can locate and you'll order a double shot. By morning (or long before) you'll be flat broke again and wake up so sick you'll have no time to hunt a job. You'll have to hustle the eye-opener and the rest that follow it. And by the end of the week you'll either be in jail again or on skid row."

There you are.

That was the spiritual awakening.

For the first time in fifty-seven years I realized that all my trouble was caused by booze.

And as I realized that fact, there came the necessary corollary. If I want to stay off skid row I must quit drinking. Not for a while, but forever.

So a few days later, when Ralph and Ed called on me at my jail residence, I was a pushover. I knew what I had to do, and they told me how to do it.

No one can ever convince me now that God in his infinite wisdom and kindness didn't send me that spiritual message. Of course, he sent it to me in his own way without benefit of a heavenly choir or other stage effects, but he got the message through to me.

Thank you, God.

P. C., Alton, Ill.

So <u>That's</u> a Spiritual Experience!
January 1977

I can remember, early in my sobriety, feeling depressed because I had not had a spiritual experience. I was sure that I alone had not undergone a sudden change of heart.

This impression came from listening to some other members describe their spiritual awakenings. They described them simply and honestly. There had been, they said, no flashing lights, no burning bushes. But there had been a moment when they experienced total surrender, a sudden change of attitude. It was, they said, an experience that immediately changed their lives.

I assumed (erroneously, I later found) that all AA members had undergone a similar experience. I was sure that those who did not speak of their moment of truth were too modest to describe it. And I was also sure that I was the only one, even among the new members, who had not experienced an instantaneous change.

I believed that my entry into AA had been different. I had come in reluctantly, and had stayed reluctant for as long as possible. Only gradually, over a period of months, did I realize that I had no place else to go. There was never any sudden, joyful acceptance of recovery. There was, instead, a gradual, sad admission that I could choose AA or die. Not what I would have called a "spiritual" experience.

Fortunately, there was a small group of us who were all new to the program and very close. It was among them that I made a series of discoveries.

First, I discovered that I was not alone. All of us agreed that, whatever a spiritual experience might be, we certainly hadn't had one. We had all been waiting for it to happen, and by now, most of us were convinced that it probably never would. We were different. Unlike the older members, we had been too "sinful" in the past and were too secular in the present to be worthy of anything "spiritual."

Our second discovery was more exciting. We discovered that most of the other members had not undergone an instantaneous change, either. We learned, by listening at meetings and talking to our sponsors, that the majority of those we admired had undergone, like us, a gradual change. We still didn't know what a spiritual experience was, and we were still pretty sure that we hadn't undergone one. But we had all experienced gradual change. So we weren't inferior. We were with the majority.

The third discovery was a blockbuster. One of us read Bill W.'s discussion of the Twelfth Step in *Twelve Steps and Twelve Traditions*. There, he explains that there are many kinds of spiritual experience. Some are like the conversions of the great religious leaders of the past; others seem purely psychological. Some are sudden or instantaneous; others are a gradual learning experience. But all of them, whatever form they take, have one effect: They make a person capable of doing something he could not do before.

As Bill puts it, "When a man or a woman has a spiritual awakening, the most important meaning of it is that he has now become able to do, feel, and believe that which he could not do before on his unaided strength and resources alone."

For all of us, this was an important discovery. I *was* now capable of doing things that had been impossible for me before; I could not deny it. The obvious example was staying sober—by this time, I had been dry for several consecutive months. Before AA, several consecutive days had been impossible.

But there were other important changes, which were harder to describe. My feelings of fear and guilt were slowly being replaced by feelings of hope and self-respect. And most important, that which had been impossible before—a trust in something or someone other than myself—had now become possible.

In other words, I had been undergoing a spiritual experience, without knowing it. My confused questioning about a Higher Power, my changed mental attitude, and even my physical recovery had all been part of a spiritual awakening. Without knowing it, I had been in contact with the source of life, whatever or whoever that might be.

Paradoxically, the realization that even I had experienced something spiritual was in itself a spiritual experience, and I am only slowly understanding its implications. What happened in the past, without my knowledge, is probably continuing now. And in the future, when tomorrow becomes today, it can go on and on. All that is required is a desire to stop drinking, and to stay stopped.

E. O., York, Pa.

Breakthrough
September 1969

Twenty years ago, the hospitals in our town were not equipped with special wards for alcoholics. When an alcoholic needed treatment, he was placed in the psycho ward with the patients who had serious mental disturbances. There were the usual safeguards: bars on the windows; a lock on the door; no cigarettes, matches, or shoelaces in the patient's possession.

This situation probably contributed to the sense of alcoholic despair which engulfed me on my fourth visit to such a ward, in 1944. I could see no chance of leading a normal life without periodic and increasingly dangerous lapses into alcoholic oblivion. I was on the verge of losing another job; my family had given up on me; it seemed that it would not be long before I was on skid row. What happened to me was of little consequence, but my children and my wife deserved a better break in life.

Two years before, I had come to Alcoholics Anonymous for help and had embraced their Twelve Steps program with enthusiasm. I attended meetings, made calls, and studied the Big Book. My three children and my wife were ecstatic. When I stayed sober, I was apparently a good husband and father. Their disappointment in my successive failures was devastating both to them and to me.

Now I had nowhere to go. If AA couldn't help me, there was no hope. I had no real conviction or belief that some remote God would interest himself in my individual problem. Perhaps, I thought, I was one of those not selected by God to be given the gift of faith.

Then occurred the incident that changed my life. On my last evening in the hospital, I had a visitor, an old man who had come to AA at the same time that I had, but who had been successful from the very first. He was calm and confident, and said he knew what my trouble was with the AA program, and if I was willing to invest an hour a day for a year in a practice that he would suggest, he was sure I would not only stay sober, but lead a happier life.

At that point, I was ready to do anything, so I quickly agreed. He went on to say that I was too busy to learn anything about the spiritual side of life; that from morning until night I rushed from one thing to another—job, family, AA calls—without a chance for solitude, for meditation, or for assessing the value of what I was doing.

He suggested that I get up an hour earlier in the morning, before the hustle and bustle of breakfast and getting the children off to school, and spend that hour in solitude, in seeking a knowledge of God and a better understanding of myself. During this hour I could read something inspirational and ponder it, or read the Bible if I wanted to. But the main purpose was to find out something about the Higher Power whose help was so obvious in the stories of successful members of AA. He suggested I start with a prayer something like this: "Dear God—if there is a God—guide me into a knowledge of thee." I was not to try to reason my way into a belief in God, but rather to find out about myself to begin with—my attitudes, capabilities, and relations with others.

The first morning when I walked into the quiet living room, it was still dark. I sat down, recited the suggested prayer, and wondered what to do next. Meditation was not as easy as I had thought. I had to fight to keep my thoughts from drifting to business troubles and to domestic difficulties, both of which were not inconsiderable.

It took several weeks of this daily struggle to even set up a procedure which seemed to lead toward some progress in the direction

I earnestly wanted to go. I found myself first reading a chapter of the New Testament and then turning to the meaning of words. Our thinking is, I believe, linked to our vocabulary; the clarity of our thought is determined by our understanding of words we use every day without questioning ourselves as to their exact meaning.

For instance, the word "love." What did I know about love? I started by listing all the words similar to or describing some phase of the emotion: affection, passion, yearning, desire, liking, adoration, and so on. I then listed all the types of love I could think of, from mother love to puppy love. All this I did to improve my understanding of the word "love." I even tried to include the poetry of love, but it is so voluminous and most times so passionate that I had to give it up as an aid to understanding. (This is no criticism of poetry per se; rather, it is a reflection of my own limitations.) Weeks passed, and each daily session showed some improvement in my comprehension. I can give you only a vague idea of my conclusions. To my mind, love is *giving*, not necessarily in material things, but in kindness, in ignoring faults, in thinking primarily in terms of the welfare and happiness of the beloved. The more you give, the more you love. Maybe that's why parents seem to love their children more than children love their parents.

During this period, I noticed that I had gradually added to the simple prayer that I started with. I added a plea for sobriety and then for guidance in my work and then for understanding in dealing with others, particularly with my family. Understand, I was still on strict probation as far as my wife and three children were concerned. They had been bitterly disappointed before and did not propose to get their hopes too high again.

The second word I took up was "fear," and I followed the same procedure of listing words of similar meaning: worry, apprehension, and so on. I followed with other words—humility, loyalty, greed—and I think I gradually improved my understanding.

Fall turned into winter and then into spring, and I faithfully continued this daily meditation. I looked forward to the peace of the early morning and the strength that it brought, for I still had troubles both at work and at home. One cannot be an alcoholic for fifteen years without creating some difficulties, a few of which take years to resolve and some of which are beyond repair.

One morning, considering a rather difficult problem, I found myself spontaneously praying, "Oh God, show me the way to meet this crisis." In that instant, the world changed for me. I felt the presence of God. These words from the Bible came to my mind as strongly as if they were spoken: "Let not your heart be troubled: ye believe in the Father, believe also in me."

My immediate reaction was that I was not worthy of this great experience. That was followed by a sense of wonder. This was truth, this was faith. This feeling was separate from reason. It concerned a part of me of which I had not previously been aware—a soul. My soul belonged to God. It was like searching for something in a dark room and suddenly seeing the light turned on and things vaguely imagined become clearly apparent.

I know that at this point the Freudians will interject "wishful thinking" or some other plausible idea to discount the depth and power of this revelation. But I *knew* there was a God, because to the depths of my soul I had been shaken. There was no possibility of doubt. For the first time in my life I was sure of something: that there is a God in the universe and I am part of that God.

My morning meditation continued—with, however, an entirely new perspective. Everything had to be related to the concept of an existent and accessible God.

Up to this time, I had not thought of churches as places to learn more about God. But certainly they had been concerned about man's soul for thousands of years. So I started going to church services, and in less than a year visited over thirty types and denominations. In some I felt the presence of God more than in others: some were concerned with one phase of religion more than another; but they were all apparently seeking the truth. Eventually, I became a communicant of a church close to my home. However, I believe that God is too big, too universal to be confined to one religion. I find much wisdom in the Koran and the Upanishads, as well as in the Bible, and these expressions of wisdom are surprising in their similarity.

Twenty-three years have passed, and God is as real to me now as he was that morning. My children did get a good education and are doing well and have children of their own. God has been good to me.

H. S., Lisle, Ill.

Traffic Goes Both Ways
March 1966

I n a quiet evening of conversation, a wise old clergyman had said something that lingered with me as I left him. He had said that there was a lower level of adversity beneath which all men become brothers. But likewise, he had observed that there was a higher level of attainment in life above which men become brothers. Then he suggested that the shortage of brotherly love in the world was probably due to the fact that most men for most of their lives stayed within the perimeter of the big grey area between these two levels.

As I reflected on this over a period, I recalled a talk which I had heard many years ago. A bright-eyed "honeymooner" in our way of life had traced his personal journey through the Twelve Steps. Finally he reached the extreme gratification of his first sponsorship, and then he said, "Why, these Twelve Steps are literally a stairway to the stars." It has never been a habit of mine to challenge a speaker, even though I may differ vehemently. However, I did ponder long over this "stairway to the stars" bit. There was no intimation that we graduate in this way of life. But there was an intimation that we move up the staircase to the top and stay there, unless we fall all the way down the stairs, of course.

As I started to put these things together, the wisdom of the clergyman, who is a devoted friend of our Fellowship, seemed to shine through the mist. We become brothers at the lower level. Through dedication to the philosophy of our Twelve Steps we become better people and reach brotherhood at the higher level in helping each other. But we must descend again to establish brotherhood with the new person who still suffers, and then we must take those steps all over again with him.

Accordingly, it seems clear that we do not have a "stairway to the stars"; what we have is a working, utilitarian stairway of life. We climb it to show our gratitude for sobriety—to become gracious receivers of this precious gift. And we move down it too, not merely to meet the newcomer, but as we recommit ourselves in surrender to our Higher Power again and again. As we meditate, pray, and seek greater conscious contact with God as we understand him. As we continue to make amends. And as we keep right on with those fearless inventories and the admissions of our continuing wrongs.

Our stairway of life is our bridge between the understanding and compassion we must maintain for the alcoholic who still suffers, and the higher level of attainment in life and brotherhood to which we aspire. In my early sobriety, I tried to catch up on a little worthwhile reading for a change. I discovered that William James also once said there was a low level beneath which all men became brothers. I strongly suspect that my minister friend had simply added a superstructure above the water level. However you look at it, these Twelve Steps must be used over and over again. There is one thing I know from experience—they never wear out.

Anonymous

Closet Atheist
April 1978

Twenty-seven years ago, I called AA. I told the girl who answered that I had a problem.

"What's your problem, alcohol?" she asked.

"Of course," I answered, "but I'm an atheist."

She said just the right words: "Oh, that's alright; we have lots of atheists in AA."

To run me off, all she would have needed to say was, "Aw, you're not an *atheist*; surely you believe in some kind of a higher power."

This was a while back, when AA was smaller, and she may have passed the word that there was going to be a new man, and let's take it easy on the spiritual. In any event, not much in the way of God was stressed at the early meetings I attended.

A little background on me. I was intensely interested in the Scopes "Monkey" Trial in Tennessee in 1925. For a few years afterward, the newspapers and Sunday supplements were filled with articles on the "missing link." I began to read Darwin, Wallace, Lamarck, Mendel. In the 1930s, I joined with other freethinkers in New York City in speaking on atheism. A group of us picketed a radio station in San Francisco, demanding (successfully) that an atheist be allowed equal time on Sunday. So much for background.

The Twelve Steps appeared to mean what they said. The members told me that I could use any concept of a higher power I liked. In Step Two, maybe it makes sense to believe that the power which is to restore my sanity is the power of the group, and in Step Three, maybe the group could do something with me if I turned my will and my life over to it. But it didn't make much sense to me. Then came Step Five. How do I admit my shortcomings to a God or something I do not believe in? Six and Seven required some mental skirmishing. I concluded, within eight or nine months, that if I couldn't reconcile my beliefs I couldn't stay sober on the program.

Since I had been a Catholic in my youth, I went to the church for instruction. For nine months, once and sometimes twice a week, a priest labored with me explaining Genesis. I argued Darwin to him. After nine months, he (and I) thought I now believed in God and the theory of creation. Because of a series of marriages and divorces, the church allowed me to attend Mass, but not to take the sacraments; this made me a sort of second-class Catholic. Talk about *resentments!*

But I stayed sober. For five years. Then I blew it. After a short stay on skid row and with the help of Goodwill, I got back uptown and back on the program. I recently celebrated my twentieth AA birthday.

I think what keeps me sober more than anything else is the AA Preamble: "Alcoholics Anonymous is a fellowship of men and women who share their experience, strength and hope with each other that they may solve their common problem..." That, I can buy, and I do buy it.

I'm a "closet atheist." I join in the Lord's Prayer, knowing it doesn't harm me, any more than it harms a Catholic to add "for thine is the kingdom," etc. When any spiritual question is under discussion, I usually pass when called upon to speak. I don't proselytize inside or outside of AA; I'm not trying to convert anyone to my way of thinking. I'd just ask some well-meaning, enthusiastic members not to come down so hard on the God question. There *are* atheists in them there foxholes; there *are* atheists in AA.

So let's have a little tolerance—tolerance perhaps of the unexpressed secret beliefs of the person next to you. We'll never know why that new member didn't come back. It's unpopular to be an atheist, and not every atheist admits it openly. So let's not run the agnostic or the rationalist off, back to the world of drinking.

I'm glad they didn't run me off!

C. C., Sacramento, Calif.

God Is Not Yourself
by Paul de Kruif
July 1951

AAs to me aren't ordinary human beings, because they've all been so near dead it seems spooky they're still alive and healthy. To me they're weird, like those rare people still living ten years after the cure of their incurable cancer. AAs are peculiar because, to keep alive and stay healthy, they've all got to get to be doctors. Without benefit of an MD, they far surpass the power of MDs over chronic alcoholism.

AAs are a strange lot, truly. Without any knowledge of enzymes, vitamins, and hormones, they've dragged over a hundred thousand far-goners out of a doom that baffles our best physicians.

Scientists speak of hormone or vitamin deficiencies as being at the bottom of alcoholism. The average AA wouldn't know a hormone from a hole in the ground; he'd flunk any medical school exam on the cause of alcoholism. How then do the AAs get to be the great alcohol doctors that they unquestionably are? The answer is as simple as it is rugged—every AA has to first nearly die of the disease of which later he becomes the master physician.

The medicine the AAs use is unique. Though it should be all-powerful, it has never been tried with any consistent success against any other major sickness. This medicine is no triumph of chemical science; has needed no billion dollar scientific foundation to discover it; does not come in capsules or syringes. It is free as air—with this provision: that the patients it cures have to nearly die before they can bring themselves to take it.

The AAs' medicine is God and God alone. This is their discovery.

New kind of people, a new kind of doctor, that's what, for me, the AAs boil down to. It has taken a rugged eight years to get this into my head clearly enough to begin to try to write about them. In this field the cards were stacked against me, due to my ignorance. I didn't believe alcoholism was curable. A rummy was a rummy, and too bad for him. And I didn't believe in God.

Twelve years ago, it happened to be necessary to help a heavy-drinking man who was making it tough for all of us. I went to one of the best brain doctors in the world, so down to earth that he was ashamed to be called a psychiatrist. "Yes, your man sounds like a real alcoholic," he said. It was this doctor's conviction that the mind is only part of the body. If you could cure the body, mightn't you fix its drunken mind?

That was my theory, not the doctor's. "If we could collar this patient, how about giving him deep insulin shock?" I asked the doctor. "The real McCoy, just this side of dying." I knew this had been used with some success on people desperately sick, mentally.

"That's been tried," said the doctor. "It doesn't seem to touch a real alcoholic." Then the good doctor gave me the works. In a low voice, confidential, he pronounced a doom. "Alcoholics? When a man is a real alcoholic, he's a louse," said the doctor. "Nothing'll touch him."

That was that. Thus ended my first search for a cure for alcoholism. We got our problem patient out of our lives. What's happened to him I do not know. This was in 1939. Then four years later I met my first AA. This was Earl; and it was in the days when AA was still obscure, and our meeting had nothing to do with AA but came about through our common interests.

Earl didn't wear his alcoholic anonymity on his chest. He didn't try subtly to sell it. That he was a remarkable man *because he was an AA*—this sneaked up on me slowly as we got to know each other better. On the surface, Earl was just a slow-spoken man, a good Joe, and such a wonderful listener that he made my stuff sound brilliant. In my job of reporting medical science, most of the human subjects are more or less exceptional, not so much as people as because they've saved human life. As people they're proud of what they've done—maybe the human brain when so constantly used tends a bit to exaggerate its own achievements. Though hunters for truth, these medical scientists are no more honest than the average. In short, they're no more or less than human.

Earl was the opposite. He was just a good salesman and certainly hadn't done anything to make him a candidate for the Nobel Prize—but he was a bit beyond human. What set him off from my scientists and doctors was his lack of vanity, his anonymity, a quality I intensely admire without being able to get very good at it myself. If people, on being introduced, don't recognize my name, I catch myself being a bit resentful.

Earl's anonymity was as natural as a fish swimming. He gave so little importance to being Earl that he had plenty of time to think of me. He radiated reliability. Like other human beings, Earl made promises easily. But he kept them. All of them. When he said he was going to be there at nine, he was there at nine and never an alibi. One morning he showed up on time on the dot but red-eyed and groggy from no sleep. It came out, reluctantly, that he'd been up all night trying to salvage a drunk. Then it appeared he'd been a drunk himself, one of those regular lice, he admitted, cheerfully; and that, though now working full time to get his business toehold, he spent at least half of his time trying to save drunks; and that he never refused a call for help, no matter how vital a business appointment he might have next day. In spite of this overload, he was always asking what he could do for me and then doing it, pronto.

This was my introduction to AA. Earl was the man I wish I could be. He was a Sermon on the Mount, walking.

Of course this might have been a coincidence; in history there have been many saints who have not been drunkards. But wait. Here was Earl's partner, Ward. He was an ex-drunk too. He was an AA, and he and Earl were twins in superhuman conduct.

"How did you guys get this way?" I kept asking Earl and Ward. "You're punctual; you're considerate; you never try to slip anything past me; I can't catch you lying. You guys don't fit the human pattern."

I don't remember which one gave the answer, but I believe it was Ward, though it doesn't matter; they both were so anonymous. Anyway one of them said, "It isn't only us. We AAs *all* had to get this way to save our lives."

It was an enigma. For years off and on I talked with both of them, trying to puzzle it out. Here they'd both been beat-up by years of terrific drinking, cruel to their wives, their children, their parents; their brains revolving, frantic, sleepless, in black despair, on the ropes, as good as in the gutter—in short, human lice. And now here they were, only a little less than angels. Maybe they'd had to get this way to save their lives. But how had they?

By this time not only Earl and Ward but the fact of some 25,000 AAs pulled out of the ashcan convinced me that my great doctor was wrong when he wrote alcoholics off as hopeless. I wanted to write this good news but couldn't. How would such fantastic cures make sense when I didn't know what the cure was? I kept probing for that with Earl, and his simple groping explanation kept stopping me cold.

It was to the simple effect that you had to admit you couldn't save yourself but could only be saved by a Higher Power, a Supreme Being. Did he mean God? Earl didn't like to use the word God. But he meant something greater than ourselves? All powerful? Yes. Well, *I* didn't believe in any God. I tried to argue with Earl that it didn't have to be any God that saved drunks. When AAs saved drunks, weren't they using Pavlov's conditioned reflexes? At their meetings didn't they keep each other from relapsing into rummydom by conditioning each other with pep talk?

Earl in his stubborn manner kept saying they'd still all be rummies if they hadn't found a Higher Power and put themselves in his hands. Earl's stuttering honesty undermined my argumentative pride of intellect. For many years, I'd considered myself a bit of an authority on Pavlov. For me that fierce old man with the beard from the North had the answers not only to the working of the human brain but the soul—if there was one.

To Earl in argument I brought up my friend, Andrew Salter. I told Earl that Salter had made a great scientific advance, bringing conditioned reflex science from the dog to man.

"Can Salter save alcoholics?" Earl asked with a smile.

"No, he can't."

"Does Salter believe in God?" asked Earl.

"Not much. Salter believes in Pavlov." It might have been added that Salter believed in himself. And Earl might have added that he knew de Kruif believed in himself, terrifically.

Earl saw I thought I was running my show and was captain of my soul, the existence of which was doubtful. Earl saw I thought I was some guy. And a heavy drinker. Yet not needing AA at all. And yet, if I went on drinking?

"Do you think I may need to join up?" I asked Earl. (Boss Kettering had said: "Paul, you haven't drunk the Johnnie Walker people dry yet, but you've got 'em working nights," and I considered that a great compliment.)

Earl smiled and said: "No, Paul, you don't need us yet."

It would be a humiliation. Then fate intervened to spare such humbling. My liver went bad. Not out and out cirrhosis but all liver-function tests haywire. Tired all the time. So damned tired. Rhea with her five feet two inches walking faster over the dunes than I could. Feeling all the time like walking against a gale of wind. Two or three times after very heavy drinking, blacking out. That scared me. Not irresponsible. Showing up at my writing table every morning. Not yet a real alcoholic, not in my brain doctor's louse category. But those blackouts and the fatigue and the gummed up liver-function tests scared me. For my pride, it was nice that it now needed no humbling before a God whose very existence I denied. It was still just a matter for medical science, not God. Rhea and Dr. Henry A. Rafsky (who says we are not as old as our arteries but as old as our livers) showed me the ominous figures of the liver-function tests. Rhea and Henry asked did I want to go on living. I looked at Rhea, so stern, so devoted, so loving. I didn't want to die.

Henry cut down my whiskey to three jiggers a day. This was two and a half years ago and the liver-function tests have reversed to normal. The tiredness is much less. In a year, enough brain energy was back for me to find out what Earl meant by that Higher Power, by God.

This discovery came about in an absolutely roundabout way, by not looking for God at all. Who had saved *me*? Not God. No. Rhea and Dr. Rafsky, plus huge daily therapeutic doses of vitamins, plus shots of crude liver extract, plus hormones and the new low alcohol intake—all these had saved me. Not God. It still seemed as impossible to understand Earl's God as it had always been to take any stock in the old hell-fire-and-damnation Dutch Reformed God of my fathers.

Then in 1950 came what looked like a threat to AA. Even though I didn't believe in God, the AA medicine, to me the AAs were great, because they had saved so many lives. Unquestionably. Even with a medicine to me nonexistent. But now AA was in danger. It was reported by Dr. James J. Smith of New York that he could control acute alcoholism and post-binge craving for alcohol by shots of adrenal cortex extract—"A.C.E." It was reported that Dr. Roger Williams of the University of Texas could change alcoholics into normal drinkers, by a high-vitamin formula.

So alcoholism was chemical. So it was simply a hormone or vitamin block?

To this seeming good news, my reaction was strange. Hadn't I always been for science and against this God business. You can weigh and measure vitamins and hormones; how can you dose God? I'd always been on the side of science, the more materialistic, the more godless the better. Now here I was worrying about my friends the AAs who had only God for a medicine.

By this time AA had about a hundred thousand ex-rummies, really doomed people but now dry, now healthy, now fine citizens—most of them exceptional. Just by faith and works. By faith in God. And by devoted work, getting to be doctors to salvage others doomed. At this, scientific medicine had failed. The AAs had succeeded; the MDs acknowledged it.

How did hormones and vitamins threaten AA? This way. If AAs thought hormones and vitamins could wipe out their craving for alcohol and make them drink normally, would they stay dry and stick to God when the pills and shots were easier?

In my confusion it seemed as if a fate was guiding me. Marc Rose of *Reader's Digest* asked me to study Dr. James J. Smith's hormone science for a possible *RD* story. That science looked so good it seemed more dangerous to AA than ever.

Dr. Smith had a few ex-drunks under control by hormones. AA had a hundred thousand under control by God. It's true Dr. Smith urged his hormone cures to stay dry. But could I take the responsibility of writing a story about hormones only? Maybe tempting AAs away from God?

Earl came to the rescue. I told him this threat of hormones demanded that, at last, I must write about AA—but how could I, not believing in their medicine? Could I compromise, by writing about both AA and hormones as a double-barreled hope? It turned out Earl wasn't against hormones at all. But with his slow smile Earl asked what I really knew about the AAs' medicine.

"Nothing but what you and Ward have told me about your Higher Power." Their thoughts of God had been too big for their mouths so I couldn't make head or tail of it.

"Have you read our book *Alcoholics Anonymous*?" Earl asked. He had given it to me many years before.

"Not really read it. Too many miracles. Too much camp meeting. No understand," I said. Earl asked me to study the book the way I dug through scientific papers.

Now came a humiliating experience—of finding clear what I should have learned years before. I shan't forget even the reading, nor the study of the AAs' book, spelling it out word by word; trying to find inconsistencies and failing; searching in every line and on every page through what I had considered sawdust-trail testimonials—to find a fantastic unanimity in what all these ex-derelicts understood by this medicine that had saved them from the gutter, from insanity, from dying.

What they understood clearly was what I'd looked for all my life. What they understood was not mystical or contradictory. In the book one ex-drunk tells his story. "We needed to ask ourselves but one short question: Do I believe, or am I willing to believe, there is a power greater than myself? If yes, a man is on his way."

I cluttered the book with marginal comments, noting: "Their God is only a positive way of saying: I can't do it by myself."

A man saved from alcoholic oblivion testified: "There is *something*. I know not what it is, but it is bigger than I. If I will acknowledge it, if I will give in.... All I had to do was believe in some power greater than myself and *knuckle down to it*."

Another ex-rummy said: "You admit you've made a mess of things trying to run them your own way.... Here it is, God, all mixed up. I don't know how to unmix it. I'll leave it to *you*."

It was like no other praying I'd ever met. In my childhood Calvinistic religion the dominies and deacons and elders had prayed for rain, for success, and against pestilence and fire and sudden death.

My childhood religious teachers knew precisely what they wanted and told God about it in no uncertain terms. In contrast in the book here was an AA, praying:

"I've made a mess of things and can't do anything about it. *You* take me and all my troubles and do what you want with me."

This made me ponder. In conventional prayer, when you pray for rain or sunshine or a new Cadillac, you are still trying to run your own show. On the contrary another AA said: "Every day I let him do all the caring. Who am I to run myself or anyone else?"

My Dutch Reformed forebears in church sang their Psalms and prayed and joined up in well-polished shoes, Prinz Albert coats, and striped pants. In contrast, here was the way a typical AA had found God. *"It is only when a man has tried everything else*, when in utter desperation and terrific need he turns to something bigger than himself, that he gets a glimpse of the way out."

The book began to make me understand Earl's strange humility. At the moment of his deepest despair, another AA said: "Suddenly it seemed to me I had the answer. These men [the ex-drunks doctoring him] of themselves were nothing and felt themselves nothing."

Their salvation was for some of them instantaneous, for others slow and painful. Earl himself had objected to what he called the "spiritual factor." A power greater than himself? At first it was only the little group of AAs helping him. Then Earl, joining them to save others, himself not yet recovered completely, saw it wasn't merely himself and the other AA men. It was something not human, it was something curiously negative. "When an alcoholic once accepts the fact that he is powerless to recover unaided, *he is hooked,*" Earl said.

Here was the strange medical technique of the AAs as told in their book; they had to make a man worse before he could get better. "The alcoholic has got to hit bottom...to be reduced to a state of complete dependence on whatever or whoever can stop his drinking...open-minded as only the dying can be."

The religious awakening was the opposite of mystical; it was really down-to-earth and simple. It is only "the act of giving up one's reliance on one's own omnipotence...the defiant individual no longer defies but accepts help...from outside."

There was a bit of science (which is only learning by experience) in the AAs' salvation. One AA, now dry for 15 years, was like any scientist convinced by his experimental protocols. "At first I had no faith. The power greater than myself was only my fellow AAs. I couldn't pray. Then I learned a little prayer: thy will not mine be done. Then I saw the results of what we were doing: men dragged from the insane asylum and the edge of the grave. *Then* I began to have faith. God was not the other AAs or myself...God is in all others. God's voice is my own conscience. All I have to do is follow my own conscience. God help me now to do what's right; thy will not mine be done. Then humility came with it. Humility equals God, because when truly humble you cannot do it yourself."

Earl and the book *Alcoholics Anonymous,* by making God simple, had made me understand him. Earl and the book had purged me of 45 years of the confusion and atheism that had haunted me ever since I'd begun to think at all. Scratch a Dutchman and you find a theologist, the saying goes. I'd read theology. It told me on the one hand that God is love and on the other that he is a Vindictive Old Man. The sects couldn't agree upon a definition of God at all. For Calvinists God was a cold determinist; for Fundamentalists God was terrifying; for Episcopalians God was a socialite presiding over afternoon tea; for Unitarians God was a mere absence of evil, an amiable vacuum.

For the AAs? *God is not yourself.*

To get that clear, what a sunrise for me. "It is only when a man has tried everything else, when in utter desperation..." It wasn't alcoholism that threatened me. But there are other disintegrations of character that can drive a man to despair. And wasn't I disintegrated? I'll say.

At the end of the study of the book of the AAs, I bowed my head in shame. What a contrast, between the AAs and me. I had gloried in the confusion among sects and what had always seemed to me the absurd contradictions of their ideas of God that divided Catholics, Anglicans, Presbyterians, Methodists, Baptists, and Jehovah's

Witnesses. But the AAs? Humble, they worked with all sects. AAs were devoid of that pride of intellect that made me deny God because about him there were thousands of different ideas.

In the spring of 1950 Earl came to Wake Robin to brief me for the writing of the *RD* story. "You're going to write it, alright," he said. I told him we'd have a good shot at it, anyway. "Why do you think you can write it?" Earl asked.

"Because I can pray now, at last," I said.

SIX

Neither Endorses
Nor Opposes Any Causes

———————— ♦ ————————

We Could Blow the Whole Thing
January 1979

Nothing in my life had prepared me for the six months through which I had just lived. Not my education, not my drinking, not my recovery in AA. I'd been assigned to the field as a representative for my company, to oversee the operation of an experimental system for mining copper in South America. It meant spending exactly 180 days cut off from civilization, living and working with a hard-drinking bunch of men from everywhere, assembled for the project.

Fresh from the office, a lovely home and family, and an active life in AA locally, I was suddenly thrust into a dark and treacherous existence in a jungle camp, thousands of miles away.

Right from the beginning, it was every man for himself. There were bosses and sub-bosses, some of whom knew only the authority born of physical violence. Cliques were everywhere, and because of the extreme isolation, nerves wore thin. Recreation ended in drunken brawls almost every night. In the morning, sick and hungover, everyone got back to work.

At the end of my stint, there was only one thought in my mind: How fast can I get to a meeting? As it happened, there was a day's layover on my trip home, and I knew there'd be a meeting somewhere nearby.

I remember the feeling of excitement as, in the rented car, I pulled out of the hotel parking lot. My *International AA Directory* was safe at my side, and my anticipation grew as I found the street, and then the address of the meeting. What a welcome sight that church was. As I walked briskly to the side door, I could almost smell the coffee, and I reached for the handle.

The door was locked. In fact, there wasn't a sign of life anywhere. I checked the directory, and it showed clearly I was in the right place. A glance at my watch told me the meeting scheduled should begin in ten minutes. I scratched my head—where was everyone?—and I walked back to the car.

I stood on the street for a few minutes more, and when no one appeared, I shrugged and got in, and turned on the light. Well, I thought, there should be another meeting somewhere nearby. Looking down the list, I found a Step group across town. Within a few minutes, I pulled up to a large church, its lights beckoning everywhere. My enthusiasm was short-lived, however. A thorough search of the parish house revealed a number of empty rooms, one vestry meeting, and no AA to be found.

The eerie feeling that had begun to grow in me now turned to anger. What the heck was going on here? I left the church and headed my car back out of town, toward my hotel. As I drove, I ranted and raved. Some way to treat a visitor! I was sure nothing like this could ever happen back home—we knew how to keep AA together a lot better! I was halfway through the blistering letter I'd fire off to the AA General Service Office upon my return home, as I pulled into the hotel lot and went to my room. Still grousing, I went to bed.

The next morning, as I stepped out of the shower, I hadn't shaken off the indignant rage that haunted me. On an impulse, I looked at my watch. It was about half past ten in New York, and I knew GSO would be open. I picked up the phone, not trusting my anger to last till I returned home, and placed the call.

The operator and I listened to the recording: "The number (you have reached is not in service at this time." My shock was indescribable. A verifying operator obtained the same message, and I hung up.

Now, for the first time, I was genuinely afraid. There was obviously something really wrong, and I wasn't sure I knew what to do. Funny, all I could think of was that old saw "Don't drink, and go to meetings." What a laugh! Later, I turned the car in at the airport and boarded a plane for home, arriving late that evening.

Naturally, the first thing I did when I was settled in with my family was to get on the phone to some of my AA friends. There was no one home anywhere I called, and I felt the oddest sensation. I was suddenly in the *Twilight Zone*. Everything I knew about the AA program, all the tools I'd been using for the past few years, were suddenly gone!

The next morning I was out early, and I drove to the roadside coffeehouse that had become the unofficial AA club. It had always provided an all-day meeting, of sorts, and surely *there* someone could tell me what was going on.

There was only one car in the parking lot. I walked inside, and I saw only George T., who owned the place, sitting at the end of the counter. He greeted me warmly. "Well, hello, buddy. Where've you been? It's been an age since I've seen you!"

I shook his hand eagerly but decided to skip the small talk. "George, what's going on?" I began at the beginning and told him of all the strange things that had happened to me.

George never really changed expression, and when I finished my tale, he just looked at me. Then, staring into his coffee, he said, "Y'know, buddy, I'll bet you're the last guy on earth to hear the news, and I'm sure sorry I gotta be the one to tell you. It's all over, buddy. It's all gone."

I stared at him. "What are you saying?"

"Just that, buddy. There is no more AA—not here, not anywhere!"

"But—but how can that be?" I stammered.

"Well now, that's a long story," George said, like a man retelling something for the umpteenth time. "It was a case of benign neglect, I guess you could say. Sorta slow, like a cancer, it was. You know, there was always lotsa groups—thousands of them—and folks to carry the message all over the place. And that GSO office in New York to send out stuff. Who'd ever think a thing like that could just fall apart? But y'know, buddy, that's just what it did. It just went to seed and died."

I couldn't speak. I just stared openmouthed at George.

After a minute, he went on. "I guess it was in the spring, just after you left on that trip of yours, that we got a letter from New York appealing to all AAs for help. They said it felt like they were under attack from all sides, and the structure was beginning to fall apart. That rash of anonymity breaks, y'know, that started last fall—and that national telethon didn't help, with all those AAs getting their faces on TV.

"Seems like all our friends at the churches just started closing out our meetings faster than we could get new places. Didn't want any part of the 'new AA,' they said!

"Then, in April, there was that last General Service Conference. Boy, it must've been something! See, there was this bloc of delegates that got together, nobody seemed to know how, and just *took over!* They said it was about time the *real* group conscience had its day. Threw out the whole board of trustees and did over the whole general service structure. Yep—they really did it, vote by vote. What a bunch of supersalesmen! Of course, they were only the tip of the iceberg. It turned out they had a regular organized bunch of drunks all over the country.

"Well, the rest was predictable. Before you could blink, they sent out a long 'restructure bulletin' from this new World AA Office, and they laid down a whole set of rules and new procedures, and began to badger the groups for pretty heavy 'donations.' In a few weeks, almost a third of all the groups in the whole Fellowship had already folded. They died like flies! The rest were all confused and couldn't cope with the load, plus all the bickering that broke out. Finally, I guess everybody just gave up. There've been some halfhearted attempts around town to keep it going, on an independent basis—y'know, in homes, here at the club—but believe me, it just ain't the same, if you know what I mean. Nobody feels like a part of anything anymore."

I was stunned. When I finally found my voice, I said, "George, what happened to the Traditions? That's why we had the Twelve Traditions!"

George blinked. "The Twelve what?" he asked...

Of course, it's all a fantasy. I'm not even a mining engineer. And one thing I've learned in AA is not to be an alarmist. Still, around the groups I attend, it *does* seem that we AAs sometimes get a little funny about the Traditions. That's what prompted me to wonder: What would happen if we *all* decided to let somebody else safeguard these twelve foundation stones?

If you woke up one morning, and found there was simply no more AA, where would that leave you?

Yeah, that's the feeling I got, too.

R. S., Queens, N.Y.

"Let the Bum Find Us"
October 1976

B ill W., on that historic day in the Akron hotel lobby, did not leave a note with the desk clerk to the effect that he would be waiting in his room reading the papers in case an inquiring alcoholic stumbled in wanting help. Today, though, much Twelfth Step work is conducted on just such a premise. "Let the bum find us" is a disturbingly pervasive attitude, and it is contrary to every historic and traditional principle established in the early days of AA.

The Big Book itself is the result of a monumental, thoroughly unlikely series of events designed to actively share what had become "the great news" for our founders. Initial motives, dreams of money and fame, are beside the point. The only important point is that our visionary predecessors courageously tackled an audacious enterprise, which gave us this incredible gift of real living.

Today, some critical, unknowledgeable AAs strongly oppose local public information use of the media and efforts to communicate with the public in person. They shout accusations of tub-banging, book-thumping evangelism at best, and charge promotion and Tradition violation at worst. Such members are seemingly unacquainted with, co-founder Bill W.'s words, "Obviously, AA had to be publicized somehow," and the fact that the most powerful magnet cannot attract the desired object without first being in specific proximity to it.

The words "attraction rather than promotion" in the Eleventh Tradition, referring to our public relations policy, assume that we *have* a public relations policy to begin with. Because our reason for existence is "to stay sober and help others to achieve sobriety," our own hard-won sobriety depends in great measure on finding means of reaching the public. The still-suffering alcoholic *is* the public until we get the message to him.

The long form of the Eleventh Tradition says we ought to avoid sensational advertising and instead depend upon our friends to recommend us. Those who do not bother to inform themselves do not know that we have, historically and practically, found it necessary to cultivate and value such friends. In *Twelve Concepts for World Service*, Bill says, "We need to be on still better terms with medicine, religion, employers, governments, courts, prisons, mental hospitals, and all enterprises in the alcoholism field. We need the increasing goodwill of editors, writers, television and radio channels. These publicity outlets need to be opened ever wider." To this list we can add educators, because of the continuing appeals for information from grade schools, high schools, and colleges.

Somebody must responsibly contact these people; God doesn't come down and whisper in the ears of editors, TV station owners, and others, telling them to get out some AA material. If that were the standard method, he would not need us. If we timidly refuse to discharge that responsibility, how can we hope to reduce the stigma on alcoholism and lessen its lethal potential for others?

Shortly after Bill W.'s well-known spiritual experience, the thought came to him that he might be able to help some of the thousands of still-suffering alcoholics, and that they in turn could help many others. AAs everywhere seem to have lost sight of the fact that, instead of fewer alcoholics out there yet to be reached, there are now many, many more.

Others in the field of alcoholism are "explaining" AA to vast numbers of people daily—because we are refusing to do it. If you've never listened to a nonmember professional explain AA, you're not keeping abreast of the state of the art. Your imagination will not even come close to the distortions and misinformation that sometimes occur.

But these professionals are not to be faulted; we are. Even Congress came close to receiving a document about us written by nonmembers and described by a GSO staff member as "a dog." By the grace of God and some dedicated public information footwork, GSO was given an opportunity to rewrite it before it went to Congress.

A traveling member recently discovered to his dismay that AA in a large Eastern city was all but a secret society. While there, he went to work tirelessly, against considerable opposition, to set up some exceedingly successful PI projects. Today in that city, thanks to the traveler's efforts, many citizens know some basic facts about AA.

With so many other enterprises, both public and private, in the field of alcoholism today, we are experiencing a widespread reduction in our usual Twelfth Step opportunities. For our own well-being and continued sobriety, we must search out every possible avenue for conducting the public information phase of Twelfth Step work.

There are well-meaning individual zealots who go out on their own with blaring sensationalism and overdramatization to "tell the AA story." Such persons can, in one fell swoop, destroy years of careful, painstaking efforts to portray AA in a dignified, sensible, explanatory, and informative way. When there is an active, responsible local PI committee that maintains close liaison with all the community and local media, the probability of such harmful acts is minimized and everyone benefits: the community, the Fellowship as a whole, and most especially the potentially offending member, who will be given a chance to recover sufficiently before making his services available.

The obvious recommendations for an AA member meeting the public are a neat, clean appearance, an absence of offensive language, and a noncritical attitude. These are vital to "attraction," but they are just the beginning of desirable qualifications. We do not appreciate vague, distorted descriptions of our Fellowship by outsiders, so we should take precautions against doing this ourselves. We should know our AA history and principles through diligent study and familiarization with *all* our material, especially the Traditions. Through them, "each member becomes an active guardian of our Fellowship." And "Moved by the spirit of anonymity, we try to give up our natural desires for personal distinction as AA members." With the public particularly, we practice the humble recognition that the only thing of real value we possess is our message.

It is my hope and prayer that instead of failing to be altogether responsible, instead of just minimally meeting the trickle of "requests" that come in, we can put some real meaning into "I Am Responsible" and "Let It Begin with Me." An honest appraisal of individual responsibility reveals something considerably beyond waiting for the answering-service phone to ring (and it is ringing less and less often). The pledge "When anyone, anywhere, reaches out..." does not require the reacher to *know* beforehand that he needs AA—nor to say so to my satisfaction. As far as possible, I must help him discover that it is AA he is reaching out for. "I want the hand of AA always to be there" means that I will try to make AA visible and available wherever "there" happens to be—in the schools, the medical societies, the prisons, the media, or wherever and however suffering people with my illness can be found. "And for that: I am responsible."

A California PI chairperson

Are We Forgetting Twelfth Step Calls?
March 1983

I was lucky! One of the first women I met in AA knew no limits when it came to reaching out to still-suffering alcoholics. Shortly after I joined the Fellowship, she became my sponsor, and her message was clear. She said that I was self-centered, that I was wallowing in self-pity, and that I could overcome this—by trying to help other alcoholics.

I had seen the movies *The Lost Weekend* and *Days of Wine and Roses*, so I was familiar with Hollywood's version of carrying the AA message, and it appealed to me. I've always liked high drama, so I enthusiastically agreed to go along with her on Twelfth Step calls early in my sobriety. We went on many calls together, armed with "care packages"—soup, honey, tea, juice, and handfuls of AA literature. The women we called on were a far cry from Lee Remick, and Hollywood forgot to mention that most alcoholics seem to have dogs that haven't been outside for days.

Alcoholics also change their minds; there were many times when we were welcomed less than graciously in spite of the fact that the alcoholic had called for help and we had canceled plans in our efforts to "go to any length." A few of the people we called on did get sober. Most did not; I hope they reached out for help later and found AA.

But my sponsor was right. It was hard for me to feel sorry for myself when my energies were focused on helping another drunk. Most important, I stayed sober. Twelfth Step calls taught me about myself and my illness. I'll always remember the help I received from an indigent woman in the alcoholic ward of the city hospital. She may have been only forty-five or fifty, but she looked very old. I was there because it was my night to make coffee for the weekly AA meeting. She was lying on her bed exposing her toothpick legs, which were covered with wine sores. She was so weak that she could barely walk, so I offered to take her to the meeting in a wheelchair. She responded, "No thanks, honey. I've never been so bad that I need the AAs."

I heard myself answer, "Thank God I was *bad* enough to need AA, and it sure has helped me."

It's been several years since I've been on what we think of as a Twelfth Step call, and I'm not sure why. Maybe it's because I've neglected to let the intergroup office know that I would welcome an opportunity to carry the message.

With AA growing at a rate of fifteen new groups daily, Twelfth Step work is still taking place, but perhaps in different forms. The AA General Service Office lists 540 area and local public information committees and more than 300 additional public information contacts [like all statistics here, these were current in 1983]. By talking to non-AAs in schools, churches, and service clubs, by providing literature displays at health fairs, and by placing AA public service announcements on TV and radio and getting articles about AA into local newspapers, these twelfth-steppers are reaching thousands of alcoholics hidden in the general public.

More than 200 committees on cooperation with the professional community are carrying the AA message to physicians, medical students, members of the clergy, psychologists, social workers, educators, and people in labor and management.

Approximately 200 institutions committees are carrying the AA message to hospitals, treatment centers, and correctional facilities.

With the proliferation of treatment facilities that took place in the 1970s, we aren't seeing many alcoholics holding half-empty cups of coffee at their first meeting because they are shaking too hard to hold full cups. Thank God, it's been at least ten years since I've seen a new member go into an alcoholic convulsion at a meeting. But there is still plenty for us to do if we want what co-founder Bill W. described as the "undreamed rewards" we receive as we try to help another alcoholic—one who is "even blinder" than we.

We can let local treatment centers know that we welcome opportunities to introduce alcoholic patients to AA, that we are available to serve as temporary or interim sponsors upon their discharge.

We can be available to meet a fellow member who found sobriety inside the walls. With 1,100 AA groups in prisons and jails, there is always a need for outside members to provide that crucial AA contact the day an inmate is released.

Corresponding with inmates, sharing with an AA Loner, making coffee, talking at a meeting, sponsoring a newcomer, serving as the link between your group and AA as a whole—there are many ways to make Twelfth Step calls.

Old-timers talk about the days when early AAs literally went to any length to help other alcoholics. There's the story about a traveling salesman from New York who once rode a bus 450 miles out of his way because the AA General Service Office had received a plea for help from someone with a drinking problem. Even today, Loners write about receiving help from another Loner who has traveled a day or more over rarely used dirt roads. Those AAs understood the meaning of "reaching out" to another alcoholic.

I think of those stories, and I feel concern about recent discussions in my home group. Much emphasis is put on reaching out—but the stress is on reaching out *for* help rather than *to* help. Many of the newcomers, and some who are not so new, talk about how AA members are letting them down. One feels "abandoned" because her sponsor is going on vacation. Another is hurt because no one invited her to go for coffee after last week's meeting. They feel unsatisfied and turned-off by AA because they reached out *for* help to deal with every conceivable problem, and did not receive the attention they were seeking. I am uncomfortable as I listen, and I know that I said those things, too. Again, I was lucky—my sponsor told me that I would get better if I stopped thinking about myself and reached out to help others, and it worked!

The primary purpose of every AA group is to carry the message to the still-suffering alcoholic. Maybe it's time to make some old-fashioned Twelfth Step calls in my own group, so that nondrinking but still-suffering alcoholics I see every week can know the joy of truly living sober.

Yes, we do have central/intergroup offices to answer calls in most of our cities and hundreds of committees on public information and cooperation with the professional community to spread the word. But let's not forget that our Fellowship got its start because a drunk named Bill sought help *for* himself by reaching out *to* help another drunk named Dr. Bob.

L.F., New York, N.Y.

Exclusive—or More Inclusive?
October 1977

S pecial-purpose groups, or groups formed by specific types of people, are not new on the AA scene. All-male or all-female groups have flourished in many places for years without incurring too much criticism within the Fellowship. Many people go along with the idea that things some alcoholics want to talk about can be aired more honestly among members of their own sex. Others may not think this is important for themselves, but they are not generally inclined to question the sincerity of purpose of those who do think it important.

In the last few years, other kinds of special-purpose groups have sprung up, mostly in large metropolitan areas, and we do hear much adverse comment about them. Although the members of these groups claim that they need to talk about things not easily discussed in regular AA meetings, this contention is not accepted as graciously as it was when made by members of all-male or all-female groups.

The special-purpose groups I refer to are of three types: the professional group, comprising doctors, lawyers, clergymen, college professors, and other persons the group accepts as "professionals"; the young people's group, usually restricted to alcoholics under thirty-five (although I know many over that age who have been sneaking in regularly); and the homosexual group, which may sometimes be further restricted to only male or only female homosexuals.

When I discussed the purpose of such groups with people who attend each or all of these types—and there is much cross attendance—they expressed a definite belief that they could not be entirely open about themselves in most regular AA groups, and that they must have a forum in AA where they can be entirely open and as comfortable as possible. Homosexuals believe that their sexual orientation and the specifics of their emotional relationships would not be understood or accepted in regular AA meetings. Young people are convinced that their lifestyles, including sexual attitudes and past involvement with drugs, are not understandable to older members. And professionals feel they get more understanding from those they consider their peers, particularly in matters relating to their conduct in their professions while they were active alcoholics.

Furthermore, there seems to be genuine concern about anonymity. People with professional standing in the community, especially where licensing is involved, are fearful of identifying themselves as alcoholics or talking about their drinking escapades in a regular AA group. Homosexuals, on the whole, do not want to reveal themselves as such in predominantly heterosexual groups. And many of the young people are loath to have their illegal involvement with drugs too widely aired.

Members of special-purpose groups are certain that many of their kind would never be able to get themselves to AA if they had to enter through a regular group.

Whether or not we agree with all this thinking, the point is that many alcoholics do believe in it. And they believe in it seriously enough to form these special groups and make them work.

If our own prejudices or fears about any of these people dominate our thinking, or if we feel excluded from meetings of such groups, we will never be able to accept their existence in the AA Fellowship with equanimity. Our problem in that case is a need to examine our own value systems, because our program tells us quite clearly that we cannot afford to live with intolerance or hatred. We must be able to place principles before personalities if any comfortable understanding is to be achieved.

In working out a comfortable attitude for myself, I had to recognize first that people do get sober and stay sober in these groups. As far as I can tell there is no more or less slippage in these groups than in any others. Next, I had to own up to the fact that regular meetings, as a rule, are not equipped to handle homosexual stories and frequently discourage the discussion of addiction to drugs other than alcohol. I also had to admit that most regular groups do include a lot of people who do not leave in the meeting place what they hear at the meeting when it is something they consider sensational, despite our tradition of anonymity. These are problems to be worked out by the group conscience of the regular AA groups.

But the special-purpose groups have their problems, too. Fortunately, their leaders are generally aware of this. They have an obligation to help one another identify more widely and so become able to move comfortably into regular AA. There is much for them to learn in regular meetings, and much for them to contribute. At some point, they should begin to address themselves primarily to their alcoholism and less to attendant or secondary problems. They must learn that their ultimate objective is to lead sober, meaningful lives in the world, not huddled among their "own kind."

The topic in every special-purpose meeting should be recovery, first and foremost, and members should be encouraged to attend and fully participate in regular meetings as well as in their own groups.

As all of us in the program move closer in consciousness to the AA ideal, the need for these special-purpose groups will diminish. Until then, let's wish them every success.

K. S., Atlanta, Ga.

Opportunity Knocks
May 1986

I have resigned from my position as bleeding deacon. I am through "viewing with alarm" the conduct of certain newcomers in our midst. I have stopped splitting hairs about terms such as "chemical dependency." I'm really too busy for any of the foregoing, because I have found a whole new opportunity to do Twelfth Step work and carry the message!

Being a typical alcoholic, I managed during the past year to work myself into a real tizzy over the invasion of AA by much younger people, many of whom are dual addicts.

It seemed to me that just overnight our group and several others were overrun with youthful mopheads who noisily occupied space but contributed nothing. They just didn't participate. Oh, they ate the doughnuts and drank the coffee. But they didn't work in the kitchen, empty ash trays, help stack chairs, or any of that good stuff. And when the basket was passed, all they did was *pass*.

The straw that gave the camel the pain in the back was the kid who showed up with a radio and attempted to have a rock and roll concert for himself during the discussion part of our meeting.

It all made me wonder. Where are these kids coming from? Had someone, somewhere, turned over a large rock? The kids seemed to have no manners, no understanding of AA, no sponsors.

I felt that the group was threatened; I even thought of leaving it although I had been a co-founder of the group over eighteen years ago. Some did leave. Others started a new group elsewhere on the same night.

Then, as has happened before in my life, my Higher Power stepped in and gave me a good rap on the knuckles. He did this by sending a young man sixteen years old to ask me if I would be his sponsor. This young man, a dual addict, was just out of treatment. He said he had been told to come to AA and to find a sponsor.

I've always tried never to say no to anything I'm asked to do in AA. So this new sponsorship experience began. It has been quite an experience! When you consider that fifty years separate us in age, you can appreciate that there is a slight generation gap! But I've been listening to this young man just as I expect him to listen to me. It has been a learning experience for both of us.

I've learned that there are a lot of young people going through treatment these days. So many, in fact, that our facilities in Cleveland cannot handle them all. Therefore, many are getting help in other cities such as Columbus and Toledo.

As a result of treatment and introduction to AA in hospitals, the young patients are encouraged to attend AA when they get home. They are told to go to AA and to find sponsors.

When you stop and think about it, where else *can* they go? AA is their only chance for continuing help, just as it is for me.

So they show up at our AA meetings. They're seeking the help they've been told they will find. They're seeking sponsors. They often bring friends, and their friends are also seeking help and sponsorship.

What a tremendous opportunity this is for us to carry the message! It's up to us to help them. It's up to us to see that they get active. It's up to us to get them to contribute. It's up to us to provide the guidance that they need.

We shouldn't be afraid of change in AA. This great program of ours has gone through change before and come through it stronger than ever. I well remember when it was thought that one had to be down and out and on skid row to be "ready" for AA.

When I came into the Fellowship in 1953 that skid row idea still existed. Some of the then old-timers looked askance at me because I still had a job and had my family. A couple of these old boys told me later that they never thought I'd make it because I hadn't been hurt enough.

Fortunately AA survived that kind of thinking. Yes, AA is capable of change. We've absorbed the high bottoms and the women and the younger and younger people. I'm sure we can absorb the kids with their addiction to alcohol, pot, and pills.

AA will survive because you and I know we can keep it only as we give it away. And here come legions of new people who have no place else to go and who need our help.

What a great opportunity!

R. L., Berea, Ohio

AAs Should Be Honest About Sex Problems
May 1961

Many people who write on the subject of sex problems feel obliged to explain that sex is basically good—that it is God's method of guaranteeing the reproduction of mankind. This startling information is usually supplied defensively, almost as if to combat the grim possibility that sex might be legislated out of existence if somebody doesn't present a worthwhile case for it. The authors, of course, are really pleading for the right to discuss sex difficulties openly. Prudery on the printed page was vanquished a long time ago, but the near-pornography which replaced it is a poor counterfeit of honesty. Truth is still mighty hard to find, and it's even harder to present.

How the outside world wishes to deal with this subject is not really our affair, but it is important that we face the matter more honestly in AA. AA has a number of supplementary pamphlets for employers, wives, and young alcoholics, but none on what is often the most critical problem in our Fellowship. Our speakers thunder eloquently about the need for absolute honesty, but only a few hardy souls ever dare to hint that sex might have been a disturbing problem area. An outsider could easily get the impression—judging by what we print and what we say—that alcoholics don't have sex troubles at all.

It's a different matter when we turn to the literature published by outside observers. AA members may wish to evade the issue, but others are more objective about it. They point to sexual confusion as a significant factor in the alcoholic's personality disturbances. Sometimes their conclusions seem hastily and unfairly drawn; when, for example, a psychiatrist uses a few representative case histories to prove that almost *all* alcoholics are afflicted with certain types of sexual abnormality. In general, however, sex facts are included as a matter of course in any scientific inquiry into the subject of alcoholism. And a psychiatrist who treats an alcoholic will most certainly concern himself with the patient's sex history.

However, if we are completely honest about it, we don't even need outside observers to tell us the extent of our sex problems. We are very familiar with the oft-repeated remark, sometimes heard after an older member has resumed drinking, "Well, the poor fellow has 'other' problems." These "other" problems usually have something to do with sex. When you hear a remark like this you don't even have to ask for further details; the emphasis on "other" conveys a world of hidden meanings. Extramarital philandering exists in AA—though probably not on a large scale—and the pretty young woman who joins a group can expect "sponsorship" of a very thorough kind.

The truth is that alcoholics do have unusually troublesome sex problems. It would be almost unbelievable if people plagued by our kind of illness did not have various sex disturbances. We may not like to admit it, just as we did not like to admit our alcoholism. But when we say that "some poor fellow who had 'other' shortcomings resumed drinking," aren't we admitting indirectly that we understand the tremendous pressures of these "other" problems? Aren't we conceding that misdirected sex is a formidable threat to sobriety? Aren't we saying that AA can help a person recover if he isn't tyrannized too severely by sex? And aren't we also saying—by implication, of course—that since we are sober ourselves we aren't troubled by these problems?

After almost eleven years of continuous sobriety in the AA program, I've found myself growing tired of the evasion and hypocrisy surrounding this subject. I have seen the elder statesmen of AA frown their disapproval when a more honest member brought up his own sex problems and discussed them with remarkable frankness and humility. I have known AA members who thought it sophisticated to laugh at an off-color joke told by a visiting speaker, but who became uneasy and embarrassed if another visiting speaker explored the relationship of sex and alcoholism. And I have seen far too many older members working overtime trying to prove that absolutely insupportable notion that alcoholics are generally "just normal folks who drank too much, too often, too long."

Evasions and hypocrisy may serve certain individuals adequately, but in the long run we progress according to the amount of truth about ourselves we are able to digest. We achieved sobriety by admitting the truth about our drinking problem, and by applying AA's recommended program of recovery. Do we believe that the truth—which rescued us so effectively in one instance—is somehow pernicious and undesirable if applied to other life problems?

What are these sex problems that defy discussion? Most likely they are a cross section of the same problems that confront society outside of AA. Many alcoholics feel sexually inadequate, and have always been troubled by fears of sexual incompetence and rejection. Oddly, this may have led to frenzied promiscuity. It may have caused an unsatisfactory sex relationship in marriage. It may also have led to sex conduct that society considers immoral or deviated. In fact, it may lead in any number of directions, but the results are always pain, misery, tension, and guilt.

These are only the beginnings of sorrows for sex-troubled alcoholics who join AA. Unless they are very fortunate, they won't find much understanding and guidance in this critical problem area. He and she will secretly fear they are sexually "different" from the majority of alcoholics, for their only trouble seems to be that "they drank too much, too often, too long." They will be urged to take the Fifth Step, but will have to search for many a moon to find an understanding ear for *all* the problems. They may achieve sobriety, but it will have the characteristics of an armed truce rather than a genuine peace development.

Really, there's no excuse for it. Sex problems are powerful and deep-seated, but they need not threaten our eligibility for true sobriety and genuine happiness. There are now many older members who have remarkable understanding on this subject. They need only to tell the truth, so that newcomers will be encouraged to face the truth themselves. This won't eliminate sex anxiety overnight, but it will be a good start.

We cannot guarantee that our AA program of recovery, even with its strong emphasis on personal inventory and spiritual help, will aid all alcoholics in solving the "other" problems that seem to be such a threat to continued sobriety. But it is not unreasonable to believe that a more candid approach may create a reservoir of understanding that we do not presently have.

I am not proposing that our AA meetings should become forums for morbid recitals of lecherous behavior. I am sure that "boudoir-to-boudoir" descriptions would eventually be as boring and pointless as many of the drink-by-drink accounts we now endure. Nor am I suggesting an open flaunting of intimate facts that might better be left to private discussions between individual members. My main plea is for a general climate of open-mindedness when this problem seems to be inviting discussion.

This would fulfill—not destroy—the spirit and principles of Alcoholics Anonymous.

M.B., Jackson, Mich.

So You Want a "Celebrity" Speaker?
March 1962

Overheard at our intergroup office, volunteer to newcomer: "There is a good meeting tonight at the B— Group. Xenophon Shrdlu is speaking—you know, the TV comedian." Telephone call from a program chairman: "Would you speak at our anniversary meeting? I'm supposed to get a celebrity as the main speaker."

I know that some people in AA are impressed and even helped by the fact that even "names" are afflicted with our disease, but statements like the two reported above make me shudder.

I'm not an unbiased observer. My husband's name is quite well known, inside and outside AA. He and I have both been active, sober AAs for years. He's willing to do any AA task that needs doing. But when I'm asked to get him to speak, and the asker says something about getting a "celebrity," I'm sorely tempted to say, "If you want him as an alcoholic, it's for free, naturally. However, if you want him as a celebrity, his fee is $2,500 for doing his act. And he doesn't mention AA in the act!"

I've even seen newspaper stories about AA conventions or banquets with such statements as "The main speaker will be a famous star of stage, TV, and movies."

Oh, that follows the *letter* of our Traditions, alright. But what about the *spirit?* Within AA, can't a "name" member not be a celebrity, but just another alcoholic who needs our love and understanding in exactly the same principles-first anonymous way it is given to the rest of us?

Once I heard a fellow say that to him anonymity means we are all nameless, faceless victims of the same illness, no one of any more importance than the other. And, he said, one greatness of AA is its ability to treat, with exactly the same fair degree of kind helpfulness, either the unknown newcomer, or the recognizable celebrity, or the recognized notorious unfortunate.

"We don't care about your past," he said, "or who you are outside of AA. Within the gates of AA you are simply another anonymous sufferer from our illness, and we want to help."

My husband and I feel that way, too.

Once my husband was asked to speak at a special open meeting planned to attract townspeople interested in community health. Just before the meeting began, the program chairman said, "We surely did want a celebrity for this meeting, and I was kind of stumped at first. The last two celebrities we had have been drinking ever since. So I'm sure glad you could come."

My husband went white, and bit his lip. He was crushed to think that his commercial fame was valued more highly by his fellow AAs than his sobriety and his membership in AA. He went through with that one, alright, but I doubt if he ever will again. It's my guess, too, that people in the audience were so curious and enthralled by seeing the celebrity in the flesh that very little of the "alcoholism is a sick-ness" message got through. I suspect that when they talked about it later, they said, "Guess *who* I heard speak, and did you know that *he* is an alcoholic?" instead of "Guess what I learned about alcoholism and Alcoholics Anonymous the other night?"

(Incidentally, an awfully nice AA gal gave a wonderful talk just before my husband went on. I wonder how she felt when, at the end of her talk, the chairman introduced the next speaker as the "star" of the evening, the one everyone was just waiting to hear?)

There are other perils, too. A celebrity can get carried away with hamminess in AA, so that he is performing rather than carrying the message. If his anonymity becomes too widely shattered by newcom-ers or visitors, this may cause him to stay away from the one place that promises sobriety. Or a newcomer may himself be frightened by the loss of anonymity, and not come again. Surely he is puzzled at having anonymity suggested then casually ignored by those who recommend it!

I'm sure this could also be rough on well-known writers, or al-coholic doctors and other professional men known within the com-munity.

Wouldn't it be more within the AA spirit for each of us, when se-curing speakers, to ask them as communicators of the AA message— not because of who they are? Shouldn't those of us who serve on con-vention or banquet committees try to resist pressures from those who say, "Let's get a 'name' speaker; we'll draw more people, and our affair will be a big success!"?

Examine those last three little words a minute, if you will. What are we here for, anyhow?

I go to an AA meeting, sit on hard chairs in a smoky room to at-tain and maintain sobriety. I must honestly say that I have heard more good solid AA from people whose names I'll never know than from any celebrity, as such. If I want to see a celebrity I can go to a theater or lecture or concert hall, or turn on TV. I know that my dis-ease is shared by all kinds of people, regardless of occupation or environment, and I want AA to be *anonymous*—inside, as well as out.

Let's let the alcoholic "names" come inside, too, and share the joys of our spiritual anonymity.

M.B., New York, N.Y.

Generalizations Can Be Dangerous
September 1984

I heard some old-timers discussing Twelfth Step work. One said, "It's like pulling people out of a river and starting them back up on solid dry ground. Then you pull the next one out. Pretty soon you notice you're pulling some of the same ones out of the river again. Someone needs to look upstream to see what's pushing them back into the drink."

I'm one of many whose second go at drowning followed prescribed medication after nine dry years. Our AA literature reminds us that the chief thing we have to offer is our own personal experience, so I'd like to share some of mine.

When I put down what I pray was my last drink, nine years ago, I still had ten months to go on three drugs for tuberculosis. Winners in AA didn't try to assure me that those particular drugs weren't mood-changing—believe me, they are. Winners told me that I had to take the drugs to save my life and that the program would help me through it. I needed a lot of meetings, often several a day. When I staggered from the drug side effects, people at meetings kissed me more—just checking. Or—until they understood they called to tell my sponsors. I appreciated that concern.

Once drug free, I became comfortable with a few meetings a week, but I still attend whenever I have time. I made lots of friends while going so often at first.

Following the winners' example, I learned to respectfully remind my doctors I'm a recovered alcoholic, and to say: "I'm just checking with you to see if I have something serious.... Please don't prescribe anything just for my symptoms....A prescription for tincture of time is quite acceptable." My doctors learned to understand, but they are so busy that they need to be reminded at each visit. I'm extra careful to tell them I won't take antihistamines or decongestants unless they think my condition is serious enough that I can be admitted to a hospital and kept there two days after the last dose.

I'm convinced that I picked up a drink after nine dry years because medication prescribed for my allergies changed my thinking. It took me fourteen years after that to find AA and get sober. Then, I watched a sober daughter almost self-destruct without drinking following a prescription from an allergist who knew she was alcoholic. Since then, she and I avoid all cold, cough, and sneezing remedies except salt water gargles or honey and lemon.

I admire the sobriety of winners who feel all painkillers are dangerous for us. They structure their diet, their rest, their attitude, and the risks they take in sports in order to *avoid* pain. They don't buy over-the-counter drugs, only vitamins. When taking a prescription drug is unavoidable, they ask someone to keep it and give each dose to them. They attend more meetings and make sure an AA friend is prepared to report stinking thinking to their doctors. I follow their example.

Because I hear AA stories of slips after dental work and other occasions for local anesthesia, my sober tooth-filling sessions so far have been drug free. A little pain for a short time beats the way I've seen AA friends feel after shots or gas. My sponsor says that after shots for dental work, she once sat in a meeting between her sponsor and her sober husband wondering, "How can I ditch these turkeys and get a drink?" Generally, the attitude change seems to be more subtle than that, but it is still obvious to a well-prepared AA friend.

I've seen AAs use holding hands and saying prayers and telling jokes to replace "anxiety" drugs before and after surgery. I want that kind of care when I need it, and I will gladly help provide it for any of you.

An AA friend of mine recently died ten years sober, from a fast-spreading cancer. He needed and received supervised narcotic pain relief but wanted his mind and emotions as clear as possible. He refused tranquilizers after one try, and he told me, "I never took pills, but I'd give that one a three-martini rating. I didn't relax —I flew all night."

Some treatment centers provide care for a short time following surgery. Our daughter was grateful for three days in a center after she had four wisdom teeth removed. Many AAs arrange to stay with a sponsor or have another AA "babysit" afterward. They don't just sit looking gloomy—they have lunch or go to a meeting or a movie.

I found the whole problem so interesting that I spent some sober years getting a degree and a license in pharmacy. At the college, I heard more lectures on drugs than medical schools have time for; but I heard and read very few cautions about drugs for recovered alcoholics, except for some warnings on narcotics and tranquilizers. The college gave me course credit for collecting experiences with prescribed or over-the-counter drugs reported by sober AAs and professional treatment people. I found AAs do have experience, strength, and hope to share with one another and with medical people who want to learn to treat us safely. When enough of us report our experiences and those we hear about, the subject will reach the medical literature.

I agree with earlier Grapevine writers that we must carefully warn one another of the dangers of sudden, unsupervised withdrawal from any drug. I also understand that a small percentage of alcoholics, in extreme cases when all else fails, must risk the side effects of mind-changing drugs and take them for a time or for life. But let's stop making dangerous generalizations from those two statements.

I get scared when I hear an AA righteously and emphatically tell a newcomer who has asked for advice: "Leave the drug decisions to the doctors"—when they're talking about relief from some passing symptom or about diet pills. Often, in that same meeting is a member who has been to hell and back on a slip after using that same drug.

I plan to go on introducing anyone who asks me about medicine to winners who have "been there," or to friends of those who didn't make it back from slips. I'm grateful to be alive and sober today because AAs do that for me.

I need you all to keep reminding me that the AA program offers a way of life that beats any "pill for every ill" advertised on television. If I really can't sleep, I can use the hours profitably with the Big Book, the Grapevine, and telephone numbers. Sobriety is our most treasured gift. Let's help one another keep it.

N.D., New Providence, N.J.

Another Vision for You
March 1986

I am not a member of Alcoholics Anonymous, but I am among the millions of people who owe our lives to the Twelve Steps of recovery. Bill W.'s vision of other societies similar to AA forming to address problems other than alcoholism is very much a reality today. Thanks to the inspiration and vision of your co-founders, and the current generosity of your Fellowship in sharing its experience, a few of these other Fellowships are becoming strong, well-developed programs of recovery, with a network of local and world services, hotlines, literature, old-timers, service centers employing special workers—all the necessary ingredients.

As a member of one of those other Fellowships, I'm writing to the Grapevine as an outside writer, but the issue I'm addressing is not an outside issue. I'm writing about addicts attending AA meetings —perhaps an issue that most of us are tired of dealing with—but one whose solution is finally at hand. After years of internal controversy in AA (and in fellowships modeled after AA), just maybe we're at a place where the turmoil can stop. The solution envisioned by Bill W., articulated in your pamphlet *Problems Other Than Alcohol,* can finally be implemented with confidence.

I am a drug addict who came to AA in 1978 looking for help. When the suggestion that I go to AA to address my drug problem was first put to me I was puzzled. "My problem is this other drug. Why would I go to AA?" It was explained to me that AA is what works, and no one could kick me out. No one has the authority to do that. "Just substitute alcohol for your drug," I was told, "and it will work."

I did that. I went to AA for a period of about four years. I learned the "passwords" that would not offend the old-timers, and I made a place for myself in your Fellowship. I was also introduced to Narcotics Anonymous from the very beginning, but in 1978 NA had very little literature, no old-timers locally to serve as sponsors, no network of services for its groups. I went to that NA meeting to identify more fully and share more fully, and I went to Alcoholics Anonymous for the substance of recovery. Those were the realities of being a recovering drug addict in the upper Midwest in the late seventies.

As I stayed around and observed both Fellowships closely, I could not miss the great dilemma that was brewing about us addicts in AA. I did not take this problem personally, because I read the words of Bill W. and they made sense. The primary purpose of every AA group is to carry its message to the *alcoholic* who still suffers. If AA groups try to carry their message to anyone else, that atmosphere of identification for the alcoholic is weakened. If an alcoholic walks into an AA meeting and encounters a discussion among junkies, gamblers, overeaters, or whatever, that alcoholic may just miss his shot at the miracle. I slowly became more and more aware that I was the outsider in AA; that old-timer who got irritated when I shared about my drug use was on his home ground, and I was straining his Traditions. It has been a tough issue for us all.

But what were the AA people to do in 1978? Throw us out? Even if that were possible in AA, who had the heart? "What would the Master do?" it says in the "Twelve and Twelve." Where would we go? Most of our NA groups were not part of a worldwide structure that could sustain us in recovery. In many places, the compromise measure seems to have been to just overlook the issue as best as we could and go on about our recovery. And the wisdom of the co-founder has been borne out again. Many AA groups have become a mix of alcoholics and people addicted to other drugs, and many of those NA groups' growth has been stunted. They were not seriously regarded as part of a separate Fellowship capable of sustaining recovery. The service of recovering addicts went into AA services. As addicts got some time in recovery, they became AA sponsors. The texture of the AA community was slowly drifting from a clear atmosphere of identification for the alcoholic, and the texture of those isolated NA groups was remaining pretty static.

With the eighties came a vast change in that scenario. More and more recovering addicts began to turn our attention to the developing Fellowship of NA. We got busy writing literature, developing our services at every level, refining our own thinking and language for our own principles of recovery. We had learned so much from our forerunners in AA, and now we were breaking some new ground.

It has been an exciting period of new hope for the addict who still suffers. And ironically, maybe it is an exciting period of renewed hope for the alcoholic who still suffers too. By going exclusively to NA, doing my service in NA, growing in my understanding of the NA message, I have left the AA groups just a little freer to focus on their own primary purpose. That is not personal. It's sound principle.

Today NA is thriving. We have our own basic text, and we're in the later stages of producing a book on our Steps and Traditions. We are experiencing the kind of booming growth that AA experienced in the forties. Our world services are coming together in a way that can only be attributed to a loving God, expressing himself in our group conscience. It has been a time of the joy and pain of rapid growth for us, and we expect this growth rate to continue for some time to come.

I guess I'm really saying a number of things. First, thank you AA, for your wisdom in taking the stand that you can best help the addict not by allowing us to become members, but by offering us the model of your program and inspiring us to build our own. Even though the realities of life have sometimes forced us all to compromise that, your Conference and your written word never lost perspective. That vision is now bearing fruit. I also want to assure you that strong, stable, long-term recovery is available today in NA, so the days of worrying that addicts are just being kicked out into the street are over. Many addicts are pointed in our direction by AA groups adhering to their own primary purpose. A fast friendship, based on "cooperation, not affiliation," is cropping up between us everywhere.

It goes without saying that these words are one member's views—I do not speak for my Fellowship any more than these other articles speak for yours. But let's all look at these issues now from the vantage point of our best spiritual vision of the future. The time for coming to rest on this issue is finally at hand.

R. H., Northridge, Calif.

SEVEN

Alcoholics Anonymous
Is a Fellowship

———— ♦ ————

The Fundamentals—In Retrospect
by Dr. Bob
September 1948

It is gratifying to feel that one belongs to and has a definite personal part in the work of a growing and spiritually prospering organization for the release of the alcoholics of mankind from a deadly enslavement. For me, there is double gratification in the realization that, more than thirteen years ago, an all-wise Providence, whose ways must always be mysterious to our limited understandings, brought me to "see my duty clear" and to contribute in decent humility, as have so many others, my part in guiding the first trembling steps of the then-infant organization, Alcoholics Anonymous. [AA began June 10, 1935, with the start of Dr. Bob's lasting sobriety. He died November 16, 1950.]

It is fitting at this time to indulge in some retrospect regarding certain fundamentals. Much has been written, much has been said about the Twelve Steps of AA. These tenets of our faith and practice were not worked out overnight and then presented to our members as an opportunist creed. Born of our early trials and many tribulations, they were and are the result of humble and sincere desire, sought in personal prayer, for divine guidance.

As finally expressed and offered, they are simple in language, plain in meaning. They are also workable by any person having a sincere desire to obtain and keep sobriety. The results are the proof. Their simplicity and workability are such that no special interpretations, and certainly no reservations, have ever been necessary. And it has become increasingly clear that the degree of harmonious living which we achieve is in direct ratio to our earnest attempt to follow them literally under divine guidance to the best of our ability.

Yet there are no shibboleths in AA. We are not bound by theological doctrine. None of us may be excommunicated and cast into outer darkness. For we are many minds in our organization, and an AA decalogue in the language of "Thou shalt not" would gall us indeed.

Look at our Twelve Traditions. No random expressions, these, based on just casual observation. On the contrary, they represent the sum of our experience as individuals, as groups within AA, and similarly with our fellows and other organizations in the great fellowship of humanity under God throughout the world. They are all suggestions, yet the spirit in which they have been conceived merits their serious, prayerful consideration as the guidepost of AA policy for the individual, the group, and our various committees, local and national.

We have found it wise policy, too, to hold to no glorification of the individual. Obviously, that is sound. Most of us will concede that when it came to the personal showdown of admitting our failures and deciding to surrender our will and our lives to Almighty God, *as we understood him*, we still had some sneaking ideas of personal justification and excuse. We had to discard them, but the ego of the alcoholic dies a hard death. Many of us, because of activity, have received praise, not only from our fellow AAs, but from the world at large. We would be ungrateful indeed to be boorish when that happens; still, it is so easy for us to become, privately perhaps, just a little vain about it all. Yet fitting and wearing halos is not for us.

We've all seen the new member who stays sober for a time, largely through sponsor-worship. Then maybe the sponsor gets drunk, and you know what usually happens. Left without a human prop, the new member gets drunk, too. He has been glorifying an individual, instead of following the program.

Certainly, we need leaders, but we must regard them as the human agents of the Higher Power and not with undue adulation as individuals. The Fourth and Tenth Steps cannot be too strongly emphasized here—"Made a searching and fearless moral inventory of ourselves.... Continued to take personal inventory and when we were wrong promptly admitted it." There is your perfect antidote for halo-poisoning.

So with the question of anonymity. If we have a banner, that word, speaking of the surrender of the individual—the ego—is emblazoned on it. Let us dwell thoughtfully on its full meaning and learn thereby to remain humble, modest, ever-conscious that we are eternally under divine direction.

Alcoholics Anonymous was nurtured in its early days around a kitchen table. Many of our pioneer groups and some of our most resultful meetings and best programs have their origin around that modest piece of furniture, with the coffeepot handy on the stove. True, we have progressed materially to better furniture and more comfortable surroundings. Yet the kitchen table must ever be appropriate for us. It is the perfect symbol of simplicity. In AA we have no VIPs, nor have we need of any. Our organization needs no titleholders nor grandiose buildings. That is by design. Experience has taught us that simplicity is basic in preservation of our personal sobriety and helping those in need.

Far better it is for us to fully understand the meaning and practice of "thou good and faithful servant" than to listen to "With 60,000 members [in 1948] you should have a sixty-stories-high administration headquarters in New York with an assortment of trained 'ists' to direct your affairs." We need nothing of the sort. God grant that AA may ever stay simple.

Over the years, we have tested and developed suitable techniques for our purpose. They are entirely flexible. We have all known and seen miracles—the healing of broken individuals, the rebuilding of broken homes. And always, it has been the constructive, personal Twelfth Step work based on an ever-upward-looking faith which has done the job.

In as large an organization as ours, we naturally have had our share of those who fail to measure up to certain obvious standards of conduct. They have included schemers for personal gain, petty swindlers and confidence men, crooks of various kinds, and other human fallibles. Relatively, their number has been small, much smaller than in many religious and social-uplift organizations. Yet they have been a problem and not an easy one. They have caused many an AA to stop thinking and working constructively for a time.

We cannot condone their actions, yet we must concede that when we have used normal caution and precaution in dealing with such cases, we may safely leave them to the Higher Power. Let me reiterate that we AAs are many men and women, that we are of many minds. It will be well for us to concentrate on the goal of personal sobriety and active work. We humans and alcoholics, on strict moral stocktaking, must confess to at least a slight degree of larcenous instinct. We can hardly arrogate the roles of judges and executioners.

Thirteen grand years! To have been a part of it all from the beginning has been reward indeed.

People and Principles
October 1971

Our Fellowship would not be where it is today if we had not benefited from the influence of some wonderful personalities—fine men and women who launched our groups and set the tone for everything that AA was to become.

We are doubly fortunate, however, that these strong personalities usually took themselves out of the picture when principle was involved, thus giving their assent to the idea of "principle before personality." Perhaps the best example of this was a noted lady member who had done significant work in a related field of alcoholism, yet decided early to retain her anonymity at the public level in the interest of protecting AA.

The motto "principle before personality" has a much broader application than in the safeguarding of anonymity, though this is where it is often applied in AA. The fact is, it really can be a spiritual guideline for every human activity.

There is a good reason why that is so. A principle is a fundamental truth, something that never changes and always works in the same way under similar conditions. It is a principle, for example, that causes water to boil at 212°F. at a certain elevation. The principle is not affected by the attitudes and opinions of human beings. Water boils just as well for the sinner as it does for the saint.

But a personality is something quite different. A personality is a human being as he happens to be at a particular time, usually the sum total of his attitudes, opinions, experiences, expectations, and other feelings. Personality changes from year to year, even from moment to moment. It is often unreliable, and it is certainly unpredictable. A personality may be pleasing and positive for a period of time, then suddenly become ugly and destructive. Personality is still one of the most difficult fields of study, and much has to be learned before it becomes an "exact" science. Psychologists and sociologists have trouble agreeing on terms primarily because they must always deal with the variables and caprices of the human personality.

But this does not make personality less interesting to most of us. Principles often leave us cold and indifferent, while personalities give life its color and magic. Albert Einstein discovered great principles, but most of us would find the man himself more interesting than his discoveries.

This attraction to personality is both a strength and a weakness. We can be led to great heights by the right kind of person—the individual who believes in the truth and practices it. Or we can be swept to the depths by following the wrong kind of person—the mistaken or selfish individual who encourages us to do something that is fundamentally wrong.

We will always be attracted to strong personalities, and we will always seek out people who seem to have answers for us. How can we balance this tendency with the wiser inclination to follow principle?

AA's guideline is very simple, yet it never fails to work. It is this: People can help us by carrying the truth to us, but they cannot cause it to become effective in our lives. Only we can do that, by accepting the truth and applying it. What then happens will be determined by our own diligence and sincerity in applying the principle, not by the personalities of those people.

Likewise, nobody can own a principle. A brilliant personality may discover a principle and pass it along to others, but he cannot later keep the principle from working for them. Once a principle is learned, it can easily be applied by anybody who cares to test it out. It is no respecter of persons, and never will be.

It was our good fortune, as sick alcoholics, to find a set of principles that can work very well in our recovery. We call these principles the Twelve Steps and the Twelve Traditions, but they are not the exclusive property of AA. They would work for any person who wanted to apply them in his life.

Wonderful as people are, not one of them can serve as an absolutely reliable guide for our own actions. We can use others as models for our own behavior, and we can go to them for advice. But we are in trouble if we do not base our own actions on truths that we know to be right. We need to understand such truths and use them, for the time may come when we will no longer have others to lean on, and will have to use our own understanding to get through a difficult situation.

In our AA lives, there is no personality who can serve as a substitute for such practices as turning our problems over to a Higher Power, taking our own inventories, and working with others. If somebody tells us that these actions are not necessary and can be sidestepped in some way, we should not take his word for it, but should check the matter out to our own satisfaction.

In our everyday living, we will be no less successful if we try to follow good principles. A businessman got into trouble, for example, because he accepted a questionable business contract from a group with shaky credit and credentials. He would have refused the contract had it not been recommended by several prominent men. His failure to heed good business principles and his willingness to listen to the siren call of personality resulted in the loss of several thousand dollars.

In another case with a far greater potential for tragedy, a beginning pilot took off with his wife and young daughter on a cross-country trip with a flying club. Visibility was marginal, with low mountains on the flight path, but the other members had laughed at the newcomer's doubts. The fog closed in shortly after takeoff, and the plane crashed into a mountain. Fortunately, all three aboard were rescued, but the experience made the man a much wiser pilot, willing to follow the principles of good flying rather than the opinions of others, who may have been willing to take foolish risks.

A third case concerned an amateur arts group which came under the sway of a dominant but opinionated board member. Largely at his insistence, the board finally dismissed a director who had been quite popular and had kept the group on a sound financial basis. This ill-advised decision, based on emotion rather than objective reasoning, plunged the group into near bankruptcy.

The lesson in all this is that people are often wrong, through either malice or ignorance. If we listen to their counsel when it goes against what we know to be right, we are placing personalities ahead of principles. We are asking for trouble, and we will be lucky if we avoid it.

Some people think that all principles, whether physical or moral in nature, come from God. Human personality also comes from God, but it is distorted by being caught up in the mixture we call "truth and error." Human beings come and go, and are constantly changing, but principles go on and on, and do not change. When we put principles first, we are really putting God first. Perhaps that is why the two great commandments suggest loving God first and then our neighbor. Our neighbor is a great guy, but he is not worthy of being our guide in all things. If we put God and his principles first, we will have things in proper order. What's more, we'll even be finer personalities!

M. B., Jackson, Mich.

Because One Man Was Lonely
January 1977

As I see it, the ever-growing, multiplying, and compounding miracle of AA is that because one man was lonely, afraid, and sick in a strange city, I need never be alone again in a strange city. Because he sought out a physician for his own incurable disease and arrested it by helping to heal the physician, there is great hope for me. Because one man—greatly gifted by his Higher Power—failed to live up to the expectations of the crowd, never scaled the heights of social, financial, or professional worlds, and never made headlines or created empires, but chose instead to share his private spiritual awakening with other sufferers, I have a life to live and share.

The miracle is that this one beautiful man—without funds or financial aid, without benefit of publicity and great advertising campaigns—quietly, *anonymously* spread a message from one man in one room in one city to reach millions of persons in thousands of rooms clear around the world. Today, more than a million of us who suffer from the disease of alcoholism have found not just the ability to live with or survive this insidious disease, but a joyful way of life as new as this morning and as old as mankind. We can gain sobriety, aspire to serenity, at no greater price than caring for our fellow sufferers and sharing with them what has been freely given to us. We can experience the true joy of love that we once tried to destroy by not giving it away, and we can learn the truth that the more we give away, the more we will have.

The miracle is that I won all this by admitting defeat. The miracle is that the whole world became mine when I had nowhere else to go. The miracle is God's greatest gift—people who care, love to share, and have honest, open hearts.

J. R., Brick Town, N.J.

It Might Have Been the Time...
by Lois W.
February 1950

It is hard to say just when Alcoholics Anonymous began. It may have been at the time a friend came to see my husband, Bill. Or it may have been at the moment of Bill's spiritual experience. Most AAs feel it is the time six months later when he met Dr. Bob in Akron and, together, they started to help other alcoholics who wanted to be rid of their addiction.

But for me it was the day I first saw the released expression on my husband's face. We had been married seventeen years, and were compatible and companionable. Our interests were similar and we both deeply desired and strove for the other's welfare. The only, but considerable, block to our happiness was Bill's uncontrolled drinking. In the early years he said that he could stop when he wanted, and I thought I'd soon be able to make life so complete for him that he would wish to quit drinking entirely. Much later when he really did want to stop, he was absolutely unable to do so, and we both then became terribly confused and frustrated. Oddly enough he had been in other matters a person of strong willpower, but his will seemed to melt away where alcohol was concerned. In his remorse and disappointment he was a tragic and heartbreaking figure. I too felt myself a failure, for despite every endeavor, I had not been able to help him in time, nor could I aid him in the least in his final struggle for freedom.

Today I can talk and write about these intimate details of our life together. While Bill was drinking, I dared not even speak to my family about it and tried to hide the fact of his alcoholism in every way possible. Now that I have learned that Bill was actually a very sick man, that awful feeling of disgrace has left me. I have also learned how much help the telling of such experiences can be to those who are going through similar ones. After fifteen years in AA, the old trying times are so faraway and foreign to Bill's and my present way of life that it seems like the experience of someone else.

After Bill left the hospital for the last time, he began to think of the thousands of alcoholics who wanted to be rid of their malady. If they could be made to feel desperate enough, they might have a releasing experience just like his. He would hold before them the medical verdict that alcoholism was hopeless. So tirelessly, day and night, we worked. Our home was filled with alcoholics in various stages of sobriety. As many as five of them lived with us at one time. But none of them stayed sober for long. They started a long process of trial and error; certain ideas were retained, but many discarded.

It was in June 1935 that Bill went to Akron, Ohio on a business trip. The venture failed. He finally contacted Dr. Bob, an Akron surgeon soon to become co-founder of Alcoholics Anonymous. Bob too wanted above all to stop drinking. He and his wife, Anne, had done everything they could.

Something passed between these two men. There was real mutuality this time. By example they showed how it worked. Thus AA spread like a chain letter.

Bill had learned a great deal. At first he had tried to put every alcoholic he met in the way of a spiritual experience just like his own. As AA grew, he realized that what had come to him in a few dramatic minutes usually dawns on others in months or years. Sometimes the alcoholic himself does not even realize his own development, though his words and actions soon speak for him, for he is doing now what, of himself, he was unable to do before. He is staying sober and helping other people as never before. He is gaining a serenity, a joy in living.

Watching Bill and the other men at the meetings, I noticed many of them had begun to grow by leaps and bounds. This made me look at myself. I had been given a sound religious upbringing and felt I had done for Bill all a good wife could do, although this was strangely mixed with a sense of failure. At first it never occurred to me that I too needed spiritual development. I did not realize that by living such an abnormal life I might have become twisted, losing a sense of true values. After awhile I saw that unless I jumped on the bandwagon too, I would be left way behind. The AA program, I found, could be most helpful to the nonalcoholic as well, a fact thousands of alcoholics' relatives and friends now apply to their own lives.

Those Clinton Street days are full of memories. Some of them are humorous, some tragic. But most of them bring back a warm glow of hope and courage, of friendship and rebirth. For the fellowship in AA is unique. Ties are made overnight that it would take years to develop elsewhere. No one needs a false front. All barriers are down. Some who have felt outcasts all their lives now know they really belong. From feeling as if they were dragging anchor through life, they suddenly sail free before the wind. For now they can be of tremendous and peculiar use to others having a dire need like their own.

Was My Leg Being Pulled?
by Jack Alexander
May 1945

Ordinarily, diabetes isn't rated as one of the hazards of reporting, but the Alcoholics Anonymous article in the Saturday Evening Post came close to costing me my liver, and maybe AA neophytes ought to be told this when they are handed copies of the article to read. It might impress them. In the course of my fact gathering, I drank enough Coca-Cola, Pepsi-Cola, ginger ale, Moxie and Sweetie to float the Saratoga. Then there was the thickly frosted cake so beloved of AA gatherings, and the heavily sweetened coffee, and the candy. Nobody can tell me that alcoholism isn't due solely to an abnormal craving for sugar, not even a learned psychiatrist. Otherwise the AA assignment was a pleasure.

It began when the Post asked me to look into AA as a possible article subject. All I knew of alcoholism at the time was that, like most other nonalcoholics, I had had my hand bitten (and my nose punched) on numerous occasions by alcoholic pals to whom I had extended a hand—unwisely, it always seemed afterward. Anyway, I had an understandable skepticism about the whole business.

My first contact with actual AAs came when a group of four of them called at my apartment one afternoon. This session was pleasant, but it didn't help my skepticism any. Each one introduced himself as an alcoholic who had gone "dry," as the official expression has it. They were good-looking and well dressed and, as we sat around drinking Coca-Cola (which was all they would take), they spun yarns about their horrendous drinking misadventures. The stories sounded spurious, and after the visitors had left, I had a strong suspicion that my leg was being pulled. They had behaved like a bunch of actors sent out by some Broadway casting agency.

Next morning I took the subway to the headquarters of Alcoholic Anonymous in downtown Manhattan, where I met Bill W. This Bill W. is a very disarming guy and an expert at indoctrinating the stranger into the psychology, psychiatry, physiology, pharmacology, and folklore of alcoholism. He spent the good part of a couple of days telling me what it was all about . It was an interesting experience, but at the end of it my fingers were still crossed. He knew it, of course, without my saying it, and in the days that followed he took me to the homes of some of the AAs where I got a chance to talk to the wives, too. My skepticism suffered a few minor scratches, but not enough to hurt. Then Bill shepherded me to a few AA meetings at a clubhouse somewhere in the West Twenties. Here were all manner of alcoholics·, many of them the nibblers at the fringe of the movement, still fragrant of liquor and needing a shave. Now I knew I was among a few genuine alcoholics anyway. The bearded, fume-breathing lads were AA skeptics, too, and now I had some company.

The week spent with Bill W. was a success from one standpoint. I knew I had the makings of a readable report but, unfortunately, I didn't quite believe in it and told Bill so. He asked why I didn't look in on the AAs in other cities and see what went on there. I agreed to do this, and we mapped out an itinerary. I went to Philadelphia first, and some of the local AAs took me to the psychopathic ward of Philadelphia General Hospital and showed me how they work on the alcoholic inmates. In that gloomy place, it was an impressive thing to see men who had bounced in and out of the ward themselves patiently jawing a man who was still haggard and shaking from a binge that wound up in the gutter.

Akron was the next stop. Bill met me there and promptly introduced me to Doc S., who is another hard man to disbelieve. There were more hospital visits, an AA meeting, and interviews with people who a year or two before were undergoing varying forms of the blind staggers. Now they seemed calm, well spoken, steady handed, and prosperous, at least mildly prosperous.

Doc S. drove us both from Akron to Cleveland one night, and the same pattern was repeated. The universality of alcoholism was more apparent here. In Akron it had been mostly factory workers. In Cleveland there were lawyers, accountants, and other professional men, in addition to laborers. And again the same stories. The pattern was repeated also in Chicago, the only variation there being the presence at the meeting of a number of newspapermen. I had spent most of my working life on newspapers and I could really talk to these men. The real clincher, though, came in St. Louis, which is my hometown. Here I met a number of my own friends who were AAs, and the last remnants of skepticism vanished. Once rollicking rumpots, they were now sober. It didn't seem possible, but there it was.

When the article was published, the reader mail was astonishing. Most of it came from desperate drinkers or their wives, or from mothers, fathers, or interested friends. The letters were forwarded to the AA office in New York and from there were sent on to the AA groups nearest the writers of the letters. I don't know exactly how many letters came in, all told, but the last time I checked a year or so ago, it was around 6,000. They still trickle in from time to time, from people who have carried the article in their pockets all this time, or kept it in the bureau drawer under the handkerchief case intending to do something about it.

I guess the letters will keep coming in for years, and I hope they do, because now I know that every one of them springs from a mind, either of an alcoholic or of someone close to him, which is undergoing a type of hell that Dante would have gagged at. And I know, too, that this victim is on the way to recovery, if he really wants to recover. There is something very heartening about this, particularly in a world which has been struggling toward peace for centuries without ever achieving it for very long periods of time.

Service Is the Reason
June 1979

From the very beginning, Alcoholics Anonymous wasted no time nor effort in trying to determine the why of alcoholism or what causes the phenomenon. We were simply advised to accept the fact of our illness and get on with the recovery program.

Not too many days gone by, I found myself thinking, "Why me?" It was not the old "Why me?" prompted by self-pity, but the realization that of all the people who were still suffering, somehow I was given sobriety. With an absolutely honest appraisal, I could in no way understand why I had been selected to enjoy the blessings of our sober life when people all around were still in the darkness of alcoholism.

I found the answer in the very Steps of recovery I was encouraged to take, in the order they were written. The prayer in the Third Step in the Big Book held the key: "Take away my difficulties, that victory over them may bear witness to those I would help..." Perhaps there *was* a reason. Just maybe, a purpose could be found right here.

Soon, I was engulfed with the problems of defects and inventory. The purpose faded for a while, until I carefully read Step Seven. I believe I was at the time in desperate need to determine what was meant by humility and to just what degree one could humbly measure one's progress in that area. In those days, too, we argued a lot about *how* God was going to remove those defects, and we worried a lot while discussing the "very serious" difference between defects and shortcomings.

There were those words in the prayer mentioned in the Big Book discussion of Step Six: "my usefulness to you and my fellows." The reason for my very existence must be to serve. Later on, that was clearly defined: "Our real purpose is to fit ourselves to be of maximum service to God and the people about us."

Service to God and my fellows is the reason I am given sobriety, and there is *no other reason.* If I fail to serve, my purpose in life will be unfulfilled, and no doubt life itself will be taken away.

Long ago, I stopped praying for sobriety, because perhaps my Maker might think, "If he does not know what he has got, why, I might as well take it back." Sooner or later, all our prayers might change from "What can you give to me?" to "What have you got for me to do?" How best can I serve?

I have always felt that if Recovery has taken place, Unity and Service must follow—completing the Three Legacies left to us by AA's co-founders. However, if Recovery is to be available in the group, Unity and Service must be part of that group. So which really comes first?

Yet for some unexplained reason, the word service is not well received in our Fellowship. Put on a service meeting, and the attendance is sparse. I wonder how many people would attend if a Regional Forum was called a "regional service meeting"? People talk about "getting involved in service." Service is looked upon in many places as something separate and to be endured by only a few.

I believe deeply in the recovery miracle of our program. I have experienced that recovery in my life. I believe we have a great obligation to tell all people that we have a program of recovery that works. In many places, I shock our own members by saying I have recovered. I am no longer sick. I can no longer use the illness of alcoholism as an excuse for anything. There is a catch, however. If I fail to use my recovery in service to others, I will become sick again. So service becomes not only the reason for recovery, but the only way there is to maintain our recovery.

When I look back on how our society outside of our Fellowship treated the alcoholic at the time of my coming to AA, I can see some progress. In all honesty, however, I don't believe we are making much progress in developing new treatment methods that will greatly reduce the numbers who suffer so tragically and do not reach us. More than ever, we have a tremendous responsibility to carry our message. More than ever, we have to realize that it is we who have to care.

Look, if you will, at the attitude in society today. Example: Recently, tremendous strides were announced in the treatment of heart disease. This breakthrough was so great that death from recurrent heart attacks could be reduced by fifty percent. This news did not even rate a cover story. *Newsweek* carried a feature story that week on "Sex on Television." More and more, we respond only to what is happening to us. So let's not expect that even in the face of our current epidemic of alcoholism, there is going to be a great public outcry. The recovery of millions of alcoholics depends upon us. That is an obligation, a responsibility that is mind-boggling.

Alcoholics Anonymous is truly a "beacon light of hope for mankind." If each member works through the group—through recovery to service—we cannot number the lives that can be touched. Few human beings will ever enjoy the privilege that is ours. At first, I did not even know we had a Third Legacy. Then I became aware that the people who were active in serving the Fellowship were the very people I thought of when I heard the words "If you want what we have..." Their example and that of countless others have led me in my journey with this great Fellowship. People like Bern Smith [one of AA's early nonalcoholic trustees] believed in giving their all. Remember Bern saying, "When they put me on the scrap heap of life, I want to be all used up."

Many times, my sponsor and I have been criticized by our mutual friends outside AA for doing what we do: nearly every weekend away from home and family; hours on end spent in airports. We discuss this, and every time we do, we come up with the same answer. We see what happens to people who do "retire," and we always say we had best keep doing what we are doing. You know, we haven't had to drink for a total of forty-six years between us.

No one will ever be able to say it any better than, nor, in fact, nearly as well as our co-founder Bill. He summed it up when he wrote: "God will constantly disclose more to you and to us. Ask Him in your morning meditation what you can do each day for the man who is still sick."

M. C., Winnipeg, Manitoba

Give My Regards to New York
May 1958

I am one of the thousands of AAs who could have been—but who was not—present at the Convention in St. Louis in July 1955. I wasn't interested.

I had been told that at this Twentieth Anniversary Convention our co-founder would, on behalf of himself and the original old-timers, formally propose that all worldwide general services should be permanently turned over to the members of Alcoholics Anonymous. I still was not interested. I couldn't see what this had to do with me.

At that time, sober a little over a year, it was difficult for me to connect general services with my own sobriety. Anything that began with the words "general service" was, if you lived on the West Coast as I did, referred to simply (and very often disparagingly) as "New York." I knew we had to have "New York," and that we were supposed to send money there to support the operation of general service Headquarters [today, the General Service Office], but the whole thing bored me. I listened with impatience on the rare occasions when a district committee member or general service representative was granted a few minutes at a regular AA meeting to make a pitch. My AA horizon embraced the group, and to a limited degree our local intergroup central office. The rest was out of sight and out of mind.

Then I became a general service representative of my group, and later a committee member. I glanced through the Third Legacy Manual [now *The AA Service Manual*], listened to our delegate's annual report on the General Service Conference, and attended committee meetings in a perfunctory manner because it was the thing to do. My group sent in its $2.00 per member to "New York." As far as I could see, this was the extent of my responsibility.

Then one day I found myself discussing an action taken by our area committee with two alert and informed AAs who had about twenty-eight years of sobriety between them—who had seen the beginning of the Third Legacy, and had given their time and their hearts to make it a success. And this was no peaceful chat, because they talked to me about principles, and about individual responsibility, and about the historic significance of the precious gift of the Legacy of Service; and I resisted all of the personal implications of what they were saying; and they got mad and shouted at me, and I got defensive and shouted back at them; and we had one hell of an afternoon.

But afterward I began to think calmly about some of the things they had said. And I took an inventory of my own personal relationship with "New York." How much did general services have to do with my own sobriety? What exactly was the extent of my *individual* responsibility for the survival of our general services? For the survival of Alcoholics Anonymous?

My own personal experiences in AA provided me with the answers.

It began on the morning when, sick and beaten, I picked up the phone and called the number I found in the telephone directory, under "Alcoholics Anonymous." I needed help. I knew no other place to look for it.

I said to the man in the central office: "I'd like to talk to someone about my drinking," and an hour later a man who lived in my own neighborhood was sharing his experience, strength, and hope with me.

So I incurred the first installment of my personal debt to general services. Because, you see, at the other end of the telephone line was a man, and an office, and money to pay the man and to keep the office open; and behind all that was a system, an organization of AA groups supporting that office and sending representatives from the groups to watch over that office and see to its operations; and behind *that* was General Service Headquarters—men and women, armed with the carefully documented experience of thousands of groups and dozens of central offices, who poured out ideas and advice and suggestions to the Los Angeles AAs who started that office, and who continue to do so when asked.

Our central office has a sponsor: "New York."

Later I went to my first meeting, sober now for a few days, and there I found the answer that has made it unnecessary for me to take another drink. After the meeting I raided the supply of free literature. I took one of everything they had, and I read all of it before I went to bed. And the next evening, at my second meeting, I bought the Big Book.

I would like to make a flat statement right here: I could never have stayed sober if it had not been for the Big Book. When nothing else and nobody else can get me out of my own way, an hour with the Big Book does the trick. I am a "Book AA." It has all the answers to all my problems.

Do you see how my debt to general services grew and grew? Without general services there would be no pamphlets, and there would be no Big Book, and for many of us there would be no sobriety. Somebody had to start a publishing company, somebody , had to write the material, and somebody had to distribute it to thousands of groups and thousands of Loners all over the world. And you know who the somebody is? "New York."

After a while, I began reading the Grapevine. I like to read the Grapevine because it raps my knuckles, slaps my back, tickles my funny bone, and shakes my hand, all at the same time. It is a critic, a guide, a good-natured friend, and an unmitigated joy. I am in love with the Grapevine, that's what I am. I love it so much I steal from it. So do my friends.

Who is responsible for editing the Grapevine? "New York." And thus my debt continued to grow.

Speaking of literature, has anybody noticed how the accuracy of newspaper and magazine articles about AA has improved lately? And the films and TV shows? It's been a long time since I've seen a syndicated article referring to AA as a "cure." And, more and more, writers are calling our disease a disease, instead of a moral weakness. This is the kind of publicity that helps to carry the message, that helps me every time I make a Twelfth Step call. It's good publicity, and I'm grateful for it.

Then, too, have you noticed that the anonymity breaks by members of AA have dropped off sharply in the press and elsewhere in the last year or two?

Why? General Service Headquarters. Thousands of letters to editors, writers, producers. "Fact Files" giving an accurate, concise explanation of what we are and what we believe and what we do, and why it is important for us to remain anonymous at the public level. Written by "New York," distributed by "New York."

Now I would like to tell about a particular personal experience with general services.

One night I attended a small discussion meeting in a desert community, and after the meeting four of us were standing around the coffee urn, and somebody said: "Wouldn't it be great if we had an open meeting down here, with guest speakers from Los Angeles?" and somebody else said: "Let's start one."

In a way this was funny, because the oldest on the program among the four of us had been sober just four and a half months. We were ignorant, we were confused, but we did have an idea. So we talked to some of the local old-timers about our idea, and they gave us a dozen good reasons why it wouldn't work; and deep discouragement set in. What to do?

Well, we wrote a letter—to General Service Headquarters. And you should have seen the reply that whistled back by airmail. A friendly, encouraging, wonderful letter, pages of it, directed to our particular local problems, answering one by one every question we had asked, and pointing out a number of things we hadn't even thought of. *Service*—from "New York"!

So we were given support and hope, and the capsuled experience of thousands of groups that had gone before us. We held our first open meeting a few weeks later, and the old-timers came and enjoyed the meeting; and recently the group marked its third anniversary, strong and well-knit and flourishing.

Thanks to "New York"!

One more story. I think the work that General Service Headquarters does is God's work. It is spiritual. Here is a personal experience to show why I think so.

A couple of years ago I flew on short notice to a small island in the British West Indies, to meet a ship that was coming north from Brazil. Before leaving the U.S., I checked with General Service Headquarters and they told me there was one AA Loner on the island, a British subject who had to guard his anonymity with care.

I arrived at the island several hours ahead of schedule. I had passed through a lot of old drinking territory on the way, and old memories were seeping into my mind, and I sure felt like talking a little AA with somebody. So I went around to the address that had been given to me, and met Clay.

I introduced myself and said: "Ann M. in New York gave me your name and address," and this man just stood there and beamed. Then he grabbed my arm and shoved me into his office, and he called his wife at home and said: "Doris, there is a man here that got my name from New York"; and he hung up and said: "She'll be right down."

So I went out to their home and spent the day with them. I met their two kids, Patrick and Prudence, and the dog, and several cats, and I looked at all the pictures in the family album, and I heard Clay's story.

Five years before, Clay had drunk himself out of his trade in England, and the only employment he could get was out of the country. His wife made the hard decision to send him off alone, because she couldn't risk it, with one small child and another on the way, and Clay's drinking, and so forth. And then, a week before the sailing date, Clay saw an ad for an AA meeting in a London newspaper. He went to the meeting, and Doris went with him, and when they got home that night she asked: "Well, what do you think?"—and he said: "I think I've found it."

On that slim hope, Doris shipped out with Clay.

That is the only AA meeting Clay has ever attended. He has never taken another drink. He told me: "I get all the bulletins and things from New York, and of course I have the Big Book. And I receive a personal letter once a month from one of the girls in the New York office." Then he grinned. "Also, my kids have got uncles."

I said: "What do you mean, uncles?"

"Well, the people in New York give my name and address to AA merchant seamen whose ships dock here, and these chaps always head straight for my place. The kids call them their uncles." Then he said, "They come here instead of hanging around the pubs in town, and it keeps them out of trouble. And they help me stay sober."

I never spent a better day than the day I spent with Clay and his family. I never saw more heartfelt gratitude—for AA, and for "New York."

So I have changed my mind about "New York." And I wish now that I had gone to the big Convention in St. Louis. I wish I had been there to hear Bill challenge 5,000 sober alcoholics: "We are ready to deliver the world services of Alcoholics Anonymous into your hands. Do you accept this gift?" And I would like to have heard the roar that thundered back at him: "YES!" from 5,000 throats.

I wasn't there that day, but the gift was accepted in my behalf. Not only the gift, but the responsibility for the gift. The lifeline of my own sobriety was delivered into my hands, together with the responsibility to guard it, support it, and extend it. And to be alert, and vigilant, and informed about it.

There is a big debt to repay—to "New York"!

J. K., Los Angeles, Calif.

Gifts from the Past
March 1985

I t was in the early 1960s that I first visited my sponsor's private rooms in Dublin, Ireland. My first impression was that Sackville M.'s natural habitat resembled an Old Curiosity Shop or, to put it bluntly, the back room of a purveyor of junk.

It was full of piles of old books, magazines, and pamphlets, often covered with dust, and a myriad of knickknacks and pieces of bric-a-brac, which seemed to have no connection with him, his personality, or his character. I knew but little, it developed. As my visits to him continued, this tangled mass of paraphernalia, which obviously meant so much to him, began bit by bit to take me over. These were his memorabilia, collected during his years of active membership in Alcoholics Anonymous. Slowly, he began to introduce me to each book, each signed photograph, each piece of his collection:

"This is a signed photograph of Bob." ... "Here is a photograph of Bill with his violin—you know, of course, that we both played the violin.".. "This prayer book was given to me by Sister Ignatia. You may care to see what she has written on the flyleaf." ... "Here is a photograph with some friends in Oklahoma visiting an Indian reservation, trying to set up a new meeting." ... "This bundle of letters came from Father Eddy Dowling. Did you know he came and spoke to us at the County Shop here in Dublin?"... "That Indian headdress was given to me on my second visit to America by the group I told you about, that we started on my first visit. Did you know they made me an honorary chief?"

During these early visits, I felt a great change coming about in me. For the very first time, *AA Comes of Age* became a living book. Bit by bit, I began to be emotionally captivated by what I had first viewed as a load of junk, until I started to handle each item with a reverence that I had never shown toward any material substance before. This pile of junk had become a storehouse of treasures. It was no longer just his; it was my roots and my history as well. For the first time, I began to feel in touch emotionally with the early members of AA. I suppose this was the beginning of my involvement with others.

Seeing that I was hooked, Sackville began to encourage me to collect, starting with simple items—menus of dinners, programs of conventions, photographs—and to make notes of the dates. I think he knew that in fact he was performing a very valuable Twelfth Step.

One of the first things I did on the death of my sponsor in 1979 was to gather all the letters, photographs, and convention and anniversary programs, together with memorabilia that I had relating to Sackville's involvement with the formation and growth of Europe's first AA group. Encouraged by what I had, I began to collect anything relating to the start of AA, not only in my own area, but also in the whole of England. I tried to contact people who I felt might be interested in joining me in this work; regrettably, there was no response.

I tried unsuccessfully to "twelfth-step" the secretary of my group into this work. She could see neither the point nor the need of gathering material. I was fortunate that year (1980) to attend the International Convention in New Orleans with her. I persuaded her to attend an early morning workshop led by Nell Wing (a nonalcoholic), archivist at the AA General Service Office. Our secretary went reluctantly—but that was the turning point. She left that workshop completely converted, full of enthusiasm for archives. I am delighted to say that in the years since, her enthusiasm has never waned.

We formed a little committee, and our work began in earnest. The following year, we were able to hold, at the Bristol Reunion, our first archives meeting. The 1982 and 1983 Bristol Reunions saw larger archives meetings, and an archives room, with our growing collection, was on display each year. As a result; we were able to involve other members in other parts of the country. We received great cooperation from our friends in Ireland and also great encouragement from Nell and from the AA who became archivist after Nell's retirement. We were really on our way.

Then came a bonus. Like most bonuses in recovery, it was never envisaged by me, never asked for, and it came as a true gift. It happened this way:

Our little committee's first priority was always to trace back a group's origins, as far as we could go. We would talk with surviving early members, tape their recollections, and piece together the pieces of the jigsaw puzzle. Rather, it was like joining together unrelated pieces of material to make what eventually has turned out to be the most exquisite patchwork quilt of recovery. Very often, the pieces were only names. We had difficulty in tracing some of them. Some had died; many were lost in the mists forever; but a few we eventually got through to in all kinds of situations.

They were living in homes for senior citizens, homes for retired officers, and geriatric hospitals. Their ages ranged from seventy-five to ninety-four. Most of them had not had active contact with the Fellowship for years. Nearly all were extremely cooperative and most willing to help our project. We just sat with them, started the cassette recorder, and gently encouraged their recall.

Slowly, it began to flow—names, places, people. Very often, names mentioned would be those of people we had already seen. Then, the old-timer would be delighted to know that they were alive and to have news of them, and nearly always asked whether it was possible to contact these other "ghosts of the present," who were still very much alive and active members of AA in the speaker's memory.

I saw miracles begin to happen before my eyes: long-forgotten members being contacted by their old groups; isolated, institutionalized members once again, through archives involvement, being stimulated in such a way that they again wanted to be a part of our whole. Because of financial and health considerations, they were sometimes unable to make direct contact themselves and used me as a messenger boy extraordinary, conveying their very special messages of experience, strength, and hope to one another. Their vitality was rekindled once they were needed.

T. C., Bristol, England

Guardian of AA—Our General Service Conference
by Bill W.
April 1958

E very AA wants to make sure of his survival from alcoholism, and his own spiritual well-being afterward. This is just as it should be. He also wants to do what he can for the survival and well-being of his fellow alcoholics. Therefore, he is bound to have a vital interest in the permanence and well-being of AA itself.

In his AA group, every good member feels deeply about this. He knows, once the miracle of sobriety has been received, that Providence expects all of us to work and to grow—to do our part in maintaining our blessings in full force. A perpetual miracle—with no effort or responsibility on our part—simply isn't in the cards. We all understand that the price of both personal and group survival is willingness and sacrifice, vigilance and work.

What is so true for each member and for each group must also be true for AA as a whole. Yet many of us have never given this self-evident proposition the thought it deserves. We are apt to take it for granted that AA, as a whole, will go on forever—no special attention or contribution being required of us. Save an occasional glow of pride in AA's size and reach, it is possible that half of AA's members and groups still have little active concern for the total welfare. That isn't negligence on their part at all. They simply haven't seen the need.

There are two good reasons for this. One is that AA as a whole has never run into any trouble. The other is that, until recently, a small group of AA's old-timers—acting as parents—have tended to the perils and problems of our whole Society without consulting the membership very much about such matters.

Never have we had a problem that cut clear across us. The public admires us; our friends love us; religion and medicine are in our corner. Nobody has seriously exploited us. We have avoided public controversy. The world's political strife hasn't touched us. We haven't had even one full-sized family quarrel. While members and groups have had just about all the woe there is, AA as a whole has never had any. This is the miracle for our twenty-three years of existence.

No wonder so many truly believe that nothing can ever happen to AA itself!

That we have been so long exempt from the pains that all nations and societies must suffer is something for the deepest gratitude. But we certainly cannot presume that this benign phenomenon will last forever. I, for one, do not think that it should last. We can never call ourselves grown-up until we have successfully met with all those temptations and problems that invariably harass every large grouping of men and women. This will be good for us—very good, I'm sure.

Someday, we may have to resist all the pressure that a destruction-bent world can put upon us in this craziest and most perilous century that the human race has ever seen. As a Fellowship, we shall always need to make whatever sacrifices are necessary to ensure AA's unity, service, and survival, *under any conditions whatever.* That is why I'm now writing to you about AA's General Service Conference, the guardian of our future.

Until recently, we have behaved like a still-young family. This family, like all families, has had parents. These parents have been the so-called old-timers and originators of AA. I was fortunate enough to have been one of them. Since the earliest days, we parents have been more concerned with the future welfare of AA than with anything else. At local levels, we old-timers used to look after things; until very recently, Dr. Bob and I, mightily assisted by dedicated alcoholic and nonalcoholic friends, have been doing the same at national and international levels.

As parents of AA, we had to see to it that our growing brood was protected against itself, and against the world outside. Very early, our family had to have principles to live by, and schooling in those principles. The good news of AA had to be spread far and wide, so that we could grow in numbers as well as in quality. Such were our responsibilities.

It was in 1937 that Dr. Bob and I first began to see what we must do. We knew there would have to be an AA text of principles and methods. Other old-timers agreed. By 1939, with lots of help, we had published the Big Book, *Alcoholics Anonymous*. This ended all doubt about AA's methods. The 300,000 Big Books today in circulation [all statistics in this article are as of 1958] constitute the platform of recovery upon which our whole Fellowship stands.

We next realized that AA would have to have publicity—lots of it, and of the right kind. We commenced work on this problem. Maybe half of today's members owe their lives and their fortunes to the telling efforts of the press and other means of communication.

From 1940 to 1950, we were beset by group problems of every sort, frightening beyond description. Out of these experiences, the Twelve Traditions of AA were forged—Traditions that now protect us against ourselves and the world outside. This effort, requiring immense office correspondence and experience, finally resulted in a whole new literature dealing with AA's unity and services. Under these influences, we grew solid.

The news of AA began to spread around the world, finally reaching into seventy lands. This brought a host of new problems and the need to publish AA literature in many tongues. Hospitals and prisons and Loners and men on ships also had to be reached and helped. AA's lifelines had to extend everywhere. AA needed a monthly magazine. Today, the AA Grapevine reaches 40,000 subscribers, plus countless thousands of others each month.

These have been the duties and privileges of our parenthood worldwide. We did our best to protect AA so that it could grow undisturbed. Not troubling the growing family about these critical matters, we acted on the principle that "Father knows best." In the early days, it was just as simple as that. It was then far too soon to throw the full weight of responsibility onto our whole Fellowship.

From the beginning, Dr. Bob and I found that we needed special help ourselves. Therefore, we called upon certain dedicated non-alcoholics to give us a lift. With these men, we formed a trusteeship for Alcoholics Anonymous. It was created way back in 1938, and we called it the Alcoholic Foundation (since renamed the General Service Board of AA). In 1940, our trustees acquired the AA book and assumed full responsibility for AA's general funds, its world service office [now the General Service Office], and its public relations.

To this body of trustees—alcoholic and nonalcoholic—must go most of the credit for making our world headquarters what it now is. In our new history book, *AA Comes of Age,* you can read what they did for us in our pioneering times as the moving drama of AA unfolded.

During the year 1948, we workers at AA's headquarters got a terrific jolt. Dr. Bob was stricken with a consuming and slowly fatal malady. This created a severe crisis in our affairs, because it made us face up to the fact that the old-time parents of AA weren't going to last forever.

We were filled with foreboding as we realized how insecure were the existing links between our headquarters and the vast sprawling Fellowship that it served. There was, of course, our small board of trustees. But not one AA in a thousand could name half of them. At the headquarters office, there were Bobbie, Ann, and Charlotte. There were Dr. Bob and myself. We few were just about the *only links* to worldwide AA!

Meanwhile, thousands of our members went serenely about their business. They knew little or nothing about AA's overall problems. They vaguely supposed that God, with maybe a slight assist from Dr. Bob and me, would go right on handling them. Thus, they were completely ignorant of the actual state of our affairs, and of the awful potential there was for an ultimate collapse.

It was a racking dilemma. Somehow, AA as such—*AA as a whole*—would have to take over the full responsibility. Without doubt, the groups would have to elect numerous delegates and send them to New York each year, where they could sit with and guide the trustees. Only by so doing could AA assume effective direction of its own policy and business. Only through these elected delegates could the increasing isolation of the trustees from the movement itself be halted. Only such a body could make binding decisions in any future crisis.

When our scheme for a joint conference of trustees and delegates was first proposed, a howl went up country-wide. At first, it looked as though the AA family didn't want any part of this new and un-expected responsibility. To them, "AA delegates" spelled nothing but politics, controversy, and confusion. "Let's keep it simple," they cried.

But after a couple of years of agitation and education, our Fellow-ship clearly realized that the ultra simplicity of the early days could be no more. Direct family responsibility there would have to be, or else AA would fold up at its very center. The erstwhile elders, fathers, and founders would have to be taken off the hook and replaced by delegates. There was no other way. The family would have to "come of age" or suffer dire penalties for failure to do so.

So we called in some seventy-five delegates from the U.S. and Can-ada. Together with the trustees and the headquarters and Grapevine staff, those delegates formed themselves into the General Service Conference of Alcoholics Anonymous. By then, it was 1951.

At first, this was an experiment, pure and simple. If it worked, it would mean that AA had truly "come of age," and could really man-age its own affairs. Through its representative Conference, it could become the guardian of its own future and the protector of its own lifelines of service.

Well, our Conference did work. Its performance, God be thanked, exceeded all our expectations. At the end of its five-year experimen-tal period, we knew that it could become a permanent part of our Fellowship.

In July of 1955, at AA's twentieth anniversary, I stood before the great St. Louis Convention. Amid a dwindling band of old-timers, and on their behalf, I delivered the destiny of AA into the hands of its chosen representatives, the General Service Conference of Alcoholics

Anonymous. I cannot remember any happier day in my life. A gaping chasm had been bridged. AA was secure at last.

Some people still ask these questions: Will the AA family send to the Conference its finest delegates? Will we continue to choose able and wise trustees? Will AAs back their Conference members, their trustees, and their world headquarters with enough funds, enough interest, and enough understanding?

For me, these are questions no longer. The history of AA shows that whenever a great need arises, that need is always met. In this respect, I'm quite sure that our history will go on repeating itself. Indeed, I can have no doubt whatever.

I think, too, that my own influence at the headquarters should continue to lessen. Through its Conference, complete authority and responsibility are now fully vested in AA. The parent who overstays his time can only hamper the growth of his offspring. This, I must not do. My proper place will soon be along the sidelines, cheering you newer ones as you carry on. Our family is now fully of age, and it should firmly remind me of that fact if I am ever again tempted to take charge.

For these all-compelling reasons, my friends, the future belongs to you. Embrace these new responsibilities eagerly; fear naught; and the grace of God will surely be yours.

The Twelve Steps

1. We admitted we were powerless over alcohol—that our lives had become unmanageable.
2. Came to believe that a Power greater than ourselves could restore us to sanity.
3. Made a decision to turn our will and our lives over to the care of God *as we understood Him.*
4. Made a searching and fearless moral inventory of ourselves.
5. Admitted to God, to ourselves, and to another human being the exact nature of our wrongs.
6. Were entirely ready to have God remove all these defects of character.
7. Humbly asked Him to remove our shortcomings.
8. Made a list of all persons we had harmed, and became willing to make amends to them all.
9. Made direct amends to such people wherever possible, except when to do so would injure them or others.
10. Continued to take personal inventory and when we were wrong promptly admitted it.
11. Sought through prayer and meditation to improve our conscious contact with God *as we understood Him*, praying only for knowledge of His will for us and the power to carry that out.
12. Having had a spiritual awakening as the result of these steps, we tried to carry this message to alcoholics, and to practice these principles in all our affairs.

The Twelve Traditions

1. Our common welfare should come first; personal recovery depends upon A.A. unity.
2. For our group purpose there is but one ultimate authority—a loving God as He may express Himself in our group conscience. Our leaders are but trusted servants; they do not govern.
3. The only requirement for A.A. membership is a desire to stop drinking.
4. Each group should be autonomous except in matters affecting other groups or A.A. as a whole.
5. Each group has but one primary purpose—to carry its message to the alcoholic who still suffers.
6. An A.A. group ought never endorse, finance or lend the A.A. name to any related facility or outside enterprise, lest problems of money, property and prestige divert us from our primary purpose.
7. Every A.A. group ought to be fully self-supporting, declining outside contributions.
8. Alcoholics Anonymous should remain forever nonprofessional, but our service centers may employ special workers.
9. A.A., as such, ought never be organized; but we may create service boards or committees directly responsible to those they serve.
10. Alcoholics Anonymous has no opinion on outside issues; hence the A.A. name ought never be drawn into public controversy.
11. Our public relations policy is based on attraction rather than promotion; we need always maintain personal anonymity at the level of press, radio and films.
12. Anonymity is the spiritual foundation of all our traditions, ever reminding us to place principles before personalities.

Alcoholics Anonymous

AA's program of recovery is fully set forth in its basic text, *Alcoholics Anonymous* (commonly known as the Big Book), now in its Fourth Edition, as well as in *Twelve Steps and Twelve Traditions, Living Sober*, and other books. Information on AA can also be found on AA's website at www.AA.ORG, or by writing to:

Alcoholics Anonymous
Box 459
Grand Central Station
New York, NY 10163

For local resources, check your local telephone directory under "Alcoholics Anonymous." Four pamphlets, "This is A.A.," "Is A.A. For You?," "44 Questions," and "A Newcomer Asks" are also available from AA.

AA Grapevine

AA Grapevine is AA's international monthly journal, published continuously since its first issue in June 1944. The AA pamphlet on AA Grapevine describes its scope and purpose this way: "As an integral part of Alcoholics Anonymous since 1944, the Grapevine publishes articles that reflect the full diversity of experience and thought found within the A.A. Fellowship, as does La Viña, the bimonthly Spanish-language magazine, first published in 1996. No one viewpoint or philosophy dominates their pages, and in determining content, the editorial staff relies on the principles of the Twelve Traditions."

In addition to magazines, AA Grapevine, Inc. also produces books, eBooks, audiobooks, and other items. It also offers a Grapevine Online subscription, which includes: new stories weekly, AudioGrapevine (the audio version of the magazine), Grapevine Story Archive (the entire collection of Grapevine articles), and the current issue of Grapevine and La Viña in HTML format. For more information on AA Grapevine, or to subscribe to any of these, please visit the magazine's website at WWW.AAGRAPEVINE.ORG or write to:

AA Grapevine, Inc.
475 Riverside Drive
New York, NY 10115